WOODWIND, BRASS, AND PERCUSSION INSTRUMENTS OF THE ORCHESTRA

GARLAND REFERENCE LIBRARY
OF THE HUMANITIES
(VOL. 458)

WOODWIND, BRASS, AND PERCUSSION INSTRUMENTS OF THE ORCHESTRA
A Bibliographic Guide

Allen B. Skei

GARLAND PUBLISHING, INC. • NEW YORK & LONDON
1985

Library of Congress Cataloging in Publication Data
Skei, Allen B.
Woodwind, brass, and percussion instruments of the
orchestra.

(Garland reference library of the humanities ; v. 458)
Includes indexes.
1. Wind instruments—Bibliography. 2. Percussion
instruments—Bibliography. I. Title. II. Series.
ML128.W5S6 1985 016.788 83-49079
ISBN 0-8240-9021-7

Cover design by Laurence Walczak

Printed on acid-free, 250-year-life paper
Manufactured in the United States of America

To the Memory of
William H. Stubbins

CONTENTS

PREFACE

Never scarce, the literature about musical instruments has grown in the past few decades at such a rate as to have become almost completely unmanageable. Growth can be seen in every area of concern yet nowhere more than in the area of wind and percussion instruments. It seems that almost every year or two a new journal or newsletter appears, while book publishers, often previously unknown to everyone but the authors whose works they print, display a remarkable readiness to bring to light the work and thought of what seems to be any percussionist or clarinet player with access to a typewriter.

Universities throughout the country, by their sponsorship of dissertations, have made additional and sometimes substantial contributions. Altogether, the result is that the body of literature about wind and percussion instruments has become enormous, so large that a guide such as this is needed but unfortunately too large—and too scattered—for any guide to be comprehensive.

The present bibliography makes no claim to comprehensiveness. Instead, it includes only a careful selection of books, articles, and dissertations concerning the wind and percussion instruments most commonly heard in classical music: in other words, the wind and percussion instruments of the orchestra throughout the length of its existence, from its origins in the early seventeenth century to the present day.

The book is intended for the use largely of musicologists, graduate students in music performance, and for teachers of instrumental music. Designed primarily as a guide to research and other serious study, it focuses mostly on the nature and historical development of instruments. Nevertheless, it includes a wide range of material—from historical discussions of the instruments to bibliographies of music to discussions of performers and performance practice. It also includes more-or-less comprehensive treatments of performance technique together with discussions of historical practice as well as special discussions of the new techniques developed in contemporary music. The only historical instrument tutors listed, however, are those readily available in reprint editions. For reasons partly of practical consideration, articles from a number of periodicals of limited availability, especially those directed players of particular instruments (for instance, *To the World's Oboists*) have largely been omitted.

The book includes discussions of all the wind and percussion instruments found in the modern orchestra. It also includes discussions of the immediate antecedents of these instruments as well as of a number of instruments, primarily from the nineteenth century, that have largely fallen out of use. The chalumeau, the serpent, and the saxhorn are, for instance, treated here, along with the cornetto and various brass instruments of the Baroque era. Possessing a history independent from that of any instrument in the modern orchestra, the recorder is treated here only incidentally. Already longer than I had planned it to be, the book would have grown disproportionately large had it been fully included.

It would also have grown considerably had it encompassed general discussions of performance practice. Instead, it includes only discussions relating to wind and percussion instruments specifically. Discussions of broader scope can easily be found by consulting the fine book edited by Mary Vinquist and Neal Zaslaw—*Performance Practice: A Bibliography* (New York: Norton, 1971)—as well as Robert Donington's *The Interpretation of Early Music* (London: Faber and Faber, 1974) and two books by Frederick Neumann: *Ornamentation in Baroque and Post-Baroque Music* (Princeton, N.J.: Princeton University Press, 1978) and *Essays in Performance Practice* (Ann Arbor, Mich.: UMI Research Press, 1982).

Although selective, the bibliography attempts, with one notable exception, to provide a guide to the most important literature in the areas with which it is concerned and also to point up something of the scope of the literature as a whole. That exception is the material found in *The New Grove Dictionary of Music and Musicians*, edited by Stanley Sadie (London: Macmillan, 1980). In twenty volumes, *The New Grove* is an indispensable resource for any musical study, and it will as a matter of course be consulted during the investigation of musical instruments (or of any other aspect of music). The inclusion of annotated entries for all the relevant articles from *Grove* therefore seems unnecessary. Likewise, only a few general articles from *Die Musik in Geschichte und Gegenwart* (Kassel: Bärenreiter, 1949–) have been cited here. It too will be consulted as a matter of course. *The New Grove* has been of considerable value in the preparation of this book, especially for its bibliographies. In addition, *RILM Abstracts of Music Literature* and a number of specialized bibliographies have been relied upon quite heavily. The annotations offered here are based primarily on an examination of the items themselves, but in some cases—especially dissertations and items written in Japanese and Eastern European languages—are based either upon the authors' abstracts or the descriptions in *RILM Abstracts*.

The discussions cited here have, for the convenience of the reader, been placed in what seem to be logical categories. Many of the discussions, though, could easily be placed in more than one, while some discussions each seem to demand a unique category. The cross references are intended to ameliorate the difficulty; the subject index should help even further, especially in regard to instruments other than those designated in chapter headings and subheadings.

I am indebted to many people for help of varied kinds in the preparation of the book. The staff at the Henry Madden Library of California State University, Fresno, have been unfailingly generous with their time and energy. Jean Tempesta, William Heinlen, and Ronald Harlan have been especially helpful, for which I'm very grateful. I'm also grateful for the assistance given me by the staffs of the music libraries of Stanford University and the University of California, Berkeley and Los Angeles.

The book would not have been possible without the support of research grants from California State University, Fresno. Additional and much-needed support, although of a different kind, has come from Dorothy and David Levinson and my long-suffering family.

Fresno, California
August 1983

Woodwind, Brass, and Percussion
Instruments of the Orchestra

I

DICTIONARIES, HISTORIES, AND DESCRIPTIONS
OF INSTRUMENTS IN GENERAL

1. Agricola, Martin. *Musica instrumentalis deudsch*. Witten-
   berg: Georg Rhau, 1529; reprint ed., Hildesheim: Olms,
   1969. 100 p.

   Important as one of the earliest printed sources of
   information about instruments, including trumpets and
   transverse flutes. English translation cited below
   as Item 17.

2. Baines, Anthony, ed. *Musical Instruments through the
   Ages*. Rev. ed. London: Faber and Faber, 1966. 344 p.

   A good historical survey. Includes chapters on woodwinds by James A. MacGillivray, on brass instruments by
   Christopher W. Monk and R. Morley Pegge, and on percussion
   instruments by James Blades.

3. Berlioz, Hector. *Treatise on Instrumentation*. Revised
   and enlarged by Richard Strauss. Translated by
   Theodore Front. New York: Kalmus, 1948. 424 p.

   The fundamental treatise. Valuable partly for its
   discussion of unusual instruments such as saxhorns,
   ophicleides, serpent, and Russian bassoon.

* Bonanni, Filippo. *The Showcase of Musical Instruments*.
   New York: Dover, 1964. 309 p.

   Cited below as Item 1169.

* Bragard, Roger, and Ferdinand J. de Hen. *Musical Instruments in Art and History*. Translated by Bill Hopkins.
   New York: Viking Press, 1968. 281 p.

   Cited below as Item 1171.

4. Buchner, Alexander. *Musical Instruments through the Ages*.
   Translated by Iris Unwin. London: Spring Books, [1956].

   Valuable for its plates, 323 in all, depicting
   instruments found mostly in Czech collections. Also
   reproduces paintings and various other illustrations of
   instruments. Includes a brief but useful historical
   introduction. Later reprinted as *Musical Instruments:
   An Illustrated History* (New York: Crown, 1973).

5. Del Mar, Norman. *Anatomy of the Orchestra*. Berkeley:
   University of California Press, 1981. 528 p.

   A comprehensive account of instrumental usage. Discusses
   notation, various instrumental effects, choice of instruments (for instance, which tuba for which part), and
   orchestral seating arrangment. Includes discussions of
   unusual instruments (ophicleides, for example).

6. Donington, Robert. *The Instruments of Music*. 3rd ed.
   London: Methuen, 1970. 262 p.

   A useful general discussion of European instruments.

7. *Encyclopédie de la musique et dictionnaire du Conservatoire*.
   Founder, Albert Lavignac; director, Lionel de la
   Laurencie. Part 2, vol. 3: *Technique instrumentale*.
   Paris: Delagrave, 1925. 1126 p.

   Provides comprehensive discussions of individual
   wind instruments and of percussion instruments as a
   group. Valuable partly for its treatment of instruments
   of French provenance: for instance, sarrusophone,
   sudrophone, cornet, and saxophone. Includes a general
   chapter on the acoustics of wind instruments.

8. Forsyth, Cecil. *Orchestration*. 2nd ed. London:
   Macmillan, 1935; reprint ed., New York: Macmillan,
   1946. 530 p.

   A comprehensive discussion of the instruments of the
   orchestra and of their use in orchestral music. For
   many years the standard treatment in English. First
   edition published in 1914.

* Gábry, György. *Old Musical Instruments*. Translated by
   Éva Rácz. Budapest: Corvina, 1969. 42 p.

   Cited below as Item 737.

9. Galpin, Francis W. *Old English Instruments of Music.*
   4th ed. Revised by Thurston Dart. London: Methuen,
   1965. 254 p.

   First edition published in 1910. A thorough
   examination of the history of musical instruments in
   England during the Middle Ages, Renaissance, and
   Baroque. A classic in the literature.

10. ————. *A Textbook of European Musical Instruments:*
    Their Origin, History, and Character. New York:
    Dutton, 1937; reprint ed., Westport, Conn.: Greenwood,
    1976. 256 p.

    The fundamental English-language treatment prior to
    the appearance of the history by Curt Sachs (1940),
    which is cited below as Item 30.

11. Gammond, Peter, *Musical Instruments in Color.* New York:
    Macmillan, 1976. 173 p.

    Includes general descriptions of the various types of
    instruments, a short list of instrument collections,
    and a glossary of instrument names. Illustrated with
    ninety-one color photographs, which represent the
    book's principal attraction.

12. Geiringer, Karl. *Instruments in the History of Western*
    Music. 3rd ed. New York: Oxford University Press,
    1978. 318 p.

    A generally reliable survey. Includes an introduction
    to the principles of musical instruments.

13. Gevaert, François-Auguste. *Nouveau traité d'instrumenta-*
    tion. Brussels: Lemoine, 1885. 339 p.

    One of the most important orchestration books of its
    day. Valuable today partly for its discussion of
    saxhorns, sarrusophones, ophicleides, and keyed bugles.

14. Heinitz, Wilhelm. *Instrumentekunde.* Handbuch der
    Musikwissenschaft, edited by Ernst Bücken, 11.
    Wildpark-Potsdam: Akademische Verlagsgesellschaft
    Athenaion, 1929; reprint ed., New York: Musurgia,
    1949. 160 p.

    A pioneering account that describes, traces the
    history, and reviews the acoustics of musical instruments.
    Well illustrated with plates.

15. Hollaway, William W. "Martin Agricola's *Musica instrumentalis deudsch*: A Translation." Ph.D. dissertation, North Texas State University, 1972. 265 p. UM 72-24, 188.

    Includes a survey and list of books from the sixteenth and early seventeenth centuries that deal with musical instruments. A facsimile reprint of the original edition of Agricola is cited above as Item 1.

16. Hulphers, Abraham Abrahamsson. *Historisk afhandling om musik och instrumenter*. Vasteras: J.L. Horrn, 1773; facsimile reprint, Amsterdam: Knuf, 1971. 328 p.

    Important mostly for the organ specifications given but valuable also for its description of other instruments. The reprint edition includes introductory essays by Thorild Lindgren and Peter Williams.

* Kagel, Mauricio. *Theatrum instrumentorum*. Cologne: Kölnischer Kunstverein, 1975. 72 p.

    Cited below as Item 441.

17. Kunitz, Hans. *Die Instrumentation*. 12 vols. Leipzig: Breitkopf und Härtel, 1956-60.

    A comprehensive overview. Introduced by a discussion of musical acoustics. Vols. 2-9 each deal with a single instrument: flute, oboe, clarinet, bassoon, horn, trumpet, trombone, tuba. Vol. 10 treats the percussion instruments, vol. 11 the harp, and vol. 12 the violin and viola. The histories of the instruments are reviewed and the most appropriate, most effective ways of scoring for them are discussed and illustrated with copious musical examples.

18. Majer, Joseph Friedrich Bernhard Caspar. *Museum musicum theoretico practicum*. Schwabisch Hall: George Michael Majer, 1732; facsimile reprint, edited by Heinz Becker, Kassel: Bärenreiter, 1954. 104 p.

    A compendium of information about musical instruments and general musical matters. Includes an explanation of musical terms, a review of musical rudiments, and general advice regarding performance.

19. Marcuse, Sibyl. *Musical Instruments, A Comprehensive Dictionary*. New York: Norton, 1975. 608 p.

Authoritative and complete. For basic information about instruments, unrivalled by any other book in English.

20. ————. *A Survey of Musical Instruments.* New York: Harper and Row, 1975. 863 p.

Comprehensive and reliable. Includes discussions of folk and non-Western instruments.

21. Mersenne, Marin. *Harmonie universelle: The Books on Instruments.* Translated by Roger E. Chapman. The Hague: Nijhoff, 1957. 596 p.

Originally published in 1635. A comprehensive treatment and the standard French source for early Baroque practice.

22. Montagu, Jeremy. *The World of Baroque and Classical Musical Instruments.* Woodstock, N.Y.: Overlook Press, 1979. 136 p.

A good general survey. Notable partly for its generous selection of photographs of instruments, many from British collections.

23. ————. *The World of Romantic and Modern Musical Instruments.* Woodstock, N.Y.: Overlook Press, 1981. 136 p.

A book of the same good quality as the one cited above as Item 22.

24. Nef, Karl. *Geschichte unserer Musikinstrumente.* 2nd ed. Basel: Amerbach, 1949. 213 p.

A historical overview. Illustrated by seventy-five plates. Second edition revised by Edgar Refardt from the edition of 1926.

25. Piston, Walter. *Orchestration.* New York: Norton, 1955. 477 p.

The standard American text.

26. Praetorius, Michael. *De organographia.* Syntagma musicum, 2. Wolfenbüttel: Holwein, 1619; facsimile reprint, edited by Wilibald Gurlitt, Kassel: Bärenreiter, 1958. 278 p.

An invaluable compendium of information about and
drawings of the musical instruments of the period.
Essential to the study of the history of musical
instruments.

27. Remnant, Mary. *Musical Instruments of the West.* New York:
St. Martin's Press, 1978. 240 p.

A good historical introduction. Especially strong in
its treatment of the early periods of instrument development. Copiously illustrated.

28. Sachs, Curt. *The History of Musical Instruments.* New
York: Norton, 1940. 505 p.

The fundamental English-language account.

29. ————. *Die modernen Musikinstrumente.* Berlin: Hesse,
1923. 172 p.

One of a series of handbooks published by Hesse that
are directed toward music students. Describes each
instrument in relatively superficial but nevertheless
accurate terms.

30. ————. *Real-Lexikon der Musikinstrumente zugleich ein
Polyglossar für das gesamte Instrumentengebiet.*
New York: Dover, 1964. 452 p.

Sets the standard for dictionaries of musical instruments. First edition published in 1913. The present
edition includes the corrections and additions subsequently made by Sachs but never before published.

31. Schlosser, Julius. *Unsere Musikinstrumente: Eine
Einführung in ihre Geschichte.* Vienna: Schroll,
1922. 80 p.

A historical survey of musical instruments from their
origins to the early twentieth century. Illustrated with
eighty-two photographs of instruments in the collection
of the Kunsthistorisches Museum in Vienna.

32. Teuchert, Emil, and Erhard W. Haupt. eds. *Musik-
Instrumentenkunde in Wort und Bild.* Leipzig:
Breitkopf und Härtel, 1911. 423 p.

Describes the instruments of the orchestra and illustrates their use through a generous selection of musical
examples. Each instrument is discussed by a performer on

that instrument. Valuable partly for its sympathetic treatment of instruments that have generally fallen out of use, such as the piccolo heckelphone.

33. Tintori, Giampiero. *Gli strumenti musicale.* 2 vols.
     Turin: Unione Tipografico Editrice Torinese, 1971.
     1143 p.

     A comprehensive discussion of musical instruments, non-European (in vol. 1) as well as European (vol. 2).
     Rich in detail and graced by good bibliographies as well as by an extensive glossary.

*   Trichet, Pierre. *Traité des instruments de musique.*
     Neuilly-sur-Seine: Société de musique d'autrefois, 1957. 186 p.

     Cited below as Item 164.

34. Valentin, Erich. *Handbuch der Musikinstrumentenkunde.*
     7th ed. Regensburg: Bosse, 1980. 384 p.

     A historical survey together with brief but good discussions of individual instruments and instrument types. Includes an overview of the acoustics of musical instruments. First edition published in 1954.

35. Virdung, Sebastian. *Musica getutscht.* Basel: Michael Furter, 1511; facsimile reprint, edited by Klaus Wolfgang Niemöller, Kassel: Bärenreiter, 1970. 118 p.

     An explanation of rudimentary music theory together with descriptions of musical instruments, including trumpet, trombone, and drums. The descriptions, the first ever printed, are accompanied by excellent woodcuts by Urs Graf. The reprint edition includes a helpful afterword by Niemöller.

*   Weigel, Johann Christoph. *Musicalisches theatrum.*
     Nuremberg: Weigel, [ca. 1722]; facsimile reprint, edited by Alfred Berner, Kassel: Bärenreiter, 1961.
     36 plates, 12 p.

     Cited below as Item 1193.

36. Zeraschi, Helmut. *Die Musikinstrumente unserer Zeit.*
     Leipzig: Deutscher Verlag für Musik, 1978. 303 p.

     A collection of essays on a range of topics--including instrument makers and the construction of instruments, and electronic instruments--together with descriptions and brief discussions of individual instruments of all kinds.

II

HISTORIES AND GENERAL DISCUSSIONS OF WIND
AND PERCUSSION INSTRUMENTS

1. Wind and Percussion Instruments in General

37. Adkins, H.E. *Treatise on the Military Band*. London:
Boosey, 1945. 312 p.

Dicusses in detail the instruments of the military
band, including their tuning, fingering, and use. Valuable partly for its discussion of the Clinton system
clarinet. Includes a lengthy section on arranging music
for military band as well as a section on conducting
bands.

38. Clappé. Arthur A. *The Wind-Band and Its Instruments:
Their History, Construction, Acoustics, Technique
and Construction*. New York: Holt, 1911; reprint
ed., Portland, Maine: Longwood, 1986. 208 p.

The pioneering American account. Comprehensive and
altogether sensible in its treatment.

39. Daubeny, Ulric. *Orchestral Wind Instruments Ancient and
Modern*. London: Reeves, 1920. 147 p.

Now outdated but for decades a standard descriptive
account. Makes no attempt to provide a detailed history
of the instruments.

40. Francoeur, Louis-Joseph. *Diapason général de tous les
instruments à vent*. Paris: De Lauriers, 1772; facsimile reprint, Geneva: Minkoff, 1971. 85 p.

A comprehensive treatment of the use of wind instruments in orchestral music. Points out the limitations
of the individual instruments, the most advantageous

keys, and the ways in which the instruments can be
employed in combination.

41. Gorgerat, Gérald. *Encyclopédie de la musique pour
    instruments à vent.* 3 vols. Lausanne: Éditions
    recontre Lausanne, 1955. 380, 452, 614 p.

    Begins with an explanation of harmony and counterpoint
    and continues with a discussion of percussion instruments
    and percussion notation. Provides, in vol. 2, histories
    and descriptions of the individual wind instruments,
    discussions of wind instrument technique, and a descrip-
    tion of instrument manufacture. Includes, in vol. 3,
    lists of repertory, a dictionary of terms, a dictionary
    of composers, a discussion of the brass band, and an
    explanation of conducting technique. Presumably
    includes everything a student might want to know.

42. Gourdet, Georges, *Les instruments à vent.* 2nd ed. Que
    sais-je? vol. 267. Paris: Presses universitaires
    de France, 1976. 128 p.

    Discusses the use of wind instruments from their
    origins to the present day. Includes lists of repertory.

43. Koechlin, Charles. *Les instruments à vent.* Paris:
    Presses universitaires de France, 1948. 128 p.

    A survey both historical and technical. Includes a
    list of tutors. Valuable partly because of the author's
    insights.

*   Levin, Semen. *Lukovye instrumenty v istorii muzykal'noi
    kul'tury.* Leningrad: Muzyka, 1973. 262 p.

    Cited below as Item 149.

44. Schneider, Willy. *Handbuch der Blasmusik: Ein Wegweiser
    für Bläser und Dirigenten.* Mainz: Schott, 1954. 87 p.

    A concise history and description of wind instruments
    followed by discussions of instrumentation, notation,
    various aspects of performance, and the literature for
    wind ensemble.

45. Seifers, Heinrich. *Systematik der Blasinstrumente. Eine
    Instrumentenlehre in Tabellenform.* Frankfurt: Das
    Musikinstrument, 1967. 21 p.

    A collection of tables that indicate something of each
    instrument's usage and design as well as its key and

register. Presents an impressive amount of information.

46. Vandenbroeck, Othon. *Traité général de tous les instru-
    ments à vent à l'usage des compositeurs.* Paris: Boyer,
    [*ca.* 1794]; facsimile reprint, Geneva: Minkoff, 1974.
    65 p.

    Includes brief discussions of the clarinet, trumpet,
    trombone, timpani, oboe, flute, bassoon, and serpent.
    Primarily a discussion of the French horn, which "has
    been ignored for a long time." Provides examples of
    difficult and easy passages. Carefully distinguishes
    between first and second horn.

2. Woodwind Instruments

47. Baines, Anthony. *Woodwind Instruments and Their History.*
    3rd ed. London: Faber and Faber, 1967. 384 p.

    Thorough and reliable. An indispensable source.

48. Baumgartner, J.F. *Von der Syrinx zum Saxophon.* Solothurn:
    Schweizer Jugend-Verlag, 1962. 58 p.

    A brief introduction to the woodwinds.

3. Brass Instruments

*   Bahnert, Heinz, Theodor Herzberg, and Herbert Schramm.
    Metallblasinstrumente. Leipzig: Fachbuchverlag
    Leipzig, 1958. 254 p.

    Cited below as Item 545.

49. Baines, Anthony. *Brass Instruments: Their History and
    Development.* London: Faber and Faber, 1976. 298 p.

    Comprehensive and authoritative. Includes a discussion
    of manufacturing processes and acoustical principles.
    The horn and trumpet families are treated in particular
    detail.

50. Mende, Emilie. *Arbre généalogique illustré des cuivres
    européens depuis le début du Moyen Age/Stammbuch der*

*europäischen Blechblasinstrumente in Bildern seit
dem frühen Mittelalter/Pictorial Family Tree of Brass
Instruments in Europe Since the Early Middle Ages.*
Moudon: Éditions BIM, 1978. 68 p.

An attractive collection of charts giving the history
of each group of brass instruments (cornetti, trumpets
and trombones, horns, as well as flugelhorns, cornets,
saxhorns, and tubas). Well illustrated with photographs.

4. Percussion Instruments

51. Averinos, Gerassimos. *Handbuch der Schlag- und Effektin-
strumente: Ein Wegweiser für Komponisten, Dirigenten,
Musiker und Instrumentenbauer.* Frankfurt: Das
Musikinstrument, 1967. 224 p.

    A comprehensive, illustrated dictionary of instrument
    names and relevant terms, including names of musical
    effects. Includes terms in all major European languages.
    Distinguished partly by good cross-references.

52. ————. *Lexikon der Pauke.* Frankfurt: Das Musikinstrument, 1964. 105 p.

    Defines and explains terms relevant to the timpani.
    Includes, under the term *Lautstarken*, the results of the
    author's investigation of the volume of sound produced
    by the timpani, which sometimes reaches dangerous levels
    for performers exposed to the sound for long periods
    of time.

*   Bahnert, Heinz, Theodor Herzberg, and Herbert Schramm.
    Metallblasinstrumente. Leipzig: Fachbuchverlag
    Leipzig. 1958. 254 p.

    Cited below as Item 545.

53. Blades, James. *Percussion Instruments and Their History.*
New York: Praeger, 1971. 576 p.

    The standard account. Provides a detailed history of
    the instruments, a discussion of the treatment of per-
    cussion instruments by contemporary composers, and a
    survey of Latin American percussion usage and jazz per-
    formance. Includes an introduction by Benjamin Britten.

54. Dupin, François. *Lexique de la percussion*. La revue
     musicale, vol. 284. Paris: Richard-Masse, 1971.
     71 p.

     An illustrated dictionary of instruments. Includes
     descriptions of performance techniques and musical effects.
     Also provides a list of instruments classified according
     to loudness. Includes an inventory of the percussion
     instruments in the Orchestre de Paris.

55. Firth, Vic. *Percussion Symposium: A Manual Defining
     and Illustrating the Complete Percussion Section*.
     New York: Carl Fischer, 1966. 48 p.

     Valuable for its photographs of unusual instruments,
     for its description of tone qualities, and for its
     advice to players.

56. Holland, James. *Percussion*. New York: Schirmer Books,
     1981. 283 p.

     An introduction to the instruments and their use in
     orchestral and chamber music. Includes a good selective
     discography. Foreword by Pierre Boulez.

57. Jakob, Friedrich. *Schlagzeug*. Bern: Hallwag, 1979.
     108 p.

     A well-illustrated survey of the percussion instruments
     employed in western music, particularly during the
     twentieth century.

58. Kotoński, Włodzimierz. *Schlaginstrumente im modernen
     Orchester*. Mainz: Schott, 1968. 96 p.

     Intended as a manual for composers, conductors, and
     performers. Includes concise descriptions of the instru-
     ments, illustrates the proper notation for each, and
     provides a brief but useful glossary of terms.

59. Peinkofer, Karl, and Fritz Tannigel. *Handbook of Per-
     cussion Intruments: Their Characteristics and Playing
     Techniques, with Illustrations and Musical Examples
     from the Literature*. Translated by Kurt and Else
     Stone. London: Schott, 1976. 257 p.

     A useful survey, comprehensive and well illustrated.
     Includes folk and non-western instruments. First
     edition published in 1969.

60. ———. *Handbuch des Schlagzeugs, Praxis und Technik.*
    2nd ed. Mainz: Schott, 1981. 282 p.

    Traces the history of the individual percussion instru-
    ments, describes them, discusses the way in which they
    are played, and cites instances of their use. Illustrated
    with photographs and musical examples.

61. Peters, Gordon B. *The Drummer: Man.* Rev. ed. Wilmette,
    Ill.: Kemper-Peters, 1975. 356 p.

    Marked by a rather diffuse focus. Includes a history
    of percussion instruments, a discussion of their acoustics,
    descriptions of various instruments, discussions of
    percussion ensembles and jazz, lists of various kinds,
    and press releases from a marimba ensemble.

62. ———. "Treatise on Percussion." M.A. thesis, Eastman
    School of Music, 1962. 431 p.

    A comprehensive treatment of instruments employed in
    western music. Includes a brief discussion of ancient
    instruments and a short chapter on acoustics. Percussion
    ensembles are also discussed. Usefulness limited by the
    scarcity of documentation.

63. Richards, Emil. *World of Percussion: A Catalog of
    300 Standard, Ethnic, and Special Musical Instruments
    and Effects.* Sherman Oaks, Calif.: Gwyn, 1972.
    94 p.

    A descriptive catalog of instruments, each of which
    is illustrated by a photograph. Includes several unique
    instruments invented by the author and by Erv Wilson.

64. White, Charles L. *Drums Through the Ages.* Los Angeles:
    Sterling Press, 1960. 215 p.

    An introduction to percussion instruments of all kinds.
    Describes the instruments, sketches their historical
    background, and offers suggestions for performance.

III

HISTORIES AND COMPREHENSIVE DISCUSSIONS
OF INDIVIDUAL WOODWIND INSTRUMENTS

1. Flute and Piccolo

65. Bate, Philip. *The Flute: A Study of Its History,
    Development and Construction*. New York: Norton, 1969.
    268 p.

    A comprehensive account of the history, acoustics,
    and construction of the flute. Includes details of the
    well-known Boehn-Gordon controversy and a section on the
    care and maintenance of the instrument.

66. Boehm, Theobald. *The Flute and Flute-Playing in
    Acoustical, Technical, and Artistic Aspects*. Trans-
    lated by Dayton C. Miller. New York: Dover, 1964.
    197 p.

    Reprinted, with a new introduction by Samuel Baron,
    from the second edition (1922), published by Miller.
    Provides the fundamental account of Boehm's improved
    flute. Also discusses flute technique and musical inter-
    pretation, Includes many helpful annotations by
    Miller.

67. Fitzgibbon, H. Macaulay. *Story of the Flute*. 2nd ed.
    London: Reeves, 1928. 292 p.

    In addition to a straightforward history of the
    instrument, includes chapters on women and the flute,
    the flute in English literature, and flute curiosities
    (walking-stick flutes, one-armed flutes, etc.).

68. Galleras, Roger. *Histoire de la flûte*. Pau: Moderne,
    1977. 89 p.

An attractive, well-illustrated survey. Includes a discussion of primitive and non-western instruments. Also includes a list of prominent performers, a brief discussion of the technique of flute playing, and a list of contest pieces from the Paris Conservatory, 1897-1976.

69. Girard, Adrien. *Histoire et richesses de la flûte.* Paris: Gründ, 1953. 143 p.

Reviews the history of the flute, describes its characteristics, extols its virtues, lists prominent flutists from the fifteenth to the twentieth century, and provides a lengthy chronological list of music. The first part of the list (to the late nineteenth century) is annotated. Illustrations include a selection of paintings depicting flutes.

70. Kölbel, Herbert. *Von der Flöte: Brevier für Flötenspieler.* 2nd ed. Kassel: Bärenreiter, 1966. 249 p.

Describes the acoustics of the flute, traces its history through Boehm, briefly discusses its playing technique, surveys the flute literature. Also sketches the biographies of prominent players from the past and offers suggestions for amateur performers. Valuable partly for its lists of music, especially eighteenth-century music.

* Le Roy, René. *Traité de la flûte, historique, technique et pedagogique.* Paris: Éditions musicales transatlantiques, 1966. 103 p.

Cited below as Item 829.

71. Rockstro, Richard S. *A Treatise on the Construction, the History, and the Practice of the Flute.* 2nd ed. London: Musica Rara, 1928; reprint ed., London: Musica Rara, 1967. 664 p.

First edition published in 1890. A remarkably thorough and comprehensive account. Includes a list of music for flute, biographical sketches of important performers, and an extended discussion of temperament and acoustics.

72. Scheck, Gustav. *Die Flöte und ihre Musik.* Mainz: Schott, 1975. 263 p.

Traces the history of the transverse flute, reviews its acoustics, describes the physiology of tone production, and discusses articulation. Also discusses finger techniques and--at considerable length--the interpretation of eighteenth-century music.

73. Sconzo, Fortunato. *Il flauto e i flautisti*. Milan:
    Hoepli, 1930. 180 p.

    A brief historical account of the flute together with
    a biographical dictionary of flutists and composers of
    music for the flute.

74. Southgate, T. Lea. "The Evolution of the Flute." *Pro-
    ceedings of the Musical Association* 34 (1907-08):
    155-75.

    Interesting as a reflection of what in the past some-
    times passed for scholarship.

75. Wetzger, Paul. *Die Flöte*. Heilbronn: Schmidt, [1905].
    78 p.

    Traces the history of the instrument up to the twentieth
    century. Briefly describes its use in the music of
    the eighteenth and nineteenth centuries.

76. Willms, Wolfgang. "Die Geschichte und Entwicklung der
    Querflöte." *Das Musikinstrument* 21, no. 2 (February
    1972): 158-60.

    A survey notable for its illustration of thirty-five
    instruments, mostly from the nineteenth century.

                    2. Oboe and English Horn

77. Bate, Philip. *The Oboe: An Outline of Its History,
    Development, and Construction*. 3rd ed. New York:
    Norton, 1975. 236 p.

    A comprehensive treatment. Contains a discussion of
    the acoustics of the oboe and provides biographical
    sketches of celebrated European performers of the past.

78. Bechler, Leo, and Bernhardt Rahm. *Die Oboe und die ihr
    verwandten Instrumente nebst biographischen Skizzen der
    bedeutendsten ihrer Meister*. Leipzig: Merseburger,
    1914; reprint eds., Wiesbaden: Sändig, 1972; Buren:
    Knuf, 1978. 98 p.

    Reviews the historical development of the oboe and
    related instruments, provides thumbnail sketches of the
    lives of prominent players of the past, and illustrates

the use of the instruments by means of musical examples
from the Classic and Romantic periods. Bound together
with Losch, cited below as Item 1092.

79. Bigotti, Giovanni. *Storia dell'oboe e sua letteratura*.
    Padua: Zanibon, 1974. 77 p.

    Traces the history and discusses the construction of
    all members of the oboe family. Notes famous performers
    and lists music for the oboe and English horn.

80. Goossens, Léon, and Edwin Roxburgh. *Oboe*. London:
    Macdonald and Jane, 1977. 236 p.

    An uncomplicated introduction to the instrument, its
    technique, and its literature. Includes a chapter by
    Roxburgh on the performance of Baroque music. Also
    includes a list of music and a discography.

81. Joppig, Günther. *Oboe & Fagott: Ihre Geschichte, ihre
    Nebeninstrumente und ihre Musik*. Bern: Hallwag,
    1981. 196 p.

    Traces the evolution of the instruments from the
    Middle Ages to the present. Includes a discussion of
    related instruments (English horn, sarrusophone, etc.)
    and a survey of important solo literature.

3. Bassoon

82. Heckel, Wilhelm. *Der Fagott*. Bierbrich am Rhein:
    Heckel, 1899. 32 p.

    Summarizes the history of the bassoon, describes its
    characteristics, and explains the advantages of the
    instrument made by Heckel. The *Nachtrag* (7pp.), published
    in 1901, describes further, more recent improvements
    to the instrument.

83. Jansen, Will. *The Bassoon: Its History, Construction,
    Makers, Players and Music*. Buren: Knuf, 1978.
    1818 p.

    Published in twelve fascicles, including two fascicles
    of plates (260 in all). Brings together an enormous
    amount of information about the history and acoustics
    of the bassoon and contrabassoon, their makers, reeds,

various elements of performance (including medical
aspects), composers, performers, and music. Includes an
extensive annotated bibliography of music as well as
a biographical dictionary of performers. Curiously
organized and published without an index.

* Joppig, Günther. *Oboe & Fagott: Ihre Geschichte, ihre
Nebeninstrumente und ihre Musik.* Bern: Hallwag, 1981.
196 p.

Cited above as Item 81.

84. Langwill, Lyndesay G. *The Bassoon and Contrabassoon.*
New York: Norton, 1965. 269 p.

The standard account. Traces the history of the
instruments, discusses their construction, and provides
sketches of the lives of prominent players, mostly
British. Includes a discography.

85. ————. *The Bassoon and Double Bassoon: A Short Illustrated History of Their Origin, Development, and
Makers.* London: Hinrichsen, [ca. 1963]. 40 p.

A useful, authoritative introduction. Includes brief
descriptions of various kinds of modern instruments--
British, Italian, and Czech as well as French and German.

4. Clarinet and Basset Horn

86. Altenburg, Wilhelm. *Die Klarinette: Ihre Entstehung
und Entwicklung bis zur Jetztzeit in akustischer,
technischer und musikalischer Beziehung.* Heilbronn:
Schmidt, 1904. 46 p.

The most comprehensive early twentieth-century
treatment. Focuses primarily on the development of
the instrument during the nineteenth century. Includes
a brief discussion of bass and contrabass clarinets
as well as of the saxophone.

87. Brymer, Jack. *Clarinet.* New York: Schirmer Books,
1977. 267 p.

Includes an account of the history and development
of the clarinet, a review of its acoustics, a selective
annotated bibliography of music, and a discography. Also
describes the various national schools of clarinet
playing. Well illustrated.

88. Drushler, Paul. *The Clarinet: Its Evolution, Literature, and Artists*. Rochester, N.Y.: Shal-u-mo Publications, 1973. 10 p.

   A collection of attractively designed charts notable partly for idiosyncratic content and spelling.

89. Eberst, Anton. *Klarnet od A do Z*. Krakow: Polskie Wydawnictow Muzyczne, 1971. 214 p.

   Surveys the history of the clarinet, discusses performance technique, and provides a comprehensive list of clarinet music.

90. Kroll, Oskar. *The Clarinet*. Translated by Hilda Morris. London: Batsford, 1968. 183 p.

   A brief history of the instrument, together with an extended discussion of its literature. Includes biographical sketches of well-known clarinetists and a list of repertory, which was prepared by Diethard Riehm.

91. Pino, David. *The Clarinet and Clarinet Playing*. New York: Scribner, 1980. 306 p.

   A comprehensive account written in a rather colloquial style. Includes an unreliable history of the instrument, a list of clarinet music, and a curious selective bibliography.

92. Rendall, F. Geoffrey. *The Clarinet: Some Notes upon Its History and Construction*. 3rd ed. Revised by Philip Bate. New York: Norton, 1971. 206 p.

   The standard discussion of the history and acoustics of the instrument. Includes a list of music and a good bibliography.

93. Richmond, Stanley. *Clarinet and Saxophone Experience*. New York: St. Martin's Press, 1972. 137 p.

   Includes clear discussions of mouthpiece lays, reed and key adjustment, embouchure, and alternate fingerings. Also includes a general discussion of acoustics. Questions relating specifically to the saxophone are touched upon infrequently.

94. Saam, Josef. *Das Bassetthorn, seine Erfindung und Weiterbildung*. Mainz: Schott, 1971. 72 p.

   Includes a descriptive list of basset horns found in various collections as well as a good discussion of Mozart's relationship to the instrument. Also includes a list of works for the instrument and a discussion of early virtuoso performers. Excerpted in *Acta Mozartiana* 17 (1970): 58-72.

95. Street, Oscar W. "The Clarinet and Its Music." *Proceedings of the Musical Association* 42 (1915-16): 89-115.

   Traces the evolution of the instrument and surveys its use from Mozart to Rimsky-Korsakov and Sir Charles Stanford.

5. Saxophone

96. Kool, Jaap. *Das Saxophon.* Leipzig: Weber, 1931. 280 p.

   A comprehensive survey of the acoustics, construction, history, and use of the saxophone. Includes a discussion of tone production. Well illustrated with drawings and photographs.

97. Perrin, Marcel. *Le saxophone, son histoire, sa technique, son utilisation.* Paris: Fischbacher, [1955]; reprint ed., Paris: Éditions d'aujourd'hui, 1977. 167 p.

   A rather curious collection of discussions of radio, motion pictures, saxophone teaching, music written for the saxophone, and twentieth-century performers, including the Quatuor de Saxophones de Paris. An unpublished English translation by Sylvia Pozarnsky Obr is available at the University of Iowa Library.

* Richmond, Stanley. *Clarinet and Saxophone Experience.* New York: St. Martin's Press, 1972. 137 p.

   Cited above as Item 93.

98. Ventzke, Karl, and Claus Raumberger. *Die Saxophone: Beiträge zur Baucharakteristik und Geschichte einer Musikinstrumentenfamilie.* Frankfurt: Das Musikinstrument, 1979. 109 p.

   The most authoritative and comprehensive account of the history, acoustics, and literature of the saxophone. Includes a biography of Adolphe Sax, a history of the saxophone up to 1846, a fascinating chapter on the saxophone in Germany, a description of the acoustics of the instrument, and a comparison--by Dietrich Hilkenbach--of an alto saxophone made by Sax in 1865 with a modern American and a modern French instrument. Also includes a list of makers.

IV

HISTORIES AND COMPREHENSIVE DISCUSSIONS
OF INDIVIDUAL BRASS INSTRUMENTS

1. Trumpet and Related Instruments

99. Arfinengo, Carlo. *La tromba e il trombone*. Ancona,
     Milan: Berben, 1973. 48 p.

     Surveys the history and construction of the instruments
     of the trumpet and trombone families. Also includes
     biographies of classical and jazz performers.

100. Bate, Philip. *The Trumpet and Trombone: An Outline of
     Their History, Development, and Construction*. 2nd ed.
     New York: Norton, 1978. 300 p.

     A comprehensive discussion. Includes a description of
     the acoustical behavior of both instruments. Discusses
     celebrated players, manufacturing techniques, musical
     capabilities, and the place of the instruments in the
     orchestra.

101. Frei-Rauber, Herbert. *Trompete und Trompeter*. Mellingen:
     Herbert Frei, 1976. 48 p.

     Traces the evolution of the instrument and its use.
     Describes the history of trumpet performance and lists
     222 contemporary performers.

102. Lasko, Richard. "The Historical Evolution of the Flugel-
     horn." *Brass World* 2 (1966): 128-36, 162-70; 3
     (1967): 211-17.

     A brief survey followed by a selection of excerpts from
     orchestral, band, and chamber literature.

103. Overton, Friend Robert. *Der Zink*. Mainz: Schott, 1981.
     260 p.

A comprehensive and probably exhaustive treatment of
the instrument, its history, repertory, construction,
and playing technique. Includes a list of instruments
preserved in European museums. Also provides biographical
information about the known performers on the instrument
and offers a bibliography of music employing it. Well
illustrated. Essential to the study of the early history
of cup-mouthpiece instruments.

104. Pietzsch, Hermann. *Die Trompete als Orchester-Instrument
     und ihre Behandlung in den verschiedenen Epochen der
     Musik/The Trumpet as Orchestral Instrument and Its
     Treatment During the Different Periods of Musical
     Culture.* Rev. ed. Ann Arbor: University Music Press,
     [1950]. 172 p.

     Reprint of 1911 edition, which was published in German
     with a facing English translation by John Bernhoff. The
     reprint edition includes a new, somewhat edited transla-
     tion by Clifford P. Lillya and Renold Schilke. Traces
     the history and use of the trumpet and provides a gener-
     ous selection of excerpts for natural and valve instru-
     ments.

105. Tarr, Edward H. *Die Trompete: Ihre Geschichte von der
     Antike bis zur Gegenwart.* Bern: Hallwag, 1977. 147 p.

     An authoritative, well-illustrated historical survey.
     Includes a recording that illustrates a variety of kinds
     of trumpet and cornet playing.

                      2. Trombone and Tuba

*   Arfinengo, Carlo. *La tromba e il trombone.* Ancona,
     Milan: Bèrben, 1973. 48 p.

     Cited above as Item 99.

*   Bate, Philip. *The Trumpet and the Trombone: An Outline
     of Their History, Development, and Construction.* 2nd
     ed. New York: Norton, 1978. 300 p.

     Cited above as Item 100.

106. Bevan, Clifford. *The Tuba Family.* London: Faber and
     Faber, 1978. 303 p.

Thorough and comprehensive. Includes a useful glossary of instrument names, a translation of Wieprecht's tuba patent, a list of music, and a good bibliography.

107. Gregory, Robin. *The Trombone: The Instrument and Its Music.* New York: Praeger, 1973. 328 p.

The standard account. Discusses the acoustics of the trombone, its use as an orchestral instrument, and recent developments in performance techniques. Describes the various types of trombones, including Baroque trombones and their modern copies. Includes a classified list of works for the trombone, including ensemble music.

*   Maxted, George. *Talking About the Trombone.* London: Baker, 1970. 63 p.

Cited below as Item 832.

108. Rischaug, Harry. "Trombonen." Ph.D. dissertation, University of Trondheim, 1973. 200 p.

Traces the history and describes the acoustics of the trombone. Also discusses the pedagogy of the instrument.

109. Sumerkin, Viktor. *Trombon.* Moscow: Muzyka, 1975. 78 p.

Reviews the history of the trombone and the development of its playing technique. Describes the history of trombone performance practice from the fifteenth century to the present. Stresses the development of the instrument in Russia.

3. Horn

110. Brüchle, Bernhard, and Kurt Janetzky. *Kulturgeschichte des Horns: Ein Bildsachbuch/A Pictorial History of the Horn.* Tutzing: Schneider, 1976. 303 p.

An exceptionally attractive selection of photographs, drawings, paintings, facsimiles of music, and documents, accompanied by succinct descriptions. The text is presented in German and English.

111. Coar, Birchard. *The French Horn.* DeKalb, Ill.: Coar, 1947. 102 p.

Traces the history of the instrument, offers a number of technical suggestions, and sets forth some principles of teaching.

112. Gregory, Robin. *The Horn: A Comprehensive Guide to the
      Modern Instrument and Its Music*. New York: Praeger,
      1969. 410 p.

      Includes a brief account of the instrument's history and
      a description of its acoustics and valve mechanisms.
      Discusses questions of technique and the role of the horn
      in orchestral and chamber music. Also provides a compre-
      hensive list of music for horn.

113. Janetzky, Kurt, and Bernhard Brüchle. *Das Horn: Eine
      kleine Chronik seines Werdens und Wirkens*. Bern:
      Hallwag, 1977. 112 p.

      A lavishly illustrated, attractively presented overview.

114. Morley Pegge, Reginald. *The French Horn: Some Notes
      on the Evolution of the Instrument and of Its Technique*.
      2nd ed. New York: Norton, 1973. 222 p.

      A careful account of the history of the instrument and
      of the evolution of the technique of horn playing.
      Includes a chapter on horn manufacture and biographical
      sketches of important players and teachers of the past.
      Also includes a list of makers and a good bibliography.
      First edition published in 1960.

115. Righini, Pietro. *Il corno*. Ancona, Milan: Berben,
      1972. 60 p.

      Traces the history of the instrument and sketches the
      biographies of several famous players of the past.

V

SPECIALIZED DISCUSSIONS REGARDING WIND
AND PERCUSSION INSTRUMENTS IN GENERAL

* Altenburg, Detlef. "Musikinstrumentenbau in Köln."
  Studien zur Musikgeschichte des Rheinlandes, vol. 4,
  edited by K.W. Neimöller (Cologne: Arno Volk, 1975),
  pp. 89-99.

  Cited below as Item 588.

116. *Art du faiseur d'instruments de musique et lutherie.*
     Geneva: Minkoff, 1972. 186 p.

     Facsimile reprint of various parts of the *Arts et
     métiers mécaniques* section of Diderot's *Encyclopédie
     méthodique*. Reflects fully the state of knowledge at
     the time. Well illustrated.

117. Baines, Anthony. "James Talbot's Manuscript (Christ
     Church Library Music MS 1187)." *Galpin Society
     Journal* 1 (1948): 9-26.

     Transcribes a seventeenth-century inventory of
     instruments, complete with descriptions and measurements.

118. ————. "Two Cassel Inventories." *Galpin Society
     Journal* 4 (1951): 30-38.

     Translates and comments upon the inventories of musical
     instruments belonging to the Cassel Hofkapelle in
     1573 and 1613. The inventories are published in Ernst
     Zulauf, *Beiträge zur Geschichte der landgräflich-
     hessischen Hofkapelle zu Cassel bis auf die Zeit Moritz
     den Gelehrten* (Kassel: L. Döll, 1902).

119. Barancev, Anatolij. "Obučenie igre na duhovyh instrumentah
     v Rossii konca XVIII-načala XX vekov." Ph.D.
     dissertation, Leningrad Conservatory, 1974.

Traces the history of the training of Russian wind players from the end of the eighteenth century to 1917. Describes Russian teaching methods and analyzes method books of the past.

120. *Bericht über die erste internationale Fachtagung zur Forschung der Blasmusik, Graz 1974.* Edited by Wolfgang Suppan and Eugen Brixel. Alta musica, vol. 1. Tutzing: Schneider, 1976. 319 p.

A major collection of essays regarding wind music, especially music for wind ensembles of various kinds. Includes articles cited here by Detlef Altenburg (Item 993), Hellmut Federhofer (Item 139), Werner J. Düring (Item 137), Walter Biber (Item 955), George Karstädt (Item 1015), Friedrich Körner (Item 354), and Jürgen Eppelsheim (Item 253).

121. *Die Blasinstrumente und ihre Verwendung sowie zu Fragen des Tempos in der ersten Hälfte des 18. Jahrhunderts: Konferenzbericht der 4. Wissenschaftlichen Arbeitstagung Blankenburg/Harz, 16./27. Juni 1976.* Edited by Eitelfriedrich Thom. Magdeburg: Rat des Bezirkes; Leipzig: Zentralhaus für Kulturarbeit, 1977. 92 p.

Includes articles cited here by Wolfgang Wenke (Item 168). Ludwig Güttler (Item 875), Karol Bula (Item 124), Lukás Matousek (Item 301), and Peter Damm (Item 404).

122. Brown, Howard Mayer. *Sixteenth-Century Instrumentation: The Music for the Florentine Intermedii.* N.p.: American Institute of Musicology, 1973. 229 p.

Includes a good discussion of the use of wind instruments in consort.

123. Brucker, Fritz. *Die Blasinstrumente in der altfranzösischen Literatur.* Giessen: Romanische Seminar, 1926. 145 p.

Surveys the treatment of wind instruments in French literature of the late Middle Ages and Renaissance. An invaluable source for information about the role of instruments during the period. Includes tables showing the combinations of instruments that were employed under various circumstances.

124. Bula, Karol. "Blasinstrumente in der polnischen Musikpraxis der ersten Hälfte des 18. Jahrhunderts." *Die*

Blasinstrumente und ihre Verwendung, edited by
Eitelfriedrich Thom. Magdeburg: Rat des Bezirkes;
Leipzig: Zentralhaus für Kulturarbeit, 1977, pp.
26-32.

Cites instances of wind instrument usage in Poland
during the late seventeenth and early eighteenth
centuries. Notes the revival of old music in Poland
today.

125. Burney, Charles. *An Eighteenth-Century Musical Tour
in France and Italy*. Edited by Percey A. Scholes.
Dr. Burney's Musical Tours in Europe, vol. 1. London:
Oxford University Press, 1959. 328 p.

The definitive edition of *The Present State of Music
in France and Italy* (1771/1773). Valuable partly for
Burney's descriptions of wind playing, including the
use of the serpent as an accompanying instrument in
church. Facsimile of the 1773 edition published New
York: AMS Press, 1976.

126. ————. *An Eighteenth-Century Musical Tour in Central
Europe and the Netherlands*. Edited by Percy A.
Scholes. Dr. Burney's Musical Tours in Europe,
vol. 2. London: Oxford University Press, 1959.
268 p.

A carefully annotated edition of Burney's *The Present
State of Music in Germany, The Netherlands, and United
Provinces* (1773/1775). Provides a number of descriptions
of wind playing.

127. Byrne, Maurice. "The Church Band at Swalcliffe."
Galpin Society Journal 17 (1964): 89-98.

Provides information about instruments and instrument
makers of the late eighteenth century.

128. Carse, Adam. *The Orchestra from Beethoven to Berlioz*.
Cambridge: Heffer, 1948. 514 p.

The standard account. Includes descriptions of the
instruments in use during the period.

129. ————. *The Orchestra in the XVIIIth Century*. Cambridge:
Heffer, 1940. 176 p.

Valuable especially for the details provided regarding
the constitution of the orchestras of the period.

130.   Castellani, Marcello.   "A 1593 Veronese Inventory."
       Galpin Society Journal 26 (1973):   15-24.

       Describes the inventory of Count Mario Bevilacqua's
       collection of instruments, which included six trans-
       verse flutes, a bassoon, and two trombones.

131.   Clemencic, René.   *Old Musical Instruments: Pleasures
       and Treasures*.   Translated by David Hermges.   New
       York: Putnam, 1968.   120 p.

       Outlines the history, construction, and tone quality
       of instruments from the Renaissance through the Classic
       period.

*   Closson, Ernest.   *La facture des instruments de musique
       en Belgique*.   Brussels: Degrace & Huy, [1935].   108 p.

       Cited below as Item 593.

132.   Crouch, Rebekah E.   "The Contributions of Adolphe Sax
       to the Wind Band."   Ph.D. dissertation, Florida
       State University, 1968.   134 p.   UM 69-587.

       Traces the evolution of the instrument of wind bands
       during the eighteenth and early nineteenth centuries.
       Notes Sax's influence in the reorganization of French
       military bands in the 1840s.   Summarized in *Journal
       of Band Research* 5, no. 2 (Spring 1969):   29-42; 6, no.
       1 (Fall 1969):   59-62.

133.   Culka, Zdeněk.   "Inventáře hudebnich nástrojů a hudebnin
       piaristicke koleje Kosmonosich."   *Přispěvky k dějinám
       ceské hudby* 2 (1972):   5-43.

       An annotated edition of two early eighteenth-century
       inventories of music and instruments from the Bohemian
       city of Kosmonosy.

134.   Dart, Thurston.   "Music and Musical Instruments in
       Cotgrave's *Dictionarie* (1611)."   *Galpin Society
       Journal* 21 (1968):   70-80.

       Reprints the definitions of musical terms and instru-
       ment names found in Randle Cotgrave's *Dictionarie of
       the French and English Tongues*.

*   Denis, Valentin.   *De Muziekinstrumenten in de Neder-
       landen en in Italie naar hun afbeelding in de 15e-
       eeuwsche kunst*.   Antwerp: Standard-Boekhandel, 1944.
       352 p.

Cited below as Item 1173.

135. Dräger, Hans-Heinz. "Blasinstrumentenbau." *Die Musik in Geschichte und Gegenwart*, edited by Friedrich Blume. Kassel: Bärenreiter, 1949- . Vol. 1 (1949-51), cols. 1894-1906.

A careful comparative survey of the form and construction of wind instruments. Includes a good bibliography.

136. Draper, F.C. *The Design and Manufacture of Musical Instruments*. London: Boosey and Hawkes, 1957. 35 p.

Deals primarily with problems of manufacture.

137. Düring, Werner Joachim. "Blasmusik am Dreikönigsgynmasium zu Köln." *Bericht über die erste internationale Fachtagung zur Erforschung der Blasmusik, Graz 1974*, edited by Wolfgang Suppan and Eugen Brixel. Alta Musica, vol. 1. Tutzing: Schneider, 1976, p. 103-07.

Sketches the history of wind music at the oldest gymnasium in Cologne during the period 1552-1798 and briefly describes musical activities at the gymnasium today.

138. Euting, Ernst. *Zur Geschichte der Blasinstrumente im 16. und 17. Jahrhundert*. Berlin: A. Schulze, 1899. 48 p.

A pioneering account. Describes briefly the construction and acoustics of wind instruments, summarizes their treatment in theoretical works from the sixteenth and seventeenth centuries, and surveys their treatment in the music of the period. Includes a table showing the instrumentation employed by various composers, from Giovanni Gabrieli to Purcell and Reiche.

139. Federhofer, Hellmut. "Blasinstrumente und Blasermusik in der Steiermark bis zum Ende des 18. Jahrhunderts." *Bericht über die erste internationale Fachtagung zur Enforschung der Blasmusik, Graz 1974*, edited by Wolfgang Suppan and Eugen Brixel. Alta musica, vol. 1. Tutzing: Schneider, 1976, p. 61-101.

Surveys wind instruments, their music and performers in Styria from the late Middle Ages to the end of the eighteenth century. Includes transcriptions of pertinent documents.

140. Fox, Lilla M. *Instruments of Processional Music.*
London: Lutterworth, 1967. 127 p.

     Surveys the development and use primarily of band
     instruments. Lists the instrumentation of various
     British bands from the sixteenth century to the pre-
     sent.

141. Haensel, Robert. "Die Stadtpfeifer und die Stadtkapelle
     in Lobenstein." *Festschrift zur Ehrung von Heinrich
     Albert (1604-1651)*, edited by Günther Kraft. Weimar:
     Uschmann, 1954, pp. 36-38.

     Briefly describes the role of the town musicians in
     Lobenstein and lists the names of twelve who are known.

142. Halfpenny, Eric. "An Eighteenth-Century Trade List
     of Musical Instruments." *Galpin Society Journal*
     17 (1964): 99-102.

     Reprints a list that represents a relatively full
     catalog of instruments in use at the time (*ca.* 1765).

143. ————. "Musicians at James II's Coronation." *Music
     and Letters* 32 (1951): 103-14.

     Provides details about the musicians who took part
     in the coronation procession. Discusses their instru-
     ments and some aspects of the playing technique.

144. Kade, Reinhard. "Die Leipziger Stadtpfeifer." *Monats-
     hefte für Musikgeschichte* 21 (1889): 194-95.

     Points out the proud Leipzig tradition of employing
     town musicians. The tradition extends at least
     as far back as 1479.

145. Kastner, Georges. *Manuel général de musique militaire
     à l'usage des armées français.* Paris: Didot, 1848;
     facsimile reprint, Geneva: Minkoff, 1973. 410 p.

     An invaluable source of information about the period.
     Includes a history of military music, a description
     of the instruments employed--among them instruments
     invented by Sax--and a collection of excerpts from
     documents related to military music. Also includes
     trumpet calls and drum cadences employed in military
     music.

146. Keller, Jindřich. "Pištelnici a trubaři. Pojednání o
     výrobe dechových hudebních nástroju v Cechách před

rokem 1800." *Sborník Národního muzea v Praze.* *Acta musei nationalis pragae* 29 (1975): 161-243.

Compiles forty inventories of instruments from the years 1644-1833. Surveys wind instrument manufactured in Bohemia before 1800. Offers information about makers. Indexes the instruments in the collection of the Prague National Museum.

* Köchel, Ludwig Ritter von. *Die kaiserliche Hof-Musikkapelle in Wien von 1543 bis 1867.* Vienna: Beck, 1869. 160 p.

Cited below as Item 658.

147. Krickeberg, Dieter. "Die Orchesterinstrumente im literarischen Werk E.T.A. Hoffmanns." *Jahrbuch des Staatlichen Instituts für Musikforschung Preussischer Kulturbesitz 1979/80.* Berlin: Merseburger, 1981, pp. 101-12.

Reports Hoffmann's descriptions of the character and sound quality of various orchestral instruments. Also notes their symbolic role in his works.

* LaRue, Jan, and Howard Brofsky. "Parisian Brass Players, 1751-1793." *Brass Quarterly* 3 (1959-60): 133-40.

Cited below as Item 663.

148. Leppert, Richard D. *The Theme of Music in Flemish Paintings of the Seventeenth Century.* 2 vols. Munich: Katzbichler, 1977. 288, 218 p.

Examines the representation of musical instruments in 770 paintings. Illustrated with 131 plates. Based on the author's Ph.D. dissertation, Indiana University, 1973.

149. Levin, Semen. *Lukhovye instrumenty v istorii muzykal'noi kul'tury.* Leningrad: Muzyka, 1973. 262 p.

Traces the history of wind instruments, mainly European, from the earliest times to the eighteenth century. Also offers a separate account of their development in Russia up to the nineteenth century.

150. MacGillivray, James A. "Woodwind and Other Orchestral Instruments in Russia Today." *Galpin Society Journal* 10 (1957): 3-9.

Surveys the types of instruments in use.

151. McLeish, Martin. "An Inventory of Musical Instruments at the Royal Palace, Madrid, in 1602." *Galpin Society Journal* 21 (1968): 108-28.

    Translates and discusses an inventory of a large and varied collection.

152. Marsh, John. "Hints to Young Composers of Instrumental Music." *Galpin Society Journal* 18 (1965): 57-71.

    Written *ca.* 1806. Includes general descriptions of instruments and gives some insight into orchestral playing of the period. Prefaced by a new introduction by Charles Cudworth.

153. Meer, John Henry van der. "Musikinstrumentenbau in Bayern bis 1800." *Musik in Bayern*, edited by Robert Münster and Hans Schmidt. Tutzing: Schneider, 1972. Vol. 2, pp. 17-38.

    Describes instrument building in Mittenwald, Fussen, Munich, Augsburg, and especially Nuremberg, which was important for its wind instruments.

154. Meyer, Jürgen. "Die Problematik der Qualitätsbestimmung bei Musikinstrumenten." *Instrumentenbau* 31 (1977): 241-28.

    Observes that the determination of the quality of instruments depends on psychological as well as objective factors.

155. Nef, Karl. "Die Stadtpfeiferei und die Instrumental-musiker in Basel (1385-1814)." *Sammelbände der Internationalen Musikgesellschaft* 10 (1908-09): 395-98.

    A brief survey based partly on archival sources.

156. Oberkogler, Friedrich. *Vom Wesen und Werden der Musikin-strumente*. Schaffhausen: Novalis, 1976. 175 p.

    Interweaves history and descriptions with attempts to define the mythic and symbolic significance of the instruments. Oberkogler appears to be strongly influenced by Rudolph Steiner.

157. Poole, H. Edmund. "A Catalogue of Musical Instruments Offered for Sale in 1839 by D'Almaine & Co., 20 Soho

Square." *Galpin Society Journal* 35 (1982): 2-36.

Reports the discovery of a sale catalog, summarizes the activities of the firm, reprints the catalog, and discusses its contents.

158. Robinson, Trevor. *The Amateur Wind Instrument Maker.* Rev. ed. [Amherst]: University of Massachusetts Press, 1980. 116 p.

Concerned largely with Renaissance and Baroque instruments. Provides diagrams, measurements, and instructions.

159. Salmen, Walter, ed. *The Social Status of the Professional Musician from the Middle Ages to the 19th Century.* Translated by Herbert Kaufman and Barbara Reisner. New York: Pendragon, 1983. 281 p.

A valuable collection of essays, including--among others--essays by Werner Braun on the *Hautboist* (cited below as Item 222), by Heinrich W. Schwab on the town musician, by Dieter Krickeberg on the folk musician, by Richard Petzoldt on the economic conditions of the musicians, and by Christoph-Hellmut Mahling on the German court orchestral musician.

160. Salzedo, Leonard, and Peter E.M. Sharp. "Designs on Music: Changing the Instruments." *Design*, no. 220 (April 1967): 24-33.

Makes the point that many orchestral instruments could be improved using the resources of modern technology and notes changes that could be made.

* Schneider, Willy. *Handbuch der Blasmusik: Ein Wegweiser für Bläser und Dirigenten.* Mainz: Schott, 1954. 87 p.

Cited above as Item 44.

* Selfridge-Field, Eleanor. "Annotated Membership Lists of the Venetian Instrumentalists' Guild, 1672-1727." *R.M.A. Research Chronicle* 9 (1971): 1-52.

Cited below as Item 678.

* Stauffer, Donald W. *Intonation Deficiencies of Wind Instruments.* Washington, D.C.: Catholic University of America Press, 1954. 191 p.

Cited below as Item 531.

161. Sterl, Raimund Walter. "Regensburgs Musikinstrumenten-
     bauer von der Mitte des 15. Jahrhunderts bis zur
     Neuzeit." *Verhandlungen des Historischen Verein für
     Oberpfalz und Regensburg* 113 (1973): 145-60.

     Includes a list of all the extant historical instru-
     ments in Regensburg. Also discusses instrument
     building in Regensburg.

162. Sundberg, Johan. "The 'Scale' of Musical Instruments."
     Svensk tidskrift for musikforskning 49 (1967):
     119-33.

     Explores the general notion of instrument scale in
     light of the measurement of the fundamental frequencies
     of various instruments.

163. Suppan, Wolfgang. *Lexikon des Blasmusikwesens*. 2nd ed.
     Freiburg im Breisgau: Schulz, 1976. 342 p.

     A handbook for conductors of wind ensembles. Includes
     a biographical dictionary of composers, a history of
     the wind ensemble and its music, and an excellent
     bibliography.

164. Trichet, Pierre. *Traité des instruments de musique*.
     Neuilly-sur-Seine: Société de musique d'autrefois,
     1957. 186 p.

     Publication of a manuscript compiled *ca.* 1640 that
     attempts to trace the etymology of the names of
     instruments. Points out the occasions when various
     instruments might suitably be employed. With notes and
     introduction by François Lesure.

165. Turrentine, Edgar M. "A Translation of Jean-Jacques
     Rousseau's *Concerning Military Music*." *Journal of
     Band Research* 8, no. 2 (Spring 1972): 40-43.

     Prefaced by a discussion of the date of the essay,
     which Turrentine places between 1748 and 1756.

166. Usov, Jurij, ed. *Metodika obučenija igre na dohuvyh
     instrumentah*, 4. Moscow: Muzyka, 1975. 225 p.

     A collection of ten essays on wind instrument per-
     formance and music, including essays by V. Petrov
     on Mozart's clarinet concerto, by V. Bujanovskij on
     the *Waldhorn*, and by V. Apatskij on an experimental

investigation of breathing and embouchure.

167. ———. *Istorija otečestvennogo ispolnitel'stva na duhovyh instrumentah.* Moscow: Muzyka, 1975. 199 p.

Traces the history of wind instrument performance in Russia. Lists Soviet teachers and their writings on performance.

168. Wenke, Wolfgang. "Die Hol- und Metallblasinstrumente der ersten Hälfte des 18. Jahrhunderts im deutschen Sprachgebeit." *Die Blasinstrumente und ihre Verwendung sowie zu Fragen des Tempos in der ersten Hälfte des 18. Jahrhunderts: Konferenzbericht der 4. Wissenschaftlichen Arbeitstagung Blankenburg/Harz. 16./27. Juni 1976,* edited by Eitelfriedrich Thom. Magdeburg: Rat des Bezirkes; Leipzig: Zentralhaus für Kulturarbeit, 1977, pp. 17-21.

Observes that the sound of eighteenth-century wind instruments was lighter and sharper than that of modern ones.

169. Winternitz, Emanuel. *Musical Instruments and Their Symbolism in Western Art: Studies in Musical Iconology.* 2nd ed. New Haven, Conn.: Yale University Press, 1979. 253 p.

A groundbreaking work. Centers on the depiction of musical instruments in Renaissance art. Includes ninety-six plates.

170. Young, Thomas Campbell. *The Making of Musical Instruments.* London: Oxford University Press, 1939; reprint ed., Freeport, N.Y.: Books for Libraries Press, 1969. 190 p.

A non-technical introduction to manufacturing techniques.

VI

SPECIALIZED DISCUSSIONS REGARDING
INDIVIDUAL WOODWIND INSTRUMENTS

1. Flute and Piccolo

171. Bate, Philip. "The Alex Murray Flute." *Galpin Society
      Journal* 26 (1973): 47-54.

      Describes with approval the new flute made by Murray,
      with the help of Albert Cooper, during the late 1950s
      and the 1960s. Also see Items 192 and 200 cited below.

172. Boehm, Theobald. *On the Construction of Flutes/Über
      den Flötenbau.* Buren: Knuf, 1982. 154 p.

      A facsimile edition of Boehm's treatise (1847)
      together with an English translation by W.S. Broadwood
      (1882) and a new introduction and notes, in German
      and in English, by Karl Ventzke.

173. Bowers, Jane M. "The French Flute School from 1700
      to 1760." Ph.D. dissertation, University of California,
      Berkeley, 1971. 491 p.

      A comprehensive discussion of instruments, technique,
      and literature.

174. ————. "New Light on the Development of the Transverse
      Flute between about 1650 and about 1770." *Journal of
      the American Musical Instrument Society* 3 (1977):
      5-56.

      Deduces that single-key flutes still extant should not
      be dated earlier than *ca.* 1680, that the single-key
      flute remained standard into the second decade of the
      eighteenth century, that the three-piece instrument
      continued to be popular through the 1720s, and that the
      design of the four-piece flute remained relatively

unaltered from the 1720s at least to 1770. Also
discusses the biographies of flute makers.

175. Byrne, Maurice. "Biglioni." *Galpin Society Journal* 24
(1971): 106.

Dates the flute in the Lindsey Mason Collection *ca*. 1820.

176. ────. "Schuchart and the Extended Foot-Joint."
Galpin Society Journal 18 (1965): 7-13.

Reports and discusses advertisements from 1756 that
shed light on the life of the instrument maker Charles
Schuchart and on the invention of an extended foot
joint for the flute.

177. Castellani, Marcello. "Two Late-Renaissance Transverse
Flutes" *Galpin Society Journal* 25 (1972): 73-79.

Provides measurements of two instruments from the
collection of the Accademia Filarmonica in Verona.

178. Du Bois, Elizabeth Ann. *A Comparison of Georg Philipp
Telemann's Use of the Recorder and the Transverse
Flute as Seen in His Chamber Works*. Emporia, Kansas:
Emporia State University, 1982. 72 p.

Originally an M.Mus. thesis. Describes the instruments
of the period, discusses Telemann's preferences as to
keys, and lists his works employing recorder and
transverse flute.

179. Eagle, David William. "A Constant Passion and a Constant
Pursuit: A Social History of Flute-Playing in England
from 1800 to 1851." Ph.D. dissertation, University of
Minnesota, 1977. 241 p. UM 78-9653.

A fascinating account of a love for flute playing that
bordered on mania. Includes a discussion of the
musical tastes of the flute players of the day. Notes
that George III, who was known partly for his flute
playing, served as a model for musical amateurs during
the period.

180. Fairley, Andrew. *Flutes, Flautists and Makers*. London:
Pan Educational Music, 1982. 140 p.

An illustrated dictionary of makers, performers, and
terms pertaining to the flute. In regard to makers and
performers, limited to those born before 1900.

181. Farup-Madsen, Inge. "Vivaldis anvendelse af fløjteinstrumenter." *Musik & Forskning* 3 (1977): 182.

     Reviews the question of the kinds of flutes called for by Vivaldi, especially in the concertos, Op. 10.

182. Fleury, Louis. "The Flute and Flutists in the French Art of the Seventeenth and Eighteenth Centuries." *The Musical Quarterly* 9 (1923): 515-37.

     Emphasizes the importance of the flute in French musical life during the late seventeenth and eighteenth centuries. Traces the development of the instrument during the period and summarizes the contributions of various performers and composers.

183. ———. "The Flute and Its Powers of Expression." *Music and Letters* 3 (1922): 382-93.

     Characterizes the eighteenth century as the "Golden Age" of the flute. Points to instances where, to the author's mind, the flute expresses melancholy, sweetness, pathos, and wit and gaiety.

184. Godwin, Joscelyn. "The Renaissance Flute." *Consort* 28 (1972) 71-81.

     Reviews the sparse information available about the Renaissance flute and its use. Provides a composite fingering chart. Summarized in *American Recorder* 13 (1972): 71-72.

185. Halbig, Hermann. "Die Geschichte der Klappe an Flöten und Rohrblattinstrumenten bis zum Beginn des 18. Jahrhunderts." *Archiv für Musikwissenschaft* 6 (1924): 1-53.

     Carefully traces the early history (to the beginning of the eighteenth century) of the design and placement of keys on flutes and double-reed instruments.

186. Halfpenny, Eric. "A Seventeenth-Century Flute d'Allemagne." *Galpin Society Journal* 4 (1951): 42-45.

     Describes the only seventeenth-century transverse flutes found in the British Isles.

187. ———. "Two Rare Transverse Flutes." *Galpin Society Journal* 13 (1960): 38-43.

     Describes a bass flute with wooden tuning slide and a flute by Bressan (*ca.* 1710-15). Includes measurements and photographs.

188. Higbee, Dale. "Michel Corrette on the Piccolo and Speculations Regarding Vivaldi's 'Flautino'." *Galpin Society Journal* 17 (1964): 115-16.

    Suggests that Vivaldi's *flautino* was a piccolo, not a sopranino recorder.

189. Hochstrasser, Gerhardt. "Die Flöte nach System 'Richard Keilwerth'." *Glareana* 24, no. 2 (June 1975): 40-43.

    Describes a conical wooden flute that ceased to be produced in 1974. The instrument had eight to fourteen keys and combined the key system of the Meyer and Schwedler-Kruspe flutes.

190. James, William N. *A Word or Two about the Flute*. Edinburgh: Charles Smith, 1826; reprint ed. London: Tony Bingham, 1982. 252 p.

    Compares the properties of German and English flutes and offers assessments of the performance and compositions of a number of flute players of the period. Reprint edition includes a valuable introduction by Stephen Preston.

191. Krickeberg, Dieter. "Studien zu Stimmung und Klang der Querflöte zwischen 1500 und 1850." *Jahrbuch des Staatlichen Institut für Musikforschung Preussischer Kulturbesitz* 1 (1968): 99 118.

    Compares the sound and intonation of eighteenth-century and nineteenth-century flutes. Reviews the varied approaches of eighteenth-century writers to enharmonic tones.

192. Kujala, Walfrid. "The Murray Flute." *Woodwind Anthology*. Evanston, Ill.: Instrumentalist, 1976, pp. 178-181.

    Describes the advantages of the instrument. Also see Items 171 and 200.

193. Lewis, Paul. "Barbiton and Chrysostom." *Galpin Society Journal* 33 (1980): 125-27.

    Describes two flutes, one named Barbiton and the other Chrysostom, owned by the well-known amateur flutist James Mathews (1827-1900). Both were made by Rudall, Rose and Carte.

194. Libin, Laurence. "Sex and the Flute." *American Recorder* 13, no. 3 (August 1972): 77-85.

Summarizes the opinions of Curt Sachs and others regarding the phallic symbolism of flutes. Discusses the etymology of the word "flute" and the role of the instrument in primitive and ancient cultures. Notes the flute's masculine image in European myth, art, and music, and suggests that through its use in jazz it might be regaining the meaning lost during the last century.

195. Lichtenwanger, William. "Another Treble Flute D'Allemagne by P-J Bressan." *Galpin Society Journal* 15 (1962): 45-48.

Describes and depicts an eighteenth-century flute in the Dayton C. Miller Collection at the Library of Congress.

196. Lorenzo, Leonardo de. *My Complete Story of the Flute.* New York: Citadel Press, 1951. 493 p.

Random comments on the flute, its history, and its music, together with brief biographical sketches of performers. Includes, in a separate section, reminiscences by the author.

197. ————. *To the Nine Muses.* Santa Barbara, Calif.: De Lorenzo, 1957. 25 p.

A strange collection of biographical sketches of flutists and composers, a list of new flute music, announcements of Southern California musical events, jokes, and assorted other trivia. Subtitled *Addenda* [sic] *Number III to My Complete Story of the Flute,* which is cited above as Item 196.

198. Meierott, Lenz. *Die geschichtliche Entwicklung der kleinen Flötentypen und ihre Verwendung in der Musik des 17. und 18. Jahrhunderts.* Tutzing: Schneider, 1974. 275 p.

An exhaustive treatment. Of primary importance in the study of the early history of the piccolo.

* Montagu, Jeremy. "A Query on the Habits of Instrument Makers." *Galpin Society Journal* 27 (1974): 135-37.

Cited below as Item 626.

199. Müller, Georg. *Friedrich der Grosse, seine Flöten und sein Flötenspiel.* Berlin: Parrhysius, [1932]. 20 p.

Briefly discusses Frederick's flute playing and describes the instruments he is known to have owned. Includes detailed measurements of two instruments.

200. Murray, Alexander. "The Murray Flute." *Woodwind World* 12, no. 1 (February 1973): 5, 10, 12.

Describes the instrument designed by the author. Also see Items 171 and 192.

201. Phelan, James, and Mitchell D. Brody. *The Complete Guide to the Flute from Acoustics and Construction to Repair and Maintenance*. Boston: Conservatory Publications, 1980. 109 p.

A clear, straightforward, non-technical treatment.

202. Reidemeister, Peter. "Zwischen Silberflöte und Traverso: Die konische Ringklappenflöte. Mögliche Bereicherung einer einförmigen Scenerie?" *Tibia* 1 (1976): 129-36.

Suggests that Boehm's conical ring-key flute of 1832 should find use today as a compromise between modern and eighteenth-century instruments.

203. Reilly, Edward R. *Quantz and His "Versuch."* [Philadelphia]: American Musicological Society, 1971. 178 p.

Includes a discussion of the early history of the flute, of Quantz's flutes, and of various aspects of performance practice.

204. Ribock, J.J.H. *Bemerkungen über die Flöte und Versuch einer kurzer Anleitung zur bessern Einrichtung und Behandlung der selben*. Stendal: Franzen und Grosse, [1784?]; facsimile reprint, Buren: Knuf, 1980. 62 p.

Important for its description of Ribock's improved flute mechanism and interesting for its complaints made against Tromlitz. Discusses flute embouchure and compares various flutes. Characterized by Rockstro (Item 71) as "prolix and tiresome." Reprint edition includes a useful introduction by Karl Ventzke.

205. Robinson, Trevor. "A Reconstruction of Mersenne's Flute." *Galpin Society Journal* 26 (1973): 84-85.

Gives the dimensions of a flute built following the design described by Mersenne.

*   Rockstro, Richard S. *A Treatise on the Construction,*
           the History, and the Practice of the Flute. 2nd ed.
           London: Musica Rara, 1928; reprint ed., London:
           Musica Rara, 1967. 664 p.

           Cited above as Item 71.

*   Schmid, Manfred Hermann. *Theobald Boehm 1794-1881:*
           Die Revolution der Flöte. Katalog der Ausstellung
           zum 100. Geburtstaf von Boehm. Tutzing: Schneider,
           1981. 192 p.

           Cited below as Item 790.

206. Schmitz, Hans-Peter. *Querflöte und Querflötenspiel in*
      Deutschland während des Barockzeitalters. Kassel:
      Barenreiter, 1952. 89 p.

      A brief but thorough account. Describes the transverse
      flute, the manner in which it was played, and the manner
      in which it was treated by Baroque composers.

207. Shepard, Mark. *How to Love Your Flute: A Guide to*
      Flutes and Flute Playing. Los Angeles: Panjandrum
      Books, 1980. 97 p.

      Includes useful chapters on flute selection and care
      as well as advice on flute playing. States that the
      flute can be "a pathway to wisdom." Intended for
      amateur players.

208. Smith, Catherine P. "Special Expressive Characteristics
      of the Pre-Boehm Transverse Flute." *Woodwind World,*
      Brass and Percussion 13, no. 4 (1974); 14, nos. 1-5
      (1975). *ca.* 15 p.

      Focuses on the qualities of the instrument that most
      directly affect performance.

209. Smith, Charles Warren. "The History and Literature
      of the Alto Flute, with a Method for the Construction
      of Cadenzas for Eighteenth-Century Solo Flute
      Concertos." D.M.A. dissertation, Peabody College,
      1974, 157 p. UM 75-12, 432.

      Recounts the history of the instrument and presents
      a list of works (solo and ensemble) written for it.

210. Thalheimer, Peter. "Der Flauto piccolo bei Johann
      Sebastian Bach." *Bach Jahrbuch* 52 (1966): 138-46.

Argues persuasively that in Bach's Cantata No. 96 the designation *flauto piccolo* indicates recorder in F (an octave higher than the alto recorder) and in Cantata No. 103 recorder in D. Pleads against the use of piccolo flute as a substitute.

211. Toff, Nancy. *The Development of the Modern Flute.* New York: Taplinger, 1979. 268 p.

A comprehensive discussion, rich in detail, that focuses mostly on the recent evolution of the instrument. Includes a short but good treatment of avant-garde notation.

212. Tromlitz, Johann George. *Ueber die Flöten mit mehrern Klappen, deren Anwendung und Nutzen.* Leipzig: Böhme, 1800; facsimile reprint, Amsterdam: Knuf, 1973. 144 p.

Describes an eight-key flute of the author's design and provides detailed instructions for playing it. Intended as a supplement to the *Unterricht* of 1791, cited below as Item 920. No examples of the instrument have been preserved.

213. Vaucanson, Jacques de. *An Account of the Mechanism of an Automaton or Image Playing on the German-Flute/Le mécanisme du flûteur automate.* London: Parker, 1742; facsimile reprint, Buren: Knuf, 1979. 46 p.

Describes a mechanical flute player made of wood that was able to play twelve different melodies. Introduced by what may be the first discussion of flute acoustics. Facsimile edition includes an excellent preface by David Lasocki.

* Veenstra, Adolf. "The Classification of the Flute." *Galpin Society Journal* 17 (1964): 54-63.

Cited below as Item 699.

214. Ventzke, Karl. *Die Boehmflöte: Werdegang eines Musikinstruments.* Frankfurt: Das Musikinstrument, 1966. 60 p.

Traces the development of the instrument in the first half of the nineteenth century, quoting liberally from sources of the period. Includes an excellent selection of plates.

215. Weber, Carl Maria von. "Neue Erfindung zur Vervollkommung der Flöte." *Allgemeine musikalische Zeitung* 13 (1811): 377-9.

Describes with approval the changes in mechanism
made by Johann Nepomuk Capeller, the teacher of Boehm.
The changes were later criticized by the Leipzig
flutist Carl Grenser (*Allgemeine musikalische Zeitung*
13, p. 778). Weber's article is discussed and presented
in English in Carl Maria von Weber, *Writings on Music*,
ed. John Warrack, trans. Martin Cooper (Cambridge:
Cambridge University Press, 1981), pp. 68-69.

*   Weber, Gottfried. "Praktische Resultate aus der ...
Akustik der Blasinstrumente." *Allgemeine musikalische
Zeitung* 19 (1817): 809-14, 825-32.

Cited below as Item 537.

216. Welch, Christopher. *History of the Boehm Flute*. 2nd
ed. London: Rudall, Carte, 1892; reprint ed., New
York: McGinnis and Marx, 1961. 270 p.

An authoritative account of the early development
of the flute. Includes a thorough analysis of the Boehm-
Gordon controversy and clearly establishes Boehm's role
in the development of the fingering system that bears
his name. Preface to second edition is a defense to
Rockstro's attack on Boehm (see Item 71, cited above).
Provides diagrams of key mechanisms and a list of Boehm's
published and unpublished works for flute.

217. Winternitz, Emanuel. "Leonardo and Music." *The Unknown
Leonardo*, edited by Ladislao Reti. London: Hutchinson,
1974, pp. 110-35.

A fascinating account of Leonardo's designs for musical
instruments, including a flute with a keyboard and
a mechanized kettledrum. Well illustrated.

218. ————. *Leonardo da Vinci as a Musician*. New Haven:
Yale University Press, 1982. 241 p.

Includes a well-illustrated discussion of Leonardo's
designs for flutes and drums.

219. Worman, Walter E. "Boehm's Design of the Flute: A
Comparison with that of Rockstro." *Galpin Society
Journal* 28 (1975): 107-20.

Discusses the placement of finger holes and mouth
holes.

2. Oboe and English Horn

* Almenräder, Carl. "Ueber die Irhaltung der Fagottrohre, für Fagottisten sowohl, als auch für Oboisten und Clarinettisten." *Caecilia* 11, no. 41 (1829): 58-62. Cited below as Item 249.

220. Bate, Philip, and Eric Halfpenny. "The Tenner Hoboy." *Galpin Society Journal* 6 (1953): 100-02.

An exchange of letters regarding Halfpenny's article cited below (Item 230) and the construction of the curved English horn.

221. Blake, Cevedra Marc. "The Baroque Oboe d'Amore." Ph.D. dissertation, University of California, Los Angeles, 1981. 677 p. UM 81-20, 919.

Includes a history of the instrument, a comprehensive list of all known eighteenth-century instruments, and an extensive list of Baroque compositions calling for oboe d'amore.

222. Braun, Werner. "The 'Hautboist': An Outline of Evolving Careers and Functions." *The Social Status of the Professional Musician from the Middle Ages to the 19th Century*, edited by Walter Salmen, translated by Herbert Kaufman and Barbara Reisner. New York: Pendragon, 1983, pp. 125-58.

A thorough, well-documented discussion of court, regimental, and town oboists in the seventeenth and eighteenth centuries. Concludes with a summary of eighteenth-century attitudes toward the instrument and a general description of its use in wind ensembles of the period.

223. Busch, David L. "A Technical Comparison of an 1802, a 1916, and a 1968 Oboe and Related Reed-Making and Performance Problems." D.M.A. dissertation, Louisiana State University, 1972. 72 p. UM 73-13, 695.

Of some value for its comparison of the dimensions of the instruments.

224. Dahlqvist, Reine. "Taille, Oboe da Caccia and Corno Inglese." *Galpin Society Journal* 26 (1973): 58-71.

Examines Bach's use of the oboes da caccia and of the designation *taille*. Concludes that *taille* was used to designate a part--the third oboe da caccia part--much in the same way the Bach used *principale* to designate the third trumpet part. Points out that prior to 1720 *taille* indicated a straight tenor oboe, not an oboe da caccia. Also discusses the early use of the English horn (*ca.* 1715-20).

*   Eliason, Robert E. "Oboe[s], Bassoons, and Bass Clarinets, made by Hartford[,] Connecticut, Makers before 1815." *Galpin Society Journal* 30 (1977): 43-51.

Cited below as Item 600.

*   Grush, James. "A Guide to the Study of the Classical Oboe." D.M.A. dissertation, Boston University, 1972. 272 p. UM 72-25, 121.

Cited below as Item 874.

225. Hailperin, Paul. "Some Technical Remarks on the Shawm and Baroque Oboe." M.A. thesis, Schola Cantorum Basiliensis, 1970. 33 p.

Compares measurements of surviving instruments with the information given by Agricola, Praetorius, Mersenne, and Talbot. Reports results of pitch tests on a number of shawms.

226. ————. "Three Oboes d'Amore from the Time of Bach." *Galpin Society Journal* 28 (1975): 26-36.

Describes and provides detailed measurements of three instruments, including one by Jacob Denner. Also offers details of a possibly original eighteenth-century reed.

227. ————. "Three Oboes d'Amore from the Time of Bach (Additions and Amendments)." *Galpin Society Journal* 30 (1977): 153-54.

Reports experiments with the bells for instruments made on the model of the instrument by Jacob Denner. Also revises statements made earlier regarding reeds for the instrument. See the article cited above as Item 226.

*   Halbig, Hermann. "Die Geschichte der Klappe an Flöten und Rohrblattinstrumenten bis zum Beginn des 18. Jahrhunderts." *Archiv für Musikwissenschaft* 6 (1924): 1-53.

Cited as Item 185.

228. Halfpenny, Eric. "The English Debut of the French
Hautboy." *Monthly Musical Record* 79 (1949): 149-53.

Points out the first mention of an oboist in England,
on the rolls of musicians performing the masque *Calisto*
(by John Crowe and Nicholas Stoggins) in 1674. The use
of the oboe appears to reflect the influence of Robert
Cambert, who supervised the production.

229. ————. "The English 2- and 3-Keyed Hautboy." *Galpin
Society Journal* 2 (1949): 10-26.

Classifies, discusses, and compares instruments from
the late seventeenth and early eighteenth centuries.
Quotes some interesting and previously unknown descriptions of oboe playing made at the end of the seventeenth
century, including the statement that "with a good
reed it [the oboe] goes as easie and soft as the Flute."

230. ————. "Oboe Fingering Charts, 1695-1816." *Galpin
Society Journal* 31 (1978): 68-93.

A close look at twenty-four charts. Includes a
collation that gives all the variant fingerings for
each note.

231. ————. "A Seventeenth-Century Oboe Consort." *Galpin
Society Journal* 10 (1957): 60-62.

Discusses a miniature carving on the bell of an oboe
from the late seventeenth century that depicts an oboe
quartet.

232. ————. "The 'Tenner Hoboy'." *Galpin Society Journal*
5 (1952): 17-27.

Describes and compares various tenor oboes. Includes
photographs and measurements. Also see Item 220, cited
above.

233. ————. "Tonality and the Baroque Oboe." *Early Music*
7 (1979): 355-57.

Discusses the pitch of the Baroque oboe and the ad-
visability of employing transposition to bring works
into the best key for the instrument, C.

* Haynes, Bruce. "Making Reeds for the Baroque Oboe."

Early Music 4 (1976): 31-34, 173-82.

Cited below as Item 884.

234. Hošek, Miroslav. "Tajemstý hobojového strojku, I-III."
      Hudebni nástroje 12 (1975): 115-17, 147-48, 180-85.

      Examines the construction of the oboe and the equip-
      ment used in its manufacture. Analyzes its defects and
      suggests remedies.

235. Jones, David. "A Three-Keyed Oboe by Thomas Collier."
      Galpin Society Journal 31 (1978): 36-43.

      Discusses an instrument made *ca.* 1775. Also see the
      letter by Eric Halfpenny in the following issue (1979),
      p. 150.

236. Joppig, Günther. *Die Entwicklung der Doppelrohrblatt-
      Instrumente von 1850 bis heute und ihre Verwendung in
      Orchester und Kammermusik.* Frankfurt: Das Musikin-
      strument, 1980. 158 p.

      Focuses on the design and construction of double
      reed instruments in the nineteenth and twentieth centuries,
      including such relative rarities as the baritone
      oboe and the rothphone. Lists illustrative compositions.
      Includes a generous selection of photographs. Also
      see Item 81, cited above.

*   Karp, Cary. "Baroque Woodwind in the Musikhistoriska
      Museet, Stockholm." *Galpin Society Journal* 25 (1972):
      80-86.

      Cited below as Item 753.

237. ————. "Structural Details of Two J.H. Eichentopf Oboi
      da Caccia." *Galpin Society Journal* 26 (1973): 55-67.

      Supplements Karp's earlier article, cited below as
      Item 753.

238. Kirkpatrick, Mary. "Another Oboe by Jonathan Bradbury:
      Restoration and Comparison." *Galpin Society Journal*
      33 (1980): 106-10.

      Reports the discovery of an early eighteenth-century
      oboe, describes its restoration, and compares its play-
      ing characteristics with those of another—and possibly
      earlier—instrument made by Bradbury.

239. Lange, Hansjürg, and Bruce Haynes. "The Importance of
Original Double Reeds Today." *Galpin Society Journal*
30 (1977): 145-49.

Reports the establishment of a register of early reeds
and provides drawings to facilitate description.

* Ledet, David A. *Oboe Reed Styles: Theory and Practice.*
Bloomington, Ind.: Indiana University Press, 1981.
212 p.

Cited below as Item 827.

240. Longyear, Rey M. "The English Horn in Classic and Early
Romantic Music." *Miscellanea musicologica* 9 (1977):
128-44.

Traces the use of the English horn from the time of
Gluck to that of Rossini and Halévy. The instrument
was favored more in Austria than elsewhere.

241. Marx, Josef. "The Tone of the Baroque Oboe." *Galpin
Society Journal* 3 (1951): 3-19.

Surveys the history of the instrument in the seventeenth and eighteenth centuries, describes what is
known about the tone of the Baroque oboe, and calls
attention to a number of misconceptions, especially that
the tone was harsh and shrill.

242. Palmer, Frederic R. "Reconstructing an 18th-Century
Oboe Reed." *Galpin Society Journal* 35 (1982): 100-
111.

Describes in detail the making of reeds modeled on a
reed in the Bate Collection at Oxford University.

* Perdue, Robert W. "Arundo donax--Source of Musical
Reeds and Industrial Cellulose." *Economic Botany*
12 (1958): 368-404.

Cited below as Item 1185.

243. Piguet, Michel. "The Baroque Oboe." *Recorder and
Music Magazine* 2 (1967): 171-72.

Describes the Baroque oboe and compares it to modern
instruments.

244. Post, Nora. "The 17th-Century Oboe Reed." *Galpin
Society Journal* 35 (1982): 54-67.

Argues that the short-stapled oboe reed, as illustrated in Diderot's *Encyclopédie*, was the norm during the Baroque period and the only reed in use during the late seventeenth century. Describes the playing characteristics of the reed.

*   Russell, Myron E. *Oboe Reed Making and Problems of the Oboe Player*. 3rd ed. Stamford, Conn.: Jack Spratt, 1960. 56 p.

Cited below as Item 838.

245. Sallagar, Walter Hermann. "Wiener Holzblasinstrumente." *Tibia* 3 (1978): 1-6.

Describes the Viennese tradition of *Harmoniemusik* and reviews the history of the Viennese oboe from 1880 on.

*   Sidorfsky, Joyce Ann. "The Oboe in the Nineteenth Century: A Study of the Instrument and Selected Published Solo Literature." Ph.D. dissertation, University of Southern Mississippi, 1974. 376 p. UM 75-9604.

Cited below as Item 988.

246. Staehelin, Martin. "Forschungen zur Musettenbass." *Glareana* 18, nos. 3-4 (December 1969): 17-19.

A discussion of the basset oboe, of which twenty-four examples are extant. Suggests that most of them were made by Jeanneret, a maker who fled France after the Edict of Nantes was revoked. The instrument was probably used to accompany psalm singing in the reformed churches of French-speaking Switzerland.

247. Ventzke, Karl. *Boehm-Oboen und die neueren französischen Oboen-Systeme*. Frankfurt: Das Musikinstrument, 1969. 48 p.

Describes the Boehm fingering system, especially as applied to the oboe. Discusses the contributions of the firms Buffet and Triébert. Includes a description of recent French oboe systems and a comparison, by Dietrich Hilkenbach, from the performer's point of view.

248. Washburn, Clinton T. "The Washburn System Oboe." *Woodwind World* 4, no. 3 (December 1960): 6-8.

Describes a new key system. A fingering chart appears in the following issue of the magazine (p. 12).

3. Bassoon

249. Almenräder, Carl. "Ueber die Irhaltung der Fagottrohre,
      für Fagottisten sowohl, als auch für Oboisten und
      Clarinettisten." *Caecilia* 11, no. 41 (1829): 58-
      62.

      Stresses the importance of good reeds and offers advice
      about preserving them. Notes that the author is able
      to use the same reed daily for up to two years, keeping
      it in fine playing condition the entire time.

*   Bartlett, Loren W. "A Survey and Checklist of Repre-
      sentative Eighteenth-Century Concertos and Sonatas for
      Bassoon." Ph.D. dissertation, University of Iowa,
      1961. 247 p. UM 61-5544.

      Cited below as Item 1071.

250. Bate, Philip. "An Unusual English Bassoon." *Galpin
      Society Journal* 1 (1948): 64.

      Describes a bassoon made *ca.* 1830 by Goulding & Co.
      that displays some markedly German traits.

251. Brindley, Giles. "The Logical Bassoon." *Galpin Society
      Journal* 21 (1968): 152-61.

      Describes a completely new baooooon that employs
      electrical circuits and finger switches. The instrument,
      according to the author, is easier to play than the
      conventional bassoon in regard to fingering and intona-
      tion, and produces a more consistent tone. It also can
      be adjusted to perform at concert pitches that differ
      as much as a quarter-tone from A=440. Well illustrated.

252. Dagrade, Marvin D. "A Translation and Study of the
      Bassoon Section of Joseph Fröhlich's *Vollständige
      Theoretisch-praktische Musiklehre* (1810-11) and
      a Performance Edition of his *Serenade* for Flute,
      Clarinet, Viola, Bassoon or Cello." D.M.A. disser-
      tation, Indiana University, 1970. 2 vols. 138 p.

      The section of Fröhlich's treatise that is translated
      includes descriptions of bassoon construction, reed
      making, and fingerings. The dissertation also offers
      a history of the development of the bassoon during
      Fröhlich's lifetime. Also see Item 912, cited below.

*   Eliason, Robert E. "Oboe[s], Bassoons, and Bass Clarinets, made by Hartford[,] Connecticut, Makers before 1815." *Galpin Society Journal* 30 (1977): 43-51.

Cited below as Item 600.

253. Eppelsheim, Jürgen. "Das 'Subkontrafagott'." *Bericht über die erste internationale Fachtagung zur Erforschung der Blasmusik, Graz 1974*, edited by Wolfgang Suppan and Eugen Brixel. Tutzing: Schneider, 1976, pp. 233-72.

Carefully examines the history of metal bassoons in the nineteenth century, correcting misstatements by Sachs and others. Concludes that the so-called sub-contrabassoon was an instrument pitched in B flat, a step lower than the normal contrabassoon and a fourth lower than the metal contrabassoon in E flat.

254. Galpin, Francis W. "The Romance of the Phagotum." *Proceedings of the Musical Association* 67 (1940-41): 57-72.

Translates and discusses a rather lengthy sixteenth-century account of the invention, by Alfranio Ambrogio, of a wind instrument from which the bassoon acquired its Italian and German names. It resembles the bagpipe more than the bassoon.

*   Halbig, Hermann, "Die Geschichte der Klappe an Flöten und Rohrblattinstrumenten bis zum Beginn des 18. Jahrhunderts." *Archiv für Musikwissenschaft* 6 (1924): 1-53.

Cited above as Item 185.

255. Halfpenny, Eric. "The Evolution of the Bassoon in England, 1750-1800." *Galpin Society Journal* 10 (1957): 30-38.

Compares the bassoon of the mid-eighteenth century with the bassoon of the early nineteenth century. Notes fingerings as indicated in six sources from 1751 to 1810. Includes photographs.

256. ————. "French and German Bassoons in London." *Galpin Society Journal* 21 (1968): 187-89.

Describes the preferences shown by British bassoonists in the 1920s.

* Heckel, Wilhelm. *Der Fagott*. Bierbrich am Rhein: Heckel, 1899. 32 p.

  Cited above as Item 82.

* Joppig, Günther. *Die Entwicklung der Doppelrohrblatt-Instrumente von 1850 bis heute und ihre Verwendung in Orchester- und Kammermusik*. Frankfurt: Das Musikinstrument, 1980. 158 p.

  Cited above as Item 236.

257. Kirkpatrick, Mary. "Register of Early Reeds: Bassoon Reeds in the Aylesbury Museum." *Galpin Society Journal* 34 (1981): 148-49.

     Describes and depicts a box of five reeds belonging to a bassoon that may date from the end of the eighteenth century.

* Lange, Hansjürg, and Bruce Haynes. "The Importance of Original Double Reeds Today." *Galpin Society Journal* 30 (1977): 145-49.

  Cited above as Item 239.

258. Lange, Hansjürg, and J.M. Thomson. "The Baroque Bassoon." *Early Music* 7 (1979): 346-50.

     Describes the making of bassoons and reeds after Baroque models.

* Lotsch, Hans. *Das grosse Rohrbuch. Systematischer Lehrgang für den Bau von Fagottrohren*. Frankfurt: Das Musikinstrument, 1974. 74 p.

  Cited below as Item 830.

259. Meyer, Jürgen. "Akustische Untersuchungen über den Klang alter und neuer Fagotte." *Das Musikinstrument* 17, no. 11 (November 1968): 1259-66.

     Reports that Baroque bassoons are dark in timbre and sound best in the low and middle ranges. Bassoons of Mozart's time are brighter than present-day instruments and sound best in the high register.

260. Oromszegi, Otto. "Bassoons at the Narodni Museum, Prague." *Galpin Society Journal* 24 (1971): 96-101.

     A descriptive list of thirty-six instruments, many from the eighteenth and early nineteenth centuries.

*   Palmer, Frederic R. "Reconstructing an 18th-Century
      Oboe Reed." *Galpin Society Journal* 35 (1982):
      100-111.

      Cited above as Item 242.

*   Peeples, Georgia Kay. "The Bassoon in America, 1800-
      1840, as Depicted in Contemporary Pedagogic Sources."
      D.M.A. dissertation, University of Maryland, 1981.
      87 p. UM 82-14, 397.

      Cited below as Item 904.

*   Perdue, Robert W. "Arundo donax--Source of Musical Reeds
      and Industrial Cellulose." *Economic Botany* 12 (1958):
      368-404.

      Cited below as Item 1185.

*   Popkin, Mark, and Loren Glickman. *Bassoon Reed Making.*
      Evanston, Ill.: Instrumentalist, 1969. 30 p.

      Cited below as Item 833.

*   Rhodes, David J. "Franz Anton Pfeiffer and the Bassoon."
      Galpin Society Journal 36 (1983): 97-103.

      Cited below as Item 675.

*   Schleiffer, J. Eric. *The Art of Bassoon Reed Making.*
      Oneonta, N.Y.: Swift-Dorr, 1974. 22 p.

      Cited below as Item 839.

261. Ventzke, Karl. "Boehm-System-Fagotte im 19. Jahrhundert."
      Tibia 1 (1976): 13-18.

      Describes instruments built by Boehm, Triébert, Tamplini
      and Ward, and Haseneier. Reports how the instruments
      were received during the period.

262. Voorhees, Jerry L. "Notes on the Fingering System of
      'Boehm' Bassoons." *Galpin Society Journal* 29 (1976):
      51-63.

      Describes and analyzes various mechanisms and fingering
      systems in use during the nineteenth and twentieth
      centuries.

*   Warner, Thoms E. "Two Late Eighteenth-Century Instructions
      for Making Double Reeds." *Galpin Society Journal* 15
      (1962): 25-33.

Cited below as Item 928.

*   Weait, Christopher. *Bassoon Reed-Making: A Basic Technique.* New York: McGinnis and Marx, 1970. 31 p.

Cited below as Item 850.

4. Clarinet and Related Instruments

263.   Ahrens, Christian. "Anmerkingen zu Birsaks Frequenz-messungen an 2 Chalumeaux." *Die Musikforschung* 28 (1975): 442-43.

Disputes Birsak's measurement of the tuning of keyed chalumeaus. See below, Item 269.

264.   Becker, Heinz. "Das Chalumeau bei Telemann." *Konferenzbericht der 3. Magdeburger Telemann-Festtage vom 22. bis 26. Juni 1967. George Philipp Telemann: Ein bedeutender Meister der Aufklärungsepoche*, edited by Günter Fleischhauer and Walther Seigmund-Schultze. Magdeburg: Rat der Stadt, 1969. Vol. 2, pp. 68-76.

Describes the origin, structure, and range of the instrument. Discusses Telemann's works for the instrument and points out that whereas Mattheson was critical of it, Telemann--and more than twenty other composers of the day--looked upon it as a virtuoso instrument.

265.   ————. "Das Chalumeau im 18. Jahrhundert." *Speculum musicae artis. Festgabe für Heinrich Husmann zum 60. Geburtstag*, edited by Heinz Becker and Reinhard Gerlach. Munich: Fink, 1970, pp. 23-46.

Thoroughly reviews the nature and use of the chalumeau. Includes a well-annotated list of works employing it.

266.   ————. "Zur Geschichte der Klarinette im 18. Jahrhundert." *Die Musikforschung* 8 (1955): 271-92.

An indispensable account. Thoroughly examines and carefully evaluates the documentary and musical evidence. Agrees with Kolneder (Item 293) and not with Lebermann (Item 298) that Vivaldi's designation *claren* means "clarinet."

267. Birsak, Kurt. "Bemerkungen zum Bau von Bassettklari-
      netten." *Mozart Jahrbuch* 16 (1970): 29-33.

      Surveys the relationship of clarinet, basset clarinet,
      and basset horn as seen in Mozart's music.

268. ————. "Das Dreiklappen-Chalumeau im Bayerischen
      National-Museum of München." *Die Musikforschung*
      26 (1973): 493-97.

      Describes the differences between the chalumeau and
      the early clarinet. Points out that a three-key
      instrument in the Bayerisches Nationalmuseum is a
      chalumeau, not a clarinet.

269. ————. "Die Stimmung des Klappenschalumeau von I.C.
      Denner. Ein Nachtrag." *Die Musikforschung* 28 (1975):
      82.

      Reports tuning measurements. Amends Birsak's article
      cited above as Item 268. Conclusions disputed by
      Ahrens (Item 263).

270. Clinch, Peter. "The Clarinet to the Nineteenth Century--
      A Documented Account." *Studies in Music* 9 (1973):
      19-40.

      A generally careful survey.

271. Collis, James. "The McIntyre System Clarinet." *Woodwind
      World* 2, no. 1 (February 1958): 12-13.

      Reports the advantages of a new fingering system.

272. Croll, Gerhard, and Kurt Birsak. "Anton Stadlers
      'Bassettklarinette' und das 'Stadler-Quintett' KV
      581. Versuch einer Anwendung." *Oesterreichische
      Musikzeitung* 24, No. 1 (January 1969): 3-11.

      Part 1 deals with an attempt to construct a basset
      clarinet for performances of the original versions of
      Mozart's clarinet concerto (K. 622) and clarinet quintet
      (K. 581). The instrument would possess the character-
      istics of Stadler's instrument as described in Bertuch's
      Journal des Luxes und der Moden (1801). Part 2 offers
      a reconstruction of the quintet method modeled after
      Ernst Hess's reconstruction of the concerto (see below,
      Item 976).

273. Cucuel, Georges. "La question des clarinettes dans
      l'instrumentation du xviiie siècle." *Zeitschrift der*

Internationalen Musikgesellschaft 12 (1910-11): 280-84.

Reviews the history of the clarinet in the orchestra of the late 1750s, the 1760s, and the 1770s. Notes especially Gossec's employment of the instrument. Points out that the word *clarini* was sometimes used to donate clarinets.

274. Dart, Thurston. "The Mock Trumpet." *Galpin Society Journal* 6 (1953): 35-40.

Describes a collection of music for the "mock trumpet" that was published *ca.* 1707. Determines that the instrument referred to in the title is a chalumeau, not a tromba marina.

275. Deaton, James W. "The Eighteenth-Century Six-Keyed Clarinet: A Study of Its Mechanical and Acoustical Properties and Their Relationship to Performance of Selected Literature." D.M.A. dissertation, University of Texas at Austin, 1972. 137 p. UM 73-7683.

Traces the history of the clarinet and describes the use of six-key instruments. Offers suggestions for the performance of eighteenth-century music.

276. Drury, Martial. "La clarinette contrebasse: son histoire--ses particularités--son emploi." *La revue musicale belge* 10, no. 1 (June 1934): 6-7.

Describes the instrument and its history, praises d'Indy's treatment of it in *Fervaal*, and notes its important role in French and Belgian bands.

* Eliason, Robert E. "Oboe[s], Bassoons, and Bass Clarinets, made by Hartford[,] Connecticut, Makers before 1815." *Galpin Society Journal* 30 (1977): 43-51.

Cited below as Item 600.

277. Eppelsheim, Jürgen. "Das Denner-Chalumeau des Bayerischen Nationalmuseums." *Die Musikforschung* 26 (1973): 498-500.

Points out that the Denner chalumeau in Munich can be played only with the reed turned downward. It had previously been assumed--incorrectly--that the upward-turned reed represented the normal arrangment on

instruments of the period and that the downward-
turned reed appeared only subsequently.

* Fitzpatrick, Horace. "Jacob Denner's Woodwinds for
  Gottweig Abbey." *Galpin Society Journal* 21 (1968):
  81-87.

  Cited below as Item 604.

278. Fröhlich, Franz Joseph. "Ueber die Verbesserung der
     Klarinette vom Hrn. Iwan Müller." *Allgemeine
     musikalische Zeitung* 19 (1817): 713-19.

     Describes Müller's improvements and mentions his
     having made an alto clarinet in F, for which Fröhlich
     sees use in outdoor music, especially janissary music.

279. Glick, David Alan. "The Five-Keyed Clarinet." D.M.A.
     dissertation, University of Rochester, 1978. 150pp.
     UM 79-15,039.

     Describes the five-key clarinet in general, surveys
     its history and use in the eighteenth century, and
     discusses performance problems. Also describes the
     restoration of an instrument made *ca.* 1800 by Ludwig
     and Johann Nicolaus Jehring.

280. Gollmick, Carl. "Ein Wort über die Verbesserung der
     Clarinette." *Allgemeine musikalische Zeitung* 47 (1845):
     379-82.

     Points out the advantages of Müller's improvements.
     Illustrated with musical examples.

281. Hacker, Alan. "Mozart and the Basset Clarinet." *The
     Musical Times* 110 (1969): 359-62.

     Reviews the history of the instrument designed by
     Theodor Lotz and improved by Anton Stadler. Lists
     suggested changes in the Mozart clarinet concerto in
     order to restore its original form. Depicts and
     describes the author's instrument, which was made by
     Edward Planas. See also the article by Croll and
     Birsak, cited above as Item 273.

282. Halfpenny, Eric. "The Boehm Clarinet in England."
     Galpin Society Journal 30 (1977): 2-7.

     Reprints excerpts from letters written in the
     1920s and early 1940s to Robin Chatwin regarding the

experiences of clarinet players in British orchestras during the late nineteenth and early twentieth centuries.

283. ———. "Castilon on the Clarinet." *Music and Letters* 35 (1954): 332-38.

Translates and discusses Castilon's article published in the supplement (1776) to Diderot and D'Alembert's *Encyclopédie*. The article points up the French bias toward the A clarinet and the fact that the instrument of the period was limited to playing mostly in the (written) keys of C and F.

284. ———. "Early English Clarinets." *Galpin Society Journal* 18 (1965): 42-56.

Describes thirteen English instruments from the late eighteenth and early nineteenth centuries, gives measurements in full, and provides a chronology of early clarinet playing in England. Includes photographs.

* Hess, Ernst. "Die ursprüngliche Gestalt des Klarinetten-konzertes KV 622." *Mozart Jahrbuch 1967*, pp. 18-30.

Cited below as Item 976.

285. Heyde, Herbert. "Ein Urahn der Klarinette?" *Deutsches Jahrbuch der Musikwissenschaft für 1970*, pp. 121-24.

Discusses the wind instruments depicted in an altar painting from *ca.* 1525. Argues that the instruments are single-reed instruments with metal mouthpieces and metal reeds and are therefore antecedents of the clarinet.

286. Hoeprich, T. Eric. "Finding a Clarinet for the Three Concertos by Vivaldi." *Early Music* 11 (1983): 61-64.

Reports that only two of the Baroque clarinets still extant (numbering altogether more than thirty) could possibly be capable of performing Vivaldi's three concertos for the instrument, (RV 556, 559, and 560). Both instruments, one by Denner and one by Boekhout, are preserved in the collection of the Brussels Conservatory. Describes the instruments, notes that only the Denner possesses one of the notes required by Vivaldi, and reports the fact that the instrument, to its detriment, has been rebored.

287. ———. "Chalumeau and Clarinet." *Early Music* 8 (1980): 366-68.

Takes exception to Colin Lawson's rejection of
Doppelmayer's claim that the clarinet was invented
by J.C. Denner (see below, Item 297). Followed by a
reply to Lawson reaffirming his earlier position.

288.   ————. "A Three-Key Clarinet by J.C. Denner." *Galpin
       Society Journal* 34 (1981): 21-32.

Describes in detail an instrument in the collection
of the University of California, Berkeley, that bears
the stamp of J.C. Denner. Concludes that the instrument,
with the possible exception of the bell, was made by
Johann Christoph Denner. Includes a fingering chart
for the instrument.

289.   Hunt, Edgar. "Some Light on the Chalumeau." *Galpin
       Society Journal* 14 (1961): 41-44.

Suggests that a suite by Christoph Graupner was
originally intended for three chalumeaus. Provides
a fingering chart for a modern German instrument.

290.   James, Richard D. "A Theoretical Determination of
       Clarinet Mouthpiece Facings by Analysis of the Tone
       Generating System." M.A. thesis, University of
       California, Los Angeles, 1973. 69 p.

Systematically establishes a theoretically optimum
facing for the clarinet mouthpiece. Provides specifications. Possibly the first investigation of the
problem from the perspective of engineering.

291.   Karp, Cary. "Chalumeaux." *Galpin Society Journal* 31
       (1978): 144-46.

Describes the playing characteristics of instruments
contained in the Musikhustoriska Museet in Stockholm
(see below, Item 753). Suggests that the reed-down
position on clarinet and chalumeau was known and used
at least as early as the beginning of the eighteenth
century. Also see Eppelsheim, cited above as Item
277.

292.   ————. "Measuring Single-Reed Mouthpieces." *Musical
       Instrument Conservation and Technology Journal* 1 (1978):
       19-23.

Offers a procedure for measuring chalumeau and clarinet
mouthpieces.

293. Kolneder, Walter. "Die Klarinette als Concertino-
     Instrument bei Vivaldi." *Die Musikforschung* 4 (1951):
     185-91.

     Argues that Vivaldi's designation *claren*, which is
     found in three concerti grossi, means "clarinet."
     Becker agrees (see Item 266), but Lebermann disagrees
     (see Item 298).

294. ———. "Noch einmal: Vivaldi und die Klarinette."
     Die Musikforschung 8 (1955): 209-11.

     Answers Lebermann's counter-arguments (Item 298)
     regarding the meaning of the word *claren*. Also see
     Becker, Item 267.

295. Kroll, Oskar. "Das Chalumeau." *Zeitschrift für Musik-
     wissenschaft* 15 (1932/33): 374-78.

     Reviews the early history of the instrument. Lists
     and briefly discusses works employing the instrument.

296. Lanning, Edward F. "The Clarinet as the Intended Solo
     Instrument in Johann Melchior Molter's Concerto 34."
     D.M.A. dissertation, University of Missouri, Kansas
     City, 1969. 62 p. UM 69-19,452.

     Determines that a concerto by D by Molter, preserved in
     manuscript in the Karlsruhe Landesbibliothek, was
     intended for clarinet, not tor clarino.

297. Lawson, Colin. "The Chalumeau, Independent Voice or
     Poor Relation?" *Early Music* 7 (1979): 351-54.

     Sketches the history of the instrument and reviews
     its use in the music of the early eighteenth century,
     comparing its treatment with that of the clarinet.
     Argues that the clarinet was not invented by J.C. Denner.
     See, however, the discussion in Item 287.

298. Lebermann, Walter. "Zur Besetzungsfrage der Concerti
     grossi von A. Vivaldi." *Die Musikforschung* 7 (1954):
     337-39.

     Argues, in opposition to Kolneder (see above, Item
     292), that the concertinos in the concertos F.XII.1, 2,
     and 14 do not include clarinets but trumpets (*clarini*).
     For Kolneder's answer to Lebermann, see Item 293. Also
     see Becker, Item 266.

*   MacGillivray, James A. "The Leblanc Saxophone and

Contrabass Clarinets. *Galpin Society Journal* 12 (1959): 68-72.

Cited below as Item 316.

299. McGinnis, C.S., and R. Pepper. "Intonation of the Boehm Clarinet." *Journal of the Acoustical Society of America* 16 (1944-45): 188-93.

Describes the deficiencies in the intonation of the instrument and reports the improved instrument designed by C.E. Potter, which, contrary to the hopes of the authors, did not attract the serious attention of a manufacturer.

300. McKee, M. Max. "The Eighteenth Century Clarinet: Origin and Development." *Journal of Band Research* 8, no. 1 (Fall 1971): 27-34.

A survey based largely on the work on Rendall (see below, Item 308).

301. Matoušek, Lukás. "Das Chalumeau-Problem." *Die Blasin-strumente und ihre Verwendung sowie zu Fragen des Tempos in der ersten Hälfte des 18. Jahrhunderts: Konferenzbericht der 4. Wissenschaftlichen Arbeitsta-gung Blakenburg/Harz, 26./27. Juni 1976*, edited by Eitelfriedrich Thom. Magdeburg: Rat des Bezirkes; Leipzig: Zentralhaus für Kulturarbeit, 1977, pp. 33-36.

Surveys the history of the chalumeau and its use in the music of the early eighteenth century. Views the clarinet only as an improvement upon the chalumeau rather than as a distinctly different instrument. Suggests that the two instruments, each capable of playing in high and low registers, were interchangeable.

302. Mazzeo, Rosario. "Clarinet Fingerings." *Galpin Society Journal* 19 (1966): 166-67.

Updates statements made in *The Mazzeo Clarinet Manual*, cited below as Item 303.

303. ————. *The Mazzeo Clarinet Manual*. Philadelphia: Elkan, 1959. 38 p.

Describes the Mazzeo System clarinet. Supplemented by the article cited above as Item 302.

304. Meer, John Henry van der. "The Chalumeau Problem." *Galpin Society Journal* 15 (1962): 89-91.

Surveys the use of the chalumeau in the early eighteenth century. Suggests that the designation *basson* or *bassone* indicated a tenor chalumeau, as did Vivaldi's *salmoè*. Agrees with Hunt that parts for the tenor and bass chalumeaus were probably written an octave lower than necessary (see above, Item 289).

305. Mouzay, Christian. "The Double-Boehm Clarinet." *Woodwind* 7, no. 2 (October 1954): 6, 14; no. 3 (November 1954): 4; no. 5 (January 1955): 8.

Describes the faults of the normal Boehm system clarinet and reports the changes made in the Double-Boehm instrument, describing in particular detail its simplification of left-hand technique. Provides fingerings and musical examples. See Item 312, cited below.

306. Nef, Walter. "Die Bass-Klarinette." *Schweizerische Musikzeitung* 84 (1944): 76-80.

Traces the evolution of the instrument and mentions approvingly the sonatas by Othmar Schoeck and Karl Heinrich David.

307. Owen, Angela M. "The Chalumeau and Its Music." *American Recorder* 8, no. 1 (Winter 1967): 7-9.

Suggests that the difficulty in pitch control and sound production as well as its raucous tone quality might account for its limited popularity.

*   Perdue, Robert W. "Arundo donax--Source of Musical Reeds and Industrial Cellulose." *Economic Botany* 12 (1958): 368-404.

Cited below as Item 1185.

308. Rendall, F. Geoffrey. "A Short Account of the Clarinet in England During the Eighteenth and Nineteenth Centuries." *Proceedings of the Royal Musical Association* 68 (1941-42): 55-86.

Surveys the careers of the most important clarinet players in England during the period. Also provides a brief history of the use of the clarinet in England of the eighteenth century.

309. Rice, Albert R. "An Eighteenth-Century Description of the Five-Key Clarinet." *Clarinet* 4, no. 2 (Winter (1977): 29-30.

Discusses an essay by John Wall Callcott that describes
a five-key clarinet and its fingerings.

310. Selfridge-Field, Eleanor. "Vivaldi's Esoteric Instru-
      ments." *Early Music* 6 (1978): 332-38.

      Reviews Vivaldi's sometimes ambiguous terminology as
      well as his employment of unusual instruments. Includes
      a brief discussion of the designations *claren* and
      salmoè, which the author takes to mean "clarinet."
      See also the letters by Colin Lawson, John Henry
      van der Meer, and Andrew Stiller in *Early Music* 7 (1979):
      135-39 as well as Selfridge-Field's reply in the same
      issue (pp. 139-40).

311. Swift, Frederic Fay. "The McIntyre Clarinet." *Woodwind
      World* 11, no. 5 (December 1972): 5, 16.

      Praises the design of the instrument.

312. Tenney, Wallace R. "The Double-Boehm System Clarinet."
      Woodwind 6, no. 2 (October 1953): 6-7.

      Describes a clarinet with a new fingering system,
      which is a modification of the standard Boehm system.
      The instrument is manufactured by the firm Double-
      Boehm of Paris, hence the name of the system. The
      manufacturer predicts that it will revolutionize
      clarinet playing. (Also see Item 305, cited above.)

*   Veselack, Marilyn Sue Warren. "Comparison of Cell and
      Tissue Differences in Good and Unusable Clarinet
      Reeds." D.A. dissertation, Ball State University,
      1979. 136 p. UM 81-2480.

      Cited below as Item 1192.

313. Weber, Gottfried. "Einiges über Clarinett und Bassetthorn."
      Caecilia 11, no. 41 (1829): 35-57.

      Describes the instruments generally. Explains clarinet
      transpositions. Suggests that the basset horn makes an
      excellent substitute for the second clarinet in the
      orchestra. Fingering charts for the six-key and nine-
      key clarinets appear following p. 96.

*   Youngs, Lowell V. "Jean Xavier Lefèvre: His Contributions
      to the Clarinet and Clarinet Playing." D.M.A. disser-
      tation, Catholic University of America, 1970. 180 p.
      UM 70-20,000.

      Cited below as Item 929.

5. Saxophone

*   Gilson, Paul. "Les géniales inventions d'Adolphe Sax."
       Adolphe Sax. Brochure programme de l'Institut
       national belge de radiodiffusion, 26. Brussels:
       Institut national belge de radiodiffusion, 1939, pp. 5-
       21.

       Cited below as Item 605.

314.   Hemke, Fred L. "The Early History of the Saxophone."
       D.M.A. dissertation, University of Wisconsin, 1975.
       577 p. UM 75-26,506.

       An account of the instrument to the end of the
       nineteenth century.

315.   McBride, William. "The Early Saxophone in Patents 1838-
       1850 Compared." *Galpin Society Journal* 35 (1982):
       112-21.

       Based upon an examination of the patents themselves.
       Emphasizes the fact that the instrument underwent
       considerable modification during the period. Well
       illustrated.

316.   MacGillivray, James A. "The Leblanc Saxophone and
       Contrabass Clarinets." *Galpin Society Journal* 13
       (1960): 94-95.

       An addendum to MacGillivray's earlier article, cited
       below as Item 317. Reports information about the saxo-
       phone derived from his experience playing it and offers
       additional remarks about the contrabass clarinets.

317.   ————. "Recent Advances in Woodwind Fingering Systems."
       Galpin Society Journal 12 (1959): 68-72.

       Describes the fingering system of a new saxophone,
       Le Rationnel, which was designed by Houvenaghel from the
       Paris Leblanc firm. Also describes Schmidt's Reform-
       Boehm clarinet. Supplemented by the article cited
       above as Item 316.

*   Perdue, Robert W. "Arundo donax--Source of Musical
       Reeds and Industrial Cellulose." *Economic Botany* 12
       (1958): 368-404.

       Cited below as Item 1185.

* Richmond, Stanley. *Clarinet and Saxophone Experience*.
New York: St. Martin's Press, 1972. 137 p.

Cited above as Item 93.

318. Rosenkaimer, Eugen. "Das Saxophon in seinen Frühzeiten
und im Urteil berühmter Musiker." *Die Musik* 20
(1928): 896-900.

Traces the early evolution of the saxophone, quoting
appreciative comments about the instrument by Berlioz
and Fétis, among others.

VII. SPECIALIZED DISCUSSIONS REGARDING INDIVIDUAL BRASS INSTRUMENTS

1. Trumpet and Related Instruments

319. Altenburg, Detlef. *Untersuchungen zur Geschichte der Trompete im Zeitalter der Clarinblaskunst (1500-1800)*. Kölner Beiträge zur Musikforschung, 75. 3 vols. Regensburg: Bosse, 1973). 427, 201, 67 p.

   Examines the history and repertory of court trumpeters prior to and following the establishment of a guild in 1623. Also describes the principal techniques of trumpet tone production during the period. Documents the history of the guild (vol. 2) and offers a typology of the instruments (vol. 3).

320. ————. "Untersuchungen zur Geschichte der Trompete im Zeitalter der Clarinblaskunst (1500-1800)." *Die Musikforschung* 28 (1975): 209-10.

   Summarizes the author's three-volume study, cited above as Item 319.

321. Altenburg, Johann Ernst. *Essay on an Introduction to the Heroic and Musical Trumpeters' and Kettledrummers' Art*. Translated by Edward H. Tarr. Nashville: Brass Press, 1974. 148 p.

   A thoroughly annotated translation of one of the principal sources of information about eighteenth-century practice. Prefaced by a brief but useful introduction. A facsimile of the original German edition (1795) is cited below as Item 322.

322. ————. *Versuch einer Anleitung zur heroisch-musikalischen Trompeter- und Paukerkunst*. Edited by Frieder Zschoch. Leipzig: Deutscher Verlag für Musik, 1973. 156 p.

A facsimile of the original edition (1795) of the work cited above (Item 321) in translation. Includes an afterword that describes the importance of Altenburg's work generally and of the book particularly. A translation by Mary Rasmussen of Chapters 8-15 appears in *Brass Quarterly* 1 (1957-58): 133-46, 201-13; 2 (1958-59): 20-30, 53-62.

323. Bagans, Karl. "Ueber die Trompete in ihrer heutigen Anwendbarkeit im Orchester." *Berliner allgemeine musikalische Zeitung* 6 (1829): 337-41.

Describes the harmonic series and discusses the intonation of the natural trumpet, especially as related to choice of keys. Notes the use of keyed and valved instruments but refers to the natural trumpet as the usual instrument. Discusses the difficulty of performing "old" church music employing high trumpet parts. The difficulty is caused partly by the fact that contemporary players are unaccustomed to playing in the highest register. The article appeared in English translation in the *American Music Journal* 1 (1834-35): 252 ff.

324. Bassett, Henry. "On Improvements in Trumpets." *Proceedings of the Musical Association* 3 (1876-77): 140-44.

Describes a trumpet invented by the author. The first two valves function normally; the third valve raised by the interval of a comma the pitch of any note produced with the first valve, thus permitting a more correct scale than usually found in valved instruments.

325. Beck, Frederick Allan. "The Flugelhorn: Its History and Literature." D.M.A. dissertation, University of Rochester, 1979. 159 p. UM 79-21,124.

Traces the history of the instrument and discusses its use as a solo instrument and in works for band, orchestra, and small ensembles of various kinds.

326. Blandford, W.F.H. "The 'Bach Trumpet'." *Monthly Musical Record* 65 (1935): 49-51, 73-76, 97-100.

Summarizes an account by Otto Lessmann (*Neue Berliner Musikzeitung* 10, no. 25 [1871]: 431) of a demonstration of clarino playing by Julius Kosleck. Surveys the revival of clarino playing in the nineteenth century and discusses the instruments employed. Also describes the careers of trumpet players from the eighteenth century.

327. Bowles, Edmund A. "Unterscheidung der Instrumente Buisine, Cor, Trompe und Trompette." *Archiv für Musikwissenschaft* 18 (1961): 52-72.

Describes brass instruments of the Middle Ages and Renaissance, clearly distinguishing one from the other. Brings together references from a number of medieval and Renaissance literary sources, including Chaucer.

328. Burkart, Richard E. "The Trumpet in the Seventeenth Century with Emphasis on its Treatment in the Works of Henry Purcell and a Biography of the Shore Family of Trumpeters. Ph.D. dissertation, University of Wisconsin, 1972. 153 p. UM 72-9111.

Describes the trumpet as found in England up to 1690, traces its use, and thoroughly examines Purcell's treatment as seen in seventeen works. Also attempts to establish the history of the famous Shore family.

329. Dahlqvist, Reine. *The Keyed Trumpet and Its Greatest Virtuoso, Anton Weidinger.* Nashville: Brass Press, 1975. 25 p.

Describes in detail the invention of the keyed trumpet in the late eighteenth century, possibly during the 1760s and certainly before the appearance of Weidinger. Surveys Weidinger's career, discusses the principal concertos written for the keyed trumpet, and notes briefly the twentieth-century revival of the instrument.

330. Downey, Peter. "A Renaissance Correspondence Concerning Trumpet Music." *Early Music* 9 (1981): 325-29.

Transcribes, translates, and discusses correspondence from 1557 between Christian III of Denmark and Augustus, the Elector of Saxony. The correspondence shows that, contrary to common belief, Renaissance trumpet players were competent musicians, able to read and write music and not just having to rely on rote learning.

331. Dudgeon, Ralph Thomas. "The Keyed Bugle, Its History, Literature and Technique." Ph.D. dissertation, University of California, San Diego, 1980. 262 p. UM 80-23,094.

Traces the history of the instrument with particular
emphasis on the period *ca.* 1830-1870. Examines its
role in various ensembles and provides biographical
information on Joseph Haliday, the inventor of the
instrument, as well as on important soloists. Includes
an annotated list of bugle method books and discusses
playing technique. Also includes a list of makers and
performers together with a discography.

332. Eichborn, Hermann. *The Old Art of Clarino Playing on
      Trumpets.* Translated by Bryan A. Simms. Denver:
      Tromba Publications, 1976. 34 p.

      A translation of *Das alte Clarinblasen auf Trompeten*
      (Leipzig: Breitkopf und Hartël, 1894). Provides an
      overview of clarino playing in the seventeenth and
      eighteenth centuries. Argues that it makes no sense to
      try to revive the art, that clarino parts can and
      should be played on modern valve instruments.

333. ————. *Die Trompete in alte und neuer Zeit. Ein
      Beitrag zur Musikgeschichte und Instrumentationslehre.*
      Breitkopf und Härtel, 1881; reprint ed., Wiesbaden:
      Sändig, 1968. 118 p.

      The pioneering historical study. Outdated but
      nevertheless interesting for its advocacy, at a
      time when the natural trumpet was all but forgotten,
      of the development of the skills necessary to play
      clarino parts once again.

334. Eliason, Robert E. "Brass Instrument Key and Valve
      Mechanisms Made in America before 1875 with Special
      Reference to the D.S. Pillsbury Collection in Green-
      field Village, Dearborn, Michigan." D.M.A. disser-
      tation, University of Missouri, Kansas City, 1969.
      225 p. UM 69-7227.

      Focuses on the keyed bugle.

335. ————. "The Dresden Keyed Bugle." *Journal of the
      American Musical Instrument Society* 3 (1977):
      57-63.

      Describes a fingering system for the keyed bugle,
      used *ca.* 1820-40, that differs from the conventional
      system.

336. ————. "Early American Valves for Brass Instruments."
      Galpin Society Journal 23 (1970): 86-96.

Describes the valves invented by the nineteenth-
century makers Nathan Adams, Thomas D. Paine, J.
Lathrop Allen, and Benjamin Quinby, all New Englanders.
Includes biographical information. Well illustrated
with photographs.

337. ————. *Keyed Bugles in the United States*. Washington,
D.C.: Smithsonian Institution, 1972. 44 p.

A well-illustrated survey of the development, manufacture, and use of the bugle in the United States.

338. Fontana, Eszter. "The Manufacture of Ivory Cornetti."
Galpin Society Journal 36 (1983): 29-36.

Briefly describes the manner in which ivory cornetti
of the sixteenth and seventeenth centuries were made.
Includes a list of the instruments that have survived.

339. Halfpenny, Eric. "British Trumpet Mouthpieces:
Addendum." *Galpin Society Journal* 20 (1967): 76-
88.

Describes mouthpieces. Includes a section drawing
of all and photographs of seven. Supplemented by the
article cited above as Item 344.

340. ————. "Four Seventeenth-Century British Trumpets."
Galpin Society Journal 22 (1969): 51-57.

A full description, including photographs and detailed
measurements.

341. ————. "Notes on Two Later British Trumpets." *Galpin
Society Journal* 24 (1971): 79-83.

Describes in detail an instrument by Hofmaster
(1750-60) and one by Shaw (1826). Illustrated with
photographs.

342. ————. "Two Oxford Trumpets." *Galpin Society
Journal* 16 (1963): 49-62.

Illustrates and fully describes two English trumpets
from the late seventeenth century, one of which was
made by the well-known maker William Bull.

343. ————. "William Bull and the English Baroque Trumpet."
Galpin Society Journal 15 (1962): 18-24.

Discusses two seventeenth-century trumpets made by
William Bull. Includes detailed measurements, diagrams,
and photographs.

344.   ———. "William Shaw's 'Harmonic Trumpet'." *Galpin
        Society Journal* 13 (1960): 7-13.

        Describes in detail a trumpet made in 1787. The
        instrument employs a unique pitch-change device
        consisting of vents, rotating sleeves, and one key.
        Illustrated.

345.   ———. "Early British Trumpet Mouthpieces." *Galpin
        Society Journal* 20 (1967): 76-88.

        Describes eighteen mouthpieces. Includes a section
        drawing of all and photographs of seven. Supplemented
        by the article cited above as Item 344.

*   Hall, Jody C. "A Radiographic, Spectrographic, and
        Photographic Study of the Non-Labial Physical Changes
        which Occur in the Transition from Middle to Low and
        Middle to High Registers during Trumpet Performance."
        Ph.d. dissertation, Indiana University, 1954. 313 p.
        UM 10,146.

        Cited below as Item 1178.

*   Henderson, Hayward. "An Experimental Study of Trumpet
        Embouchure." *Journal of the Acoustical Society of
        America* 14 (1942-43): 58-64.

        Cited below as Item 821.

346.   Henderson, Hubert. "A Study of the Trumpet in the
        17th Century: Its History, Resources and Use."
        M.A. thesis, University of North Carolina, 1949.
        125 p.

        Valuable partly for its examination of the technical
        resources of the Baroque trumpet as determined from
        an investigation of seventeenth-century music. Also
        discusses music that calls for two or more trumpets.

*   Heyde, Herbert. "Eine Geschäftskorrespondenz von Johann
        Wilhelm Haas aus dem Jahre 1719." *Aufsätze und
        Jahresbericht 1976 für die Freunde des Musikinstru-
        menten-Museums der Karl-Marx-Universität*, edited by
        Helmut Zeraschi. Leipzig: Direktorat für Forschung
        der Karl-Marx-Universität, 1977, pp. 32-38.

        Cited below as Item 613.

347.   ———. "Die Unterscheidung von Klarin- und Prinzipal-
        trompete. Zum Problem des Klarinblasens." *Beiträge zur
        Musikwissenschaft* 9 (1967): 55-61.

Describes and distinguishes between clarino and principal trumpets. Points out that clarino playing requires a technique of blowing different from that used in principal trumpet playing. Supports the explanation provided earlier by Hofmann (see below, Item 822).

348. Hoover, Cynthia Adams. "The Slide Trumpet of the Nineteenth Century." *Brass Quarterly* 6 (1963): 159-78.

Describes a slide trumpet once used by the English trumpeter Thomas Harper (1786-1853), which is now in the collection of the Smithsonian Institution. Also traces the history of slide trumpet playing during the nineteenth century.

* ————. "The Trumpet Battle at Niblo's Pleasure Garden." *The Musical Quarterly* 55 (1969): 384-95.

Cited below as Item 655.

349. Hyatt, Jack H. "The Soprano and Piccolo Trumpets: Their History, Literature, and a Tutor." D.M.A. dissertation, Boston University, 1974. 238 p. UM 74-20,473.

Traces the history of the piccolo valve instruments and discusses their use in detail. Includes an original tutor for the instruments.

350. Karstädt. Georg. "Das Instrument Gottfried Reiches: Horn oder Trompete?" *Bericht über den internationalen musikwissenschaftlichen Kongress Kassel 1962.* Kassel: Bärenreiter, 1963, pp. 311-13.

Discusses the instrument shown in Elias Gottlieb Haussmann's famous portrait of the Lepzig trumpet player Gottfried Reiche and concludes that it is a corno da caccia and not a trumpet. Suggests that a horn was chosen out of deference to the feelings of court and military trumpeters. Smithers (Item 368) argues, however, that the instrument is indeed a trumpet.

351. Keller, Jindřich. "Alte Trompetendämpfer." *Glareana* 18, no. 1 (March 1969): 2-9.

Describes in detail eighteen trumpet mutes from the Prague National Museum. Notes that they raise the pitch of the trumpet by a major second and suggests

that seemingly bitonal passages in Monteverdi operas
may imply the use of such mutes.

352. Kent, Earle L. "Wind Instrument of the Cup Mouthpiece
      Type." U.S. Patent No. 2, 987, 950 (June 13, 1961).

      Describes a trumpet designed and built according
      to a mathematical model. The instrument has no practi-
      cal value owing partly to the smallness of the mouth-
      piece cup, and it has never been manufactured.
      Reprinted in Kent, *Musical Acoustics*, cited below as
      Item 462.

353. Kirchmeyer, Helmut. "Die Rekonstruktion der Bachtrom-
      pete." *Neue Zeitschrift fur Musik* 122 (1966):
      137-45.

      Reports the manufacture by Finke of a coiled
      trumpet modeled after the instrument depicted in
      Haussmann's portrait of Gottfried Reiche. Describes
      in detail the acoustical principles of the instrument,
      which has two finger holes placed according to Otto
      Steinkopf's design. Karstädt, however, has argued
      strongly that the instrument in the portrait is a
      horn, not a trumpet (see above, Item 350).

354. Körner, Friedrich. "Instrumentenkundliche Untersuch-
      ungsmethoden in der Erforschung der Blechblasinstrument."
      *Bericht über die erste internationale Fachtagung
      zur Erforschung der Blasmusik, Graz 1974*, edited by
      Wolfgang Suppan and Eugen Brixel. Tutzing: Schneider,
      1976, pp. 217-32.

      Notes the relative absence of fundamental research
      studies on brass instruments. Compares the physical
      and playing characteristics of five modern instruments,
      using the trumpet part of Handel's "The Trumpet Shall
      Sound" as the basis for comparison.

355. Lampl, Hans. "Michael Praetorius on the Use of Trumpets."
      Brass Quarterly 2 (1958-59): 3-7.

      A translation, with brief commentary, of Chapter 8
      of Vol. 3 of the *Syntagma musicum*.

356. Mahling, Christoph-Hellmut. "Münchener Hoftrompeter
      und Stadtmusikanten im späten 18. Jahrhundert."
      Zeitschrift für bayerische Landesgeschichte 31 (1968):
      649-70.

      An account of the conflicting appeals of court and
      city musicians for the right to play the trumpet. Includes
      lengthy quotations from documents of the period.

357. Malek, Vincent F. "A Study of Embouchure and Trumpet-
     Cornet Mouthpiece Measurements." Ph.D. disserta-
     tion, Northwestern University, 1953. 184 p.
     UM 6219.

     Determines, through interviews with professional
     performers, the most preferable mouthpieces.

358. Menke, Werner. *History of the Trumpet of Bach and
     Handel.* Translated by Gerald Abraham. London:
     Reeves, [1934]. 128 p.

     Argues, in opposition to Eichborn (see above,
     Item 332), that the trumpet parts of Bach and Handel
     are practicible. Describes the trumpets, mouthpieces,
     and trumpet playing of the eighteenth century. Also
     describes and illustrates valve trumpets designed by
     Menke for performing Baroque music.

*   Morisset, Michel. "Étude sur la musique pour trompette
     en France de Lully à Rameau." *Recherches* 13 (1973):
     35-55.

     Cited below as Item 1017.

359. Osthoff, Wolfgang. "Trombe sordine." *Archiv für
     Musikwissenschaft* 13 (1956): 77-95.

     Surveys the use of the muted trumpet in the music
     of the seventeenth and eighteenth centuries. Argues
     persuasively that for composers during the period,
     including Haydn and Mozart, it served as a funereal
     symbol.

*   Overton, Friend Robert. *Der Zink.* Mainz: Schott,
     1981. 260 p.

     Cited above as Item 103.

360. Peress, Maurice. "A Baroque Trumpet Discovered in
     Greenwich Village." *Brass Quarterly* 4 (1960-61):
     121-28.

     Reports the discovery of a trumpet made by Johann
     Wilhelm Haas of Nuremburg (1649-1723). Describes
     the instrument fully.

361. Rasmussen, Mary. "Bach-Trumpet Madness; or A
     Plain and Easy Introduction to the Attributes,
     Causes and Cure of a Most Mysterious Musicological
     Malady." *Brass Quarterly* 5 (1961-62): 37-40.

Argues against the use of the new Steinkopf-Finke
trumpet as a solution to the problems of playing
clarino parts. The trumpet, constructed with a
hole to damp out the odd-numbered partials, has, for
Rasmussen, no historical validity. For a different
view of the instrument, see above, Item 353.

362. ————. "New Light on Some Unusual Seventeenth-
Century French Trumpet Parts." *Brass Quarterly*
6 (1962-63): 9.

Proposes that French trumpet parts of the seventeenth
century were sometimes written for double trumpets,
instruments--like the modern horn--that could alterna-
tively be pitched in two keys.

363. Remsen, Lester E. "A Study of the Natural Trumpet
and Its Modern Counterpart." D.M.A. dissertation,
University of Southern California, 1960. 183 p.

Reviews the history of the natural trumpet, compares
the physical properties of natural and valve trumpets,
and discusses performance problems. Includes an
extensive list of Baroque music employing trumpet.

364. Rhodes, Emile. *Les trompettes du roi*. Paris:
Picard, 1909. 71 p.

Describes the role of military trumpet players and
of players in the *Grande écurie* during the period
from the sixteenth through the eighteenth century.
Includes lists of court trumpet players. Discusses
their pay, official duties, and attire. Well
illustrated and documented with copious quotations
from documents.

365. Sachs, Curt. "Chromatic Trumpets in the Renaissance."
The Musical Quarterly 36 (1950): 62-66.

Discusses a fifteenth-century triptych that depicts
angels playing trumpets. Argues that the instruments
are slide trumpets capable of playing chromatically,
somewhat like the trombone.

*   Schünemann, Georg, ed. *Trompeterfanfaren, Sonaten und
Feldstücke nach Aufzeichnungen deutscher Hoftrom-
peter des 16./17. Jahrhunderts*. Das Erbe deutscher
Musik, series 1: Reichsdenkmale, vol. 7. Kassel:
Bärenreiter, 1936. 80 p.

Cited below as Item 1020.

366. Smithers, Don L. "The Baroque Trumpet after 1721--
Some Preliminary Observations, I: Science and
Practice." *Early Music* 5 (1977): 177-83.

Discusses the question of authenticity in the making
and playing of the classic trumpet. Discusses Fantini's
treatise (cited below as Item 870), the instrument
shown in the famous portrait of Reiche, and the logic
of Bach's trumpet parts. Regarding the Reiche
instrument, see the articles cited above as Items 350
and 366.

367. ————. "The Baroque Trumpet after 1721 -- Some
Preliminary Observations, II: Function and Use."
Early Music 6 (1978): 356-61.

Primarily a discussion of Bach's trumpet parts and
their performance during his own day. Argues and
presents evidence that the instrument shown in
Reiche's portrait is a small Italian trumpet, a *tromba
da caccia*, and not a horn, as stated by Karstädt (see
above, Item 350).

368. ————. "The Hapsburg Imperial *Trompeter* and *Heerpaucker*
Privileges of 1653." *Galpin Society Journal* 24 (1971):
84-95.

An English translation, briefly introduced, of
mandates issued by Emperor Ferdinand III regarding the
behavior of trumpeters and kettledrummers.

369. ————. *The Music and History of the Baroque Trumpet
before 1721*. London: Dent, 1973. 323 p.

Not so much a discussion of the instrument as an
account of its use. Thorough and authoritative. Includes a lengthy list of works, published and unpublished, for Baroque trumpet. The bibliography of
books and articles is excellent.

370. Sprint, J.E. "The Fellowships of the Minstrels."
Brass Bulletin, no. 8 (1974): 65-84.

An account of the music guilds and a description
of the special status of trumpet players. Accompanied
by a good selection of plates. An excerpt, translated
by E. Mende, from Sprint's *Van vedelaars, trommers
en Pijpers* (Utrecht, 1969).

371. Štĕdroň, Bohumir. "Die Landshafts-Trompeter und
      -Tympanisten im alten Brünn." *Die Musikforschung*
      21 (1968): 438-58.

      Describes the role of provincial trumpeters and
      timpanists in Brno during the seventeenth and early
      eighteenth centuries. Notes the different roles of
      city musicians (*Turmmusiker*). Quotes regulations from
      1653 pertaining to provincial musicians and provides
      biographical information about eighteenth-century
      performers.

372. Sternfeld, Frederick W. "The Dramatic and Allegorical
      Function of Music in Shakespeare's Tragedies."
      Annales musicologiques 3 (1955): 265-82.

      Includes a brief discussion of Shakespeare's refer-
      ences to and use of trumpets.

373. Tarr, Edward H. "The Baroque Trumpet, the High Trumpet,
      and the So-Called Bach Trumpet." *Brass Bulletin*, no.
      2 (1972): 25-29; no. 3 (1972): 44-48.

      Reviews the musical requirements placed upon players
      in the seventeenth and eighteenth centuries and points
      out that Austrian composers of the late eighteenth
      century made especially difficult demands. Surveys
      the revival of high trumpet playing in the nineteenth
      and twentieth centuries, describes the instruments used,
      ·and notes a number of important differences between
      Baroque and modern trumpet playing.

374. Titcomb, Caldwell. "Baroque Court and Military
      Trumpets and Kettledrums: Technique and Music."
      Galpin Society Journal 9 (1956): 56-81.

      A thoughtful, authoritative survey of instrumental
      practice.

375. ————. "Carrousel Music at the Court of Louis XIV."
      *Essays on Music in Honor of Archibald Thompson
      Davidson by His Associates*. Cambridge, Mass.:
      Harvard University, Department of Music, 1957, pp.
      205-14.

      Describes the spectacular equestrian ballets held
      during the reign of Louis XIV, giving particular atten-
      tion to the role played by mounted kettledrummers
      and trumpeters. Briefly discusses a suite written
      by Lully for the carrousel of 1686.

376. Urban, Darrell Eugene. "*Stromenti da tirarsi* in the
     cantatas of J.S. Bach." Ph.D dissertation, Washington
     University, 1977. 643 p. UM 77-21,042.

     Surveys the history of brass instruments in the
     Renaissance and Baroque and examines the fourteen
     cantata movements by Bach in which *tirarsi* instruments
     are called for. Also examines additional parts assigned
     to *tirarsi* instruments by Terry and others.

377. Van Nuys, Robert C. "The History and Nature of the
     Trumpet as Applied to the Sonatas of Giuseppe Torelli."
     D.M.A. dissertation, University of Illinois, 1969.
     180pp. UM 70-1013.

     Reviews the characteristics of the Baroque trumpet,
     describes its importance in the music of Bologna, and
     discusses the techniques required for performing the
     Torelli sonatas.

378. Vogel, Martin. "Eine enharmonische Trompete." *Das
     Orchester* 12, no. 2 (1964): 41-45.

     Reviews the intonation problems of trumpets and
     describes a trumpet of new design, praising its purity
     of intonation. The instrument is also discussed in
     Item 379, cited below.

379. ————. *Die Intonation der Blechbläser*. Dusseldorf:
     Gesellschaft zur Forderung der systematischen
     Musikwissenschaft, 1961. 103 p.

     Explains the problems of intonation inherent in valve
     instruments. Describes a new trumpet, manufactured
     by Alexander, which makes possible greatly improved
     intonation. The instrument has three rotary valves and
     an ingenious mechanism for adjusting tuning slides.
     It is also described in Item 378, cited above.

380. Webb, John. "Bradshaw's Serpentine Valved Cornopean."
     Galpin Society Journal 35 (1982): 154-56.

     Describes a cornet made by Robinson and Bussell *ca.*
     1850, based on the design of Robert Bradshaw. The
     instrument features relatively slender pistons and an
     ingenious valve system.

381. Wheeler, Joseph. "Further Notes on the Classic Trumpet."
     Galpin Society Journal 18 (1965): 14-22.

     Describes two trumpets (from 1715) by John Harris,
     two (from 1800) by John Smith, and three (from 1800) by
     William Shaw.

382. Wörthmüller, Willi. "Die Instrumente der Nürnberger
      Trompeten- u. Posaunemacher." *Mitteilungen des
      Vereins für Geschichte der Stadt Nürnberg* 46 (1955):
      372-480.

      Describes the physical characteristics of the instruments
      and the manner in which they were made. Provides a
      comprehensive descriptive catalog of the instruments
      that are extant. Also see the article cited below
      as Item 638.

      2. Trombone, Tuba, and Related Instruments

383. Baines, Anthony. "Cimbasso." *Galpin Society Journal* 28
      (1975): 133.

      Suggests that *cimbasso*, a term used by Verdi, meant
      a kind of Russian Bassoon "with the head of a serpent."
      Also see Items 392 and 393, cited below.

384. Bate, Philip. "A *Serpent d'Église*: Notes on Some
      Structural Details." *Galpin Society Journal* 29
      (1976): 47-50.

      Describes aspects of the reconstruction of a broken
      twelve-key English serpent.

*   Besseler, Heinrich. "Die Entstehung der Posaune." *Acta
      musicologica* 22 (1950): 8-35.

      Cited below as Item 999.

385. ———. "Some Further Notes on Serpent Technology."
      Galpin Society Journal 32 (1979): 214-29.

      Continues the discussion of the reconstruction of
      a serpent.

386. Draper, F.C. *Notes on the Boosey & Hawkes System of
      Automatic Compensation of Valved Brass Wind Instru-
      ments.* [Rev. ed.] London: Boosey and Hawkes, 1954.
      36 p.

      Describes in detail the intonation errors found in
      euphoniums and tubas without compensating valves and
      notes the significant reduction of error in instruments
      with compensating valves.

387. Ehmann, Wilhelm. *Tibilustrium: Das geistliche Blasen, Formen und Reformen.* Kassel: Bärenreiter, 1950. 175 p.

     Traces the evolution of the use of brass instruments in the church, stressing the role of the trombone choir. Discusses the proper use of brass instruments in services, the proper playing technique, and the literature available for brass choir.

*   Eliason, Robert E. "Early American Valves for Brass Instruments." *Galpin Society Journal* 23 (1970): 86-96.

     Cited above as Item 336.

388. Farrington, Frank. "Dissection of a Serpent." *Galpin Society Journal* 22 (1969): 81-96.

     Describes the reconstruction of a four-key English instrument. Includes drawings, photographs, a fingering chart, and notes on playing technique.

389. Galpin, Francis W. "The Sackbut, Its Evolution and History." *Proceedings of the Musical Association* 33 (1906-07): 1-25.

     A clear, concise examination. Well documented and still cited as a source of information. Errs in calling the *tromba da tirarsi* a "discant trombone."

*   Jaeger, Jürgen. "Zu Grundfragen des Blechbläseransatzes am Beispiel der Posaune." *Beiträge zur Musikwissenschaft* 13 (1971): 56-73.

     Cited below as Item 823.

390. Keays, James Harvey. "An Investigation into the Origins of the Wagner Tuba." D.M.A. dissertation, University of Illinois, 1977. 97 p. UM 78-4044.

     Examines the early history of the instruments. Discusses Wagner's original concept and his attempts to have the instruments built in time for the first performance of the *Ring*.

391. Lane, George B. *The Trombone in the Middle Ages and the Renaissance.* Bloomington, Ind.: Indiana University Press, 1982. 230 p.

     A thorough, well-documented account of the instrument

and its music. Includes an excellent bibliography.
Based on the author's D.M.A. dissertation (University
of Texas, 1976).

392. Leavis, Ralph. "More Light on the Cimbasso." *Galpin
     Society Journal* 34 (1981): 151-52.

     Quotes Verdi on the subject of the *cimbasso*, which
     he calls for in *Aida*. Suggests that the instrument is
     a serpent and notes Bellini's use of the term in *Norma*
     and possibly also in *Adelson e Salvini*. Also see
     Item 383, cited above.

393. Lewy, Rudolph. "Cimbasso--Verdi's Bass." *Das
     Musikinstrument* 30 (1981): 1132.

     Asserts that the word *cimbasso* is Verdi's invention
     and that the instrument intended is the bass trombone.
     Also see Items 383 and 392, cited above.

*   Merewether, Richard. *The Horn, the Horn*. London:
     Paxman, 1978. 54 p.

     Cited below as Item 417.

394. Morley Pegge, Reginald. "The 'Anaconda'." *Galpin
     Society Journal* 12 (1959): 53-56.

     Describes an exceptionally large serpent made *ca.* 1840
     by the Wood brothers of Yorkshire. Probably unique,
     the instrument is 15'7" long, approximately twice
     the length of the normal serpent.

395. Nicholson, Joseph M. "A Historical Background of the
     Trombone and Its Music." D.M.A. dissertation,
     University of Missouri, Kansas City, 1967. 52 p.
     UM 68-3573.

     Traces the evolution of the instrument from its
     origins through the eighteenth century and analyzes
     a number of solo works.

396. Pacey, Robert. "An Unusual Serpent." *Galpin Society
     Journal* 33 (1980): 132-33.

     Describes an unusual three-key serpent made in 1831.

*   Pechstein, Klaus. "Die Merkzeichentafel der Nürn-
     berger Trompeten- und Posaunemacher von 1640."
     *Mitteilungen des Vereins für Geschichte der Stadt
     Nürnberg* 59 (1972): 198-202.

     Cited below as Item 630.

397. Smith, David. "The Effects of Mouthpiece Design upon the Tone Color of Sixteenth and Seventeenth Century Trombones." M.A. thesis, Stanford University, 1978. 47 p.

 Concludes that mouthpiece design has little importance for the timbre of brass instruments. Also discusses the trumpet.

* ————. "Trombone Technique in the Early Seventeenth Century." D.M.A. dissertation, Stanford University, 1981. 98 p.

 Cited below as Item 917.

398. Weston, Stephen. "Improvements to the Nine-Keyed Ophicleide." *Galpin Society Journal* 36 (1983): 109-14.

 Reviews the changes in key mechanism and system made by Halary, Robertson, Macfarlane, Hughes, and others. Characterizes Hughes's system as the most perfect.

* Wörthmüller, Willi. "Die Instrumente der Nürnberger Trompeten- u. Posaunenmacher." *Mitteilungen des Vereins für Geschichte der Stadt Nürnberg* 46 (1955): 372-480.

 Cited above as Item 382.

3. Horn

399. Baines, Anthony. "The William Bull Horn." *Galpin Society Journal* 35 (1982): 157-58.

 Comments on the instrument found in the Carse Collection. Suggests that the bell is not original.

400. Bate, Philip. "Callcott's Radius French Horn: An English 'Cor Omnitonique'." *Galpin Society Journal* 2 (1949): 52-54.

 Describes an instrument made in Dublin during the nineteenth century. By means of a rotating slide that joins a 6' crook coil at various places, the instrument can be tuned to any of twelve different keys (from B natural chromatically downward an octave, with B flat omitted). Also see Item 418, cited below.

401. Blandford. W.F.H. "Some Observations on 'Horn Chords:
      An Acoustical Problem'." *The Musical Times* 67 (1926):
      128-31.

      Notes the possibility of the playing of chords on
      the horn, comments favorably on Kirby's article on the
      subject (cited below as Item 411), and mentions notable
      horn players of the day.

402. ————. "Studies on the Horn." *The Musical Times* 63
      (1922): 544-47, 622-24, 693-97; 66 (1925): 29-32,
      124-29, 221-23.

      Surveys the early history of the horn in England,
      reviews Wagner's treatment of the natural horn in his
      early operas, points out the impact made by the valve
      horn, and discusses the use of the horn in *Lohengrin*.
      Also discusses in detail the problematic fourth horn
      part in Beethoven's Ninth Symphony.

*   Bowles, Edmund A. "Unterscheidung der Instrumente Buisine,
      Cor, Trompe und Trompette." *Archiv für Musikwissen-
      schaft* 18 (1961): 52-72.

      Cited above as Item 327.

403. Damm, Peter. "Das Horn in der ersten Hälfte des 18.
      Jahrhunderts. Versuche der Interpretation hoher
      Hornpartien." *Die Blasinstrumente und ihre Verwendung*,
      edited by Eitelfriedrich Thom. Magdeburg: Rat des
      Bezirkes; Leipzig: Zentralhaus für Kulturarbeit,
      1977, pp. 37-41.

      Points out the differences in construction and
      sound between the modern and the Baroque horn. Recommends
      that Baroque parts be played on horns in F alto with
      an appropriately small mouthpiece.

404. ————. "300 Years of the Horn." *Brass Bulletin*, no.
      31 (1980): 19-33; no. 32 (1980): 19-41.

      A survey that places special emphasis upon the
      employment of the horn in the Dresden Court Orchestra.
      Parallel texts in German, French, and English.

405. Eichborn, Hermann. *Der Dämpfung beim Horn oder Die
      musikalische Natur des Horns*. Leipzig: Breitkopf
      und Härtel, 1897. 39 p.

      Argues the necessity of keeping the right hand in the
      bell of the valve horn. Characterizes the differences
      among French, German, and Italian players, praising the
      Germans.

* Eliason, Robert E. "Early American Valves for Brass Instruments." *Galpin Society Journal* 23 (1970): 86-96.

  Cited above as Item 336.

406. Fitzpatrick, Horace. "Blasinstrumente in Mozarts Instrumentalmusik (Instrumentenbau und Spieltechnik). Das Waldhorn der Mozartzeit und seine geschichtliche Grundlage." *Mozart Jahrbuch 1968-70*, 21-27.

  Surveys horn playing during the eighteenth century and the achievements of prominent players of the time. Describes the traits of the Viennese school of playing, characterizes the qualities of valveless horns in various keys, and praises Mozart's writing for the instrument.

407. ————. *The Horn and Horn-Playing and the Austro-Bohemian Tradition from 1680 to 1830*. London: Oxford University Press, 1970. 256 p.

  First full-scale study of its kind. Not altogether reliable in every respect but nevertheless essential to the study of the history of the instrument and its use. Includes a seven-inch recording.

408. ————. "Notes on the Vienna Horn." *Galpin Society Journal* 14 (1961): 49-51.

  Describes the distinctive features of the *Wiener Pumpenhorn*, an instrument--now falling out of use--that employes Uhlmann valves. Includes photographs.

409. ————. "Some Historical Notes on the Horn in Germany and Austria." *Galpin Society Journal* 16 (1963): 33-48.

  Transcribes and translates four repair invoices from Balthasar Furst, an eighteenth-century horn maker. The invoices shed light on the nomenclature in use at the time as well as on the instruments themselves. Also describes two Viennese horn mouthpieces from the period.

* Horvath, Helmuth. "Die physikalischen Aspekte der Blasinstrumente." *Oesterreichische Musikzeitschrift* 27 (1972): 649-57.

  Cited below as Item 461.

410. Howe, Marvin C. "A Critical Survey of Literature,
      Materials, Opinions, and Practices Related to
      Teaching the French Horn." Ph.D. dissertation,
      University of Iowa, 1967. 398 p. UM 67-2633.

      Traces the development of the horn and describes
      the evolution of horn playing as evident from the
      music.

*   Karstädt, Georg. "Die Verwendung der Horner in der
      Jagdmusik." *Bericht über die erste internationale
      Fachtagung zur Erforschung der Blasmusik, Graz 1974*,
      edited by Wolfgang Suppan and Eugen Brixel. Tutzing:
      Schneider, 1976, pp. 197-215.

      Cited below as Item 1015.

411. Kirby, Percival R. "Horn Chords: An Acoustical Problem."
      The Musical Times 66 (1925): 811-13.

      Notes the capability of the instrument to produce
      chords and sketches the acoustical background of the
      phenomenon.

412. Kling, Henri. "Le cor de chasse." *Rivista musicale
      italiana* 18 (1911): 95-136.

      A pioneering account of the history of the hunting
      horn and its early use in the orchestra. Quotes
      a detailed fourteenth-century description of hunting
      calls, fourteen in all.

413. Körner, Friedrich. "Ein Horn von Michael Nagel in
      Graz." *Historisches Jahrbuch der Stadt Graz* 2 (1969):
      87-96.

      Describes the discovery of the oldest surviving instru-
      ment from Nagel's workshop, made in 1647.

414. Lesure, François. "Pierre Trichet's *Traité des instru-
      ments de musique*: Supplement." *Galpin Society
      Journal* 13 (1962): 70-81; 16 (1963): 73-84.

      Quotes Trichet's remarks (*ca.* 1640) on *cornets de
      chasse et autres semblables instruments*. The treatise
      is cited above as Item 165.

415. Mansur, Paul. "Mansur's Answers." *The Horn Call* 13,
      No. 2 (April 1983): 13-16.

      Describes and illustrates a double French horn
      newly designed by Milos Kravka that features inlet

and outlet valves and which produces the kind of sound characteristics of natural horns.

416. Meer, John Henry van der. "Wide Sockets on 18th-Century Horns." *Galpin Society Journal* 36 (1983): 128.

Makes the point that a wide tube entrance on the horn does not indicate that the instrument was played with crooks.

417. Merewether, Richard. *The Horn, the Horn*. London: Paxman, 1978. 54 p.

Describes the acoustics of the instrument in detail and offers advice on maintenance and repair. Also includes a brief discussion of Wagner tubas, notably the kind designed by the author for the Paxman company.

418. Morley Pegge, Reginald. "Callcott's Radius French Horn." *Galpin Society Journal* 3 (1950): 49-51.

Briefly traces the history of the omnitonic horn and provides supplementary information about John Callcott and his invention. According to the author, the instrument is unique. His description of the instrument differs from Bate's (Item 400).

*   Pizka, Hans. *Das Horn bie Mozart/Mozart and the Horn*. Kirchheim: Pizka, 1980. 276 p.

Cited below as Item 1186.

419. Ricks, Robert. "Russian Horn Bands." *The Musical Quarterly* 55 (1969): 364-71.

Describes the origin, early history, and repertory of the bands. Also see Item 421, cited below.

420. Schneider, Friedrich. "Wichtige Verbesserung des Waldhorns." *Allgemeine musiklische Zeitung* 19 (1817): 814-816.

Points out that limitations of the natural horn and describes with approval Stölzel's new horn with two valves.

421. Seaman, Gerald. "The Russian Horn Band." *Monthly Musical Record* 89 (1959): 93-99.

Surveys the evolution of the band, describes its

repertory, the instruments employed, and the peculiar notation of rests. Also see the article cited above as Item 419.

422. Smith, Nicholas Edward. "The Horn Mute: An Acoustical and Historical Study." D.M.A. dissertation, University of Rochester, 1980. 91 p. UM 80-19,070.

Explains the acoustics of the mute, describes the muted horn parts in the music of the Second Viennese School, and traces the history of the mute.

*   Vandenbroeck, Othon. *Traité général de tous les instruments à vent à l'usage des compositeurs.* Paris: Boyer, [*ca.* 1794]; facsimile reprint, Geneva: Minkoff, 1974. 65 p.

Cited above as Item 46.

VIII

SPECIALIZED DISCUSSIONS REGARDING
PERCUSSION INSTRUMENTS

*   Altenberg, Johann Ernst. *Essay on an Introduction to the Heroic and Musical Trumpeters' and Kettledrummers' Art.* Translated by Edward H. Tarr. Nashville: Brass Press, 1974. 148 p.

Cited above as Item 321.

*   ————. *Versuch einer Anleitung zur heroisch-musikalischen Trompeter- und Paukerkunst.* Edited by Frieder Zschoch. Leipzig: Deutscher Verlag für Musik, 1973. 156 p.

Cited above as Item 322.

423.   Arbeau, Thoinot [pseud.]. *Orchèsographie.* Langres: I. de Preyz, 1596; facsimile reprint, Geneva: Minkoff, 1972. 208 p.

The most important dance manual of the Renaissance. Includes a brief description of drums in use at the time and a comprehensive list of drumming patterns employed in dance accompaniment. First published in 1588. Facsimile reprint published with a preface by François Lesure. English translations cited below as Items 424 and 425. Another facsimile reprint of the 1596 edition (Geneva: Slatkine Reprints, 1970) includes a valuable introduction by Laure Fonta.

424.   ————. *Orchesography.* Translated by Mary Stewart Evans. New York: Dover, 1967. 266 p.

Includes an introduction and notes by Jula Sutton as well as a transcription of dances in Labanotation made by Mireilee Backer and Julia Sutton. Evans's translation first published New York: Kamin, 1948. Facsimile reprint of Arbeau's original cited above as Item 423.

425.   ————. *Orchesography*. Translated by Cyril W.
       Beaumont. London: Beaumont, 1925; reprint ed.,
       New York: Dance Horizons, [1966]. 174 p.

       Includes a preface by the composer Peter Warlock
       (Philip Heseltine). Facsimile reprint of Arbeau's
       original cited above as Item 423.

426.   Aretz, Isabel. "Zur Erforschung lateinamerikanischer
       Musikinstrumente." International Musicological
       Society. *Report of the Eleventh Congress. Copenhagen
       1972*, edited by Henrik Glahn, Søren Sørensen, and
       Peter Ryom. Copenhagen: Hansen, 1974, pp. 138-40.

427.   Armas Lara, Marcial. *Origen de la marimba, su
       desenvolvimiento y otros instrumentos músicos.*
       Guatemala City: Centroamericana, 1970. 116 p.

       Argues that the marimba is indigenous to Guatemala.

428.   Benvenga, Nancy. "August Knocke's Timpani." *Percussion-
       ist* 16 (1978-79): 33-34.

       Describes machine timpani invented around 1840 by
       a Munich firearms manufacturer.

429.   ————. "Machine Timpani from Frankfurt-am-Main."
       Galpin Society Journal 33 (1980): 130-32.

       Depicts and describes a drum from 1884 manufactured
       probably by Johann Heinrich Lechner of Frankfurt.
       The drum seems similar to the timpani described by
       Victor de Pontigny in 1876.

430.   ————. *Timpani and the Timpanist's Art: Musical
       and Technical Evolution in the 19th and 20th
       Centuries*. Gothenburg: n.p., 1979. 160 p.

       Traces in detail the development of machine
       timpani, sticks, heads, and playing technique. Describes
       the evolution of the musical treatment of the timpani.
       Notes that the most important change in playing technique
       has been the development of pedalling technique.

431.   Blades, James, and Jeremy Montagu. *Early Percussion
       Instruments: From the Middle Ages to the Baroque.*
       London: Oxford University Press, 1976. 77 p.

       Traces the early history of percussion instruments.
       Describes their usage in the Renaissance and Baroque

and offers suggestions of the performance of early
music.

432. Bowles, Edmund A. "Nineteenth-Century Innovations in
      the Use and Construction of the Timpani." *Percussion-
      ist* 19, no. 2 (March 1982): 6-75.

      A full, authoritative, and well-documented account.
      Well illustrated with photographs, drawings, diagrams,
      and musical examples.

433. ―――. "On Using the Proper Tympani in the Performance
      of Baroque Music." *Journal of the American Musical
      Instrument Society* 2 (1976): 56-68.

      Describes the design and tone of the Baroque instrument.

434. Brown, Barclay. "The Noise Instruments of Luigi
      Russolo." *Perspectives of New Music* 20 (1981-82):
      31-49.

      Discusses Russolo's advocacy of music consisting
      partly of noise. Outlines Russolo's categories of noise,
      depicts some of the instruments he employed (none
      of which have survived), and describes a number of the
      instruments.

435. Caba, G. Craig. *United States Military Drums, 1745-
      1865.* Harrisburg, Penn.: Civil War Antiquities and
      Americana, 1977. 147 p.

      Illustrates and describes more than seventy instruments.
      Reprints a military drum manual from the period. Lists
      the principal drum makers and suppliers of the period.

436. Farmer, Henry George. *Handel's Kettledrums and Other
      Papers on Military Music.* London: Hinrichsen, 1950;
      reprint ed., London: Hinrichsen, 1965. 109 p.

      Includes chapters on the history of various British bands,
      drum and fife calls, the tenor drum, Handel's use of the
      great artillery kettledrums, and the importance of kettle-
      drums as military trophies.

437. Finger, G. "The History of the Timpani." *Percussionist*
      11 (1974): 101-06.

      Traces the development of the timpani from the
      Babylonian *tabus* to the *Heerpauken*.

438. Goldsmith, David S. "Foot-Operated Muffler-Dampers for
      Timpani." *NACWPI Journal* 23, no. 3 (Spring 1975):
      10-13.

      Describes a new device that facilitates muting.

439. Howard, Joseph H. *Drums in the Americas.* New York:
      Oak Publications, 1967. 319 p.

      Describes and discusses the most popular drums in
      the Western Hemisphere. Includes rattles and other
      percussion instruments associated with drums.

440. Howland, Howard. "The Vibraphone: A Summary of
      Historical Observations with a Catalog of Selected
      Solo and Small-Ensemble Literature." *Percussionist*
      14 (1976-77): 77-92; 15 (1977-78): 20-39.

      A careful historical survey. Includes a useful
      bibliography and a list of music arranged according to
      number of performances reported in *Percussive Notes.*

441. Kagel, Mauricio. *Theatrum instrumentorum.* Cologne:
      Kölnischer Kunstverein, 1975. 72 p.

      Illustrates, with photographs and diagrams, a large
      number of unusual new instruments, notably percussion
      instruments.

442. Longyear, Rey M. "Altenburg's Observations (1795) on
      the Timpani." *Percussionist* 7 (1969-70): 90-93.

      Summarizes and discusses the chapter on timpani in
      Altenburg's *Versuch* (cited above as Item 322).

443. Meyer, Jacqueline. "Early History and Development of
      the Vibes." *Percussionist* 13 (1976): 38-47.

      Covers the period from 1961 to 1936. Compares
      instruments manufactured by Leedy, Deagan, Premier,
      and Ludwig. Illustrated with photographs.

444. "Die neuen Pauken des Herrn Einbiegler...." *Allgemeine
      musikalische Zeitung* 47 (1845): 159-61.

      Points to the increased importance of timpani in
      the orchestra and praises the drums made by Einbiegler.
      Article signed "C.G."

445. Ortiz, Fernando. "La afroamericana *marimba.*" *Guatemala
      indigena* 6, no. 4 (December 1971): 9-43.

      A reprint of a study published in 1954. Calls
      attention to historical references to the marimba,
      describes its geographical distribution, reviews the
      names by which it is known, and describes the contexts
      in which it has been and is used.

446. Smith Brindle, Reginald. *Contemporary Percussion.*
     London: Oxford University Press, 1970. 217 p.

     Examines the treatment of percussion instruments in
     the music of the recent past. Describes the less
     common instruments, offers suggestions for notation,
     and explains the various roles percussion instruments
     can play.

*   Smithers, Don L. "The Hapsburg Imperial *Trompeter* and
     Heerpaucker Privileges of 1653." *Galpin Society
     Journal* 24 (1971): 84-95.

     Cited above as Item 368.

447. Spinney, Bradley. *Encyclopaedia of Percussion Instru-
     ments and Drumming.* 2 vols. Hollywood: Hollywood
     Percussion Club, 1955-59. 33, 40 p.

     Lists and explains terms from A (vol. 1) to B (vol. 2).
     Includes the names of some composers and performers.
     Illustrated.

*   Štědroň, Bohumir. "Die Landshafts-Trompeter und
     -Tympanisten im alten Brünn." *Die Musikforschung* 21
     (1968): 438-58.

     Cited above as Item 371.

448. Taylor, Henry W. *The Art and Science of the Timpani.*
     London: Baker, 1964. 76 p.

     Examines the acoustics of the timpani, discusses
     tuning, compares various kinds of sticks, and makes
     a number of observations on composers and specific works.

*   Titcomb, Caldwell. "Baroque Court and Military Trumpets
     and Kettledrums: Technique and Music." *Galpin
     Society Journal* 9 (1956): 56-81.

     Cited above as Item 374.

*   ————. "Carrousel Music at the Court of Louis XIV."
     *Essays on Music in Honor of Archibald Thompson
     Davison by His Associates.* Cambridge, Mass.: Harvard
     University, Department of Music, 1957, pp. 205-14.

     Cited above as Item 375.

449. Tobischek, Herbert. *Die Pauke. Ihre spiel- und bautech-
     nische Entwicklung in der Neuzeit.* Tutzing: Schneider,
     1977. 311 p.

A thorough historical account together with a
description of the acoustics of the timpani and a
discussion of the contributions of important makers
from the nineteenth and twentieth centuries. Includes
a good bibliography.

450. Torrebruno, Luigi. *Il timpano*. Milan: Ricordi, 1954.
      56 p.

      Intended as a guide to notation and usage for
      composers and arrangers. Includes a brief history of
      the instrument. Insists that it be referrred to in
      the singular (*timpano*) and not in the plural (*timpani*).

*   Winternitz, Emanuel. "Leonardo and Music." *The Unknown
        Leonardo*, edited by Ladislao Reti. London: Hutchinson,
        1974, pp. 110-35.

        Cited above as Item 217.

*   ————. *Leonardo da Vinci as a Musician*. New Haven:
        Yale University Press, 1982. 241 p.

        Cited above as Item 218.

IX

STUDIES IN ACOUSTICS

1. General

451. Backus, John. *The Acoustical Foundations of Music.*
2nd ed. New York: Norton, 1977. 368 p.

Perhaps the most popular American textbook on the
subject. Includes an excellent bibliography.

452. Benade, Arthur H. *Fundamentals of Musical Acoustics.*
New York: Oxford University Press, 1976. 596 p.

Comprehensive and detailed, yet accessible to readers
who lack extensive backgrounds in physics and mathematics.

453. Benade, Arthur H., and Daniel J. Gans. "Sound Production
in Wind Instruments." *Annals of the New York Academy
of Sciences* 155 (1968): 247-63.

A good summary. Now somewhat outdated by subsequent
research. Reprinted in Kent, cited below as Item 462.

454. Blaikley, D.J. "The Development of Modern Wind
Instruments." *Proceedings of the Musical Association*
12 (1885-86): 125-38.

A general survey that reflects accurately the state
of acoustical knowledge at the time.

455. ————. "On Quality of Tone in Wind Instruments."
Proceedings of the Musical Association 6 (1879-80):
70-90.

Reports the relative prominence of overtones in
various pitches produced by the clarinet and by brass
instruments. The investigation helps to confirm
Helmholtz's theory of compound tones.

456. Bouasse, Henri. *Instruments à vent*. 2 vols. Paris:
      Delagrave, 1929-30. 411, 387 p.

      A collection of technical essays on acoustics,
      including (but not limited to) the acoustics of wind
      instruments. The second volume is prefaced by a
      biting attack on French scientific education.

457. Culver, Charles A. *Musical Acoustics*. 4th ed. New York:
      McGraw-Hill, 1956. 305 p.

      First published in 1941 and thereafter revised only
      slightly. One of the first textbooks on the subject
      to receive wide acceptance in the United States.

458. Drake, Alan H. "Acoustical Research on Intensity and
      Loudness and Its Practical Application to Wind
      Instrument Performance." *Journal of Band Research* 6,
      no. 2 (Spring 1970): 5-12.

      A general survey based upon the work of Seashore,
      Mursell, Culver, Wood, and others. Deals partly with
      the question of the relationship of pitch to perceived
      loudness.

459. Hague, Bernard. "The Tonal Spectra of Wind Instruments."
      Proceedings of the Royal Musical Association 74 (1947-
      48): 67-83.

      Reviews the acoustics of wind instruments in generally
      non-technical language. Focuses partly on their character-
      istic tonal qualities.

460. Helmholtz, Hermann L.F. *On the Sensations of Tone as
      a Physiological Basis for the Theory of Music*. Trans-
      lated by Alexander J. Ellis. 2nd ed. New York:
      Dover, 1954. 576 p.

      The fundamental discussion of musical acoustics,
      tuning and temperament, and the perception of sound.
      Reprinted from the edition of 1885. Includes a new
      introduction by Henry Margenau, together with a
      bibliography of Helmholtz's work.

461. Horvath, Helmuth. "Die physikalischen Aspekte der
      Blasinstrumente." *Oesterreichische Musikzeitschrift*
      27 (1972): 649-57.

      Discusses the acoustics of wind instruments in
      relatively general terms. Also compares the sound quality

and playing characteristics of the Viennese single
horn and the double French horn in widespread use
elsewhere.

462. Kent, Earle L., ed. *Musical Acoustics: Piano and
Wind Instruments*. Benchmark Paper in Acoustics, vol.
9. Stroudsburg, Penn.: Dowden, Hutchinson and
Ross, 1977. 367 p.

A collection of thrity-one papers and patent
descriptions together with general comments by Kent.
Includes an excellent bibliography. The papers on
brass and woodwind instruments are cited here individually.

463. Levarie, Siegmund, and Ernst Levy. *Tone: A Study in
Musical Acoustics*. Kent, Ohio: Kent State University
Press, 1968. 248 p.

A good general introduction that views acoustics from
a musical and artistic perspective. Mathematical
calculations are held to a minimum.

464. Mahillon, Victor-Charles. *Éléments d'acoustique musicale et instrumentale*. Brussels: C. Mahillon, 1874.
270 p.

A historically important survey. Includes a discussion
of temperament and tuning.

* Meyer, Jürgen. "Die Problematik der Qualitätsbestimmung
bei Musikinstrumenten." *Instrumentenbau* 31 (1977):
241-28.

Cited above as Item 154.

465. Moritz, Camillo. *Die Orchester-Instrumente in akustischer
und technischer Betrachtung*. Berlin: Parrhysius,
1942. 174 p.

A comprehensive survey emphasizing general acoustics
as well as the acoustics of individual instruments.
Intended mainly for musicians (not for physicists) and
for technicians employed in the manufacture of musical
instruments.

466. *The Physics of Music*. San Francisco: W.H. Freeman, 1978.
98 p.

A collection of essays from *Scientific American*,
including the articles cited here as Item 482 and 546.

467. Rayleigh, John William Strutt, Baron. The Theory of
      Sound. 2nd ed. 2 vols. in 1. New York: Dover,
      1945. 480, 504 p.

      Reprinted, with a new introduction by Robert B.
      Lindsay, from the edition of 1929, which is only slightly
      revised from the edition published in 1896. A treatise
      of fundamental significance to the study of musical
      acoustics. Lindsay's introduction provides a valuable
      summary of Rayleigh's contributions.

468. Richardson, E.G. The Acoustics of Orchestral Instru-
      ments and of the Organ. London: Arnold, 1929. 158 p.

      A non-technical account based upon a series of
      lectures. Includes an explanation of the mathematical
      theory of fingering on woodwinds.

469. Roederer, Juan G. Introduction to the Physics and
      Psychophysics of Music. 2nd ed. New York: Springer,
      1975. 200 p.

      An integrated discussion of the physics and perception
      of sound. A fundamental treatment.

470. Rossing, Thomas D. "Musical Acoustics." American
      Journal of Physics 43 (1975): 944-53.

      A good annotated bibliography of books and articles.
      Available as a separate publication (Resource Letter
      MA-1) from the American Association of Physics Teachers.

471. Scheminzky, Ferdinand. Die Welt des Schalles. 2nd ed.
      Salzburg: Verlag Das Bergland-Buch, 1943. 820 p.

      A comprehensive survey of musical acoustics, including
      a discussion of the acoustics of rooms. Also discusses
      electronic amplification and reproduction as well as
      physiology of hearing.

472. Strong, Willia, and Melville Clark. "Perturbations of
      Synthetic Orchestral Wind-Instrument Tones." Journal
      of the Acoustical Society of America 41 (1967): 277-
      85.

      Evaluates the relative significance of spectral and
      temporal envelopes.

*   Sundberg, Johan. "The 'Scale' of Musical Instruments."
      Svensk tidskrift for musikforskning 49 (1967): 119-33.

Cited above as Item 162.

473. Wood, Alexander. *The Physics of Music*. 7th ed. Revised
     by J.M. Bowsher. London: Chapman and Hall, 1975.
     258 p.

     A popular textbook. Assumes relatively little mathe-
     matical background on the part of the reader. Seventh
     edition only slightly changed from the sixth, which
     appeared in 1962.

2. Woodwind Instruments

474. Aschoff, Volker. "Experimentelle Untersuchungen an
     einer Klarinette." *Akustische Zeitschrift* 1 (1936):
     77-93.

     Measures and reports the frequencies of overblown
     pitches and describes the action of the reed as observed
     experimentally.

475. Backus, John. "Acoustical Investigations of the Clarinet."
     Sound 2, no. 3 (May-June 1963): 22-25.

     Reviews the results of the author's research at the
     University of Southern California.

476. ————. "Resonance Frequencies of the Clarinet." *Journal
     of the Acoustical Society of America* 43 (1968): 1272-81.

     Describes the relationship between resonance frequencies
     and harmonic frequencies. Points out that, contrary to
     statements by other writers, even-numbered harmonics are
     clearly present in clarinet tones. Notes that the
     resonance curves for instruments of different manufacture
     and material are very much alike.

477. ————. "Small-Vibration Theory of the Clarinet."
     Journal of the Acoustical Society of America 35 (1963):
     305-13.

     Develops a theory of the clarinet based upon the fact
     that for soft tones the vibrations of the reed and of
     the air column are sinusoidal. Reprinted in Kent, Item
     462, cited above.

478. ————. "Variation with Loudness of the Harmonic Structure
     of Clarinet and Bassoon Tones." *Journal of the
     Acoustical Society of America* 34 (1962): 717.

Reports that the higher harmonics in clarinet and
bassoon tones decrease markedly as the tones become
softer. This is more true of the clarinet than of the
bassoon.

479. ————. "Vibrations of the Air Column and the Reed in
the Clarinet." *Journal of the Acoustical Society
of America* 33 (1961): 806-09.

Investigates the motion of the reed and the vibration
of the air column for loud and soft tones. Concludes,
in part, that for loud tones the aperture between reed
and mouthpiece is almost completely closed some of the
time.

480. Benade, Arthur H. "On the Mathematical Theory of
Woodwind Finger Holes." *Journal of the Acoustical
Society of America* 32 (1960): 1591-1608.

Systematically explores the effects of closed and
open holes on woodwind instruments. Reprinted in
Kent, cited above as Item 462. The reprint includes
new appendices and a list of errata found in the original
article.

481. ————. "On Woodwind Instrument Bores." *Journal of
the Acoustical Society of America* 31 (1959): 137-46.

Considers bore shape apart from the reed system.
Reprinted in Kent, cited above as Item 462. The reprint
includes corrections made by the author.

482. ————. "The Physics of Woodwinds." *Scientific American*
204, no. 4 (October 1960): 145-54.

Centers on the effect on tone tones on the vibration
of the air column. A non-technical, easily readable
account. Well illustrated. Reprinted in Kent, Item
462.

483. Brindley, Giles. "A Method for Analysing Woodwind
Cross-Fingerings." *Galpin Society Journal* 22 (1969):
40-46.

Describes a method of analyzing the manner in which
high pitches can be produced on the recorder. The
method is applicable to other instruments as well.

484. ————. "The Standing Wave-Patterns of the Flute."
Galpin Society Journal 24 (1971): 5-15.

A highly technical description of the wave patterns produced on an 1867-system wooden flute by Carte.

485. Burton, James L. "Bassoon Bore Dimensions." D.M.A. dissertation, University of Rochester, 1975. 266 p. UM 75-26,152.

Investigates the bore shape of sixty-five bassoons. Finds that the playing characteristics of the instruments are improved if the bores are altered to conform to the contour patterns found in Heckel bassoons.

486. Castellengo, Michele. "La flûte traversière." *Bulletin du Groupe d'acoustique musicale* 35 (April 1968): 1-37.

Reviews the acoustical aspects of the instrument.

487. Coltman, John W. "Acoustics of the Flute." *Woodwind Anthology*. Evanston, Ill.: Instrumentalist, 1976, pp. 158-66.

A detailed yet, even for non-specialists, easily readable account.

488. ————. "Effect of Material on Flute Tone Quality." *Journal of the Acoustical Society of America* 49 (1971): 520-23.

Determines that the material out of which the body of the flute is made has no effect on tone quality. Reprinted in *Woodwind World* 11, no. 2 (april 1972): 20, 26.

489. ————. "The Intonation of Antique and Modern Flutes." *Woodwind Anthology* (Evanston, Ill.: Instrumentalist, 1976), pp. 232-43.

Describes the deviations in intonation of a sample number of flutes from the early eighteenth century to the present. Observes that the intonation of modern flutes is superior but that they suffer unnecessarily from design flaws carried over from earlier instruments, which result in a somewhat sharp upper register. Reports favorably on the Murray flute.

490. ————. "Mouth Resonance Effects in the Flute." *Journal of the Acoustical Society of America* 54 (1973): 417-20.

Observes that changes in mouth resonance, which occur around 1000 Hz, affect frequency by approximately ten cents.

491. Crow, E.J. "Remarks on Certain Peculiarities in
     Instruments of the Clarinet Family." *Proceedings
     of the Musical Association* 11 (1884-85): 19-32.

     Reports experiments by William Rowlett in which
     a basset horn was played with a bassoon reed and, less
     successfully, a clarinet with an oboe reed. In both
     cases, the instruments produced the octave harmonic on
     overblowing, leading Rowlett to conclude that single
     reeds cause instruments to produce the harmonic of the
     twelfth. Rowlett's reasoning and conclusions are
     challenged by D.J. Blaikely in an ensuing discussion
     (pp. 25-32).

492. Elliott, Charles A. "The Effect of the Mouthpiece Upon
     the Intonational Characteristics of the Scale of the
     Baritone Saxophone." *Journal of Band Research* 8, no. 1
     (Fall 1971): 35-36.

     Reports a limited study that leads to the conclusion
     that the mouthpiece has no effect on the intonation of
     the instrument.

493. Fajardo, Raoul J. "New Flute Embouchure." *Early Music*
     1 (1973): 152-53.

     Describes and depicts three head joints patented and
     made by the author. Also illustrates and describes a
     new device to study the acoustical properties of
     open and closed pipes.

494. Fletcher, Neville H. "Acoustical Correlates of Flute
     Performance Technique." *Journal of the Acoustical
     Society of America* 57 (1975): 233-37.

     Reports that amplitude variations in flute playing
     are largely confined to the upper partials and that
     vibrato usually consists of an amplitude modulation of
     those partials. Reprinted in Kent, Item 462, cited
     above.

495. ———. "Some Acoustical Principles of Flute
     Technique." *Instrumentalist* 28, No. 7 (February
     1974): 57-61.

     Analyzes lip position and blowing pressure in relation
     to octave selection, pitch modification, volume, tone,
     and vibrato. Based partly on laboratory experiments.

496. Guillaume, Dennis A. "Acoustics and the Saxophone
     Mouthpiece Chamber." *Journal of Band Research* 9,

no. 1 (Fall 1972): 40-47.

A preliminary report showing, unsurprisingly, significant differences in tone quality produced by two mouthpieces of different chamber shape.

497. Halfpenny, Eric. "The Tonality of Wood-wind Instruments." *Proceedings of the Royal Musical Association* 75 (1948-49): 23-38.

Advances the hypothesis of a seven-hole scale common to all woodwind instruments.

498. Heine, Alois. *Akustische Phänomene: Untersuchungen und Experimente mit der Klarinette und Einführung in die Ausatztechniken zur Erzeugung von Überblasetönen, Untertönen und Akkordklängen*. Munich: Katzbichler, 1978. 87 p.

Describes the principles of overtones on the clarinet and offers a guide to the performance of multiphonics. Provides fingerings for the Boehm system clarinet as well as for the Oehler or German system instrument.

499. Hilton, Lewis B. "An Introduction to the Acoustics and Operating Principles of the Woodwind Instruments." *Woodwind World* 10, no. 1 (February 1971): 10-16; 10, no. 2 (April 1971): 11-15.

Explains simply the rudiments of the acoustics of woodwinds and the fundamental principles of fingering.

500. Jost, Ekkehard. *Akustische und psychometrische Untersuchungen an Klarinetteklängen*. Cologne: Arno Volk, 1967. 99 p.

Examines the relationship between aural impressions and the physical stimuli.

501. Kruger, Walther. "Zur Stimmung von Klarinetten." *III. Akusztikai Konferencia, Budapest*. Budapest: Optikai, Akusztikai és Filmtechnikal Egyesület, 1967, pp. 225-30.

Discusses the mistuning of the first overtone of the clarinet and points out that the tuning can be corrected by changes in the cross-section of the instrument.

502. Lanier, James M. "An Acoustical Analysis of Tones Produced by Clarinets Constucted of Various Materials." *Journal of Research in Music Education* 8 (1960): 16-22.

Reports the variation in tone produced by clarinets
of different materials--metal, wood, and ebonite.
Generally the wood clarinets produced tones with stronger
third and fifth partials than the other instruments.

503.　Lawson, Charles E.　"A Comprehensive Performance Project
in Clarinet Literature with an Essay on an Investigation
to Determine if the Oral Cavity Acoustically Influences
the Radiated Wave Form of the Clarinet."　D.M.A. dissertation, University of Iowa, 1974.　180 p.　UM 75-13,853.

Reports the results of experiments showing that the
resonance in the oral cavity is not important to tone
quality.　Manipulations of the oral cavity can, however,
affect the air pressure and flow.

504.　Lehman, Paul R.　"Harmonic Structure of the Bassoon."
Journal of the Acoustical Society of America 36 (1964):
1649-53.

Drawn from Item 503, cited below.

505.　————.　"The Harmonic Structure of the Tone of the
Bassoon."　Ph.D. dissertation, University of Michigan,
1962.　211 p.　UM 63-390.

An analysis of bassoon tone that determines that the
first partial generally tends to be rather weak and that
fewer partials are present at the pianissimo level than
at fortissimo.　Notes significant differences in the
sound spectra of different players' tones.

506.　Mather, Roger.　"The Choice of Flute Tube Material and
Thickness."　*Woodwind World* 13, no. 2 (April 1974):
24-27; 13, no. 3 (Summer 1974): 19-21, 27-28.

Describes what the author perceives as the differences
in tone quality created by different materials and
thicknesses.　Also see Item 507, cited below.

507.　————.　"The Influence of Tube Material and Thicknesses
on Flute Tone Quality."　*Woodwind World* 11, no. 4
(September 1972): 6-7.

Questions the tests conducted by Coltman and the
validity of the results obtained.　See above, Item 488.

508.　McDaniel, William Theodore Jr.　"A Synthesis of Selected
Research Studies Relating to the Physical-Acoustical

Phenomena of the Clarinet." *Journal of Band Research* 10, no. 2 (Spring 1974): 33-40.

A brief but useful summary.

509. McGinnis, C.S., and C. Gallagher. "The Mode of Vibration of A Clarinet Reed." *Journal of the Acoustical Society of America* 12 (1940-41): 529-31.

Concludes that during the sounding of any note the flow of air into the mouthpiece is completely cut off by the reed. Also see Item 479, cited above.

510. McGinnis, C.S., H. Hawkins, and N. Sher. "An Experimental Study of the Tone Quality of the Boehm Clarinet." *Journal of the Acoustical Society of America* 14 (1942-43): 228-37.

A thorough investigation showing the relative strength of harmonics for each note in the normal range of the clarinet. Offers a scientific explanation for the differences in timbre of the three registers of the instrument.

* McGinnis, C.S., and R. Pepper. "Intonation of the Boehm Clarinet." *Journal of the Acoustical Society of America* 16 (1944-45): 188-93.

Cited above as Item 299.

511. Meyer, Jürgen. *Akustik der Holzblasinstrumente in Einzeldarstellungen*. Frankfurt: Das Musikinstrument, 1966. 90 p.

Brings together five essays and technical reports relating particularly to the clarinet and bassoon. The chapters are cited here separately as Items 514, 515, 516, 518, and 519.

512. ————. "Akustische Untersuchungen an Klarinetten." *Studia instrumentorum musicae popularis*, vol. 2, edited by Erich Stockmann. Stockholm: Musikhistoriska museet, 1972, pp. 103-11.

Summarizes the results of a careful scientific investigation, reporting that air pressure has very little effect on pitch, that the influence of lip pressure is greatest in the middle register, and that air pressure should not be greater for high notes than for low notes.

513.   ———. "Akustische Untersuchungen über den Klang alter
        und neuer Fagotte." *Das Musikinstrument* 17, no 11
        (November 1968): 1259-66.

        Reports that Baroque bassoons are dark in timbre and
        sound best in the low and middle ranges. Bassoons of
        Mozart's time are brighter than present-day instruments
        and sound best in the high register.

514.   ———. "Die Deutung von Klangspektren." *Akustik der
        Holzblasinstrumente in Einzeldarstellungen.* Frankfurt:
        Das Musikinstrument, 1966, pp. 33-47.

        Identifies, illustrates (with graphs), and discusses
        the components of woodwind tone color.

515.   ———. "Die Klangspektren von Fagotten." *Akustik der
        Holzblasinstrumente in Einzeldarstellungen.* Frankfurt:
        Das Musikinstrument, 1966, pp. 49-65.

        A systematic, detailed overview of bassoon tone quality,
        showing the influence of various factors.

516.   ———. "Die Klangspektren von Klarinetten." *Akustik
        der Holzblasinstrumente in Einzeldarstellungen.* Frank-
        furt: Das Musikinstrument, 1966, pp. 67-89.

        A detailed, technical overview of the relationship of
        various elements--dynamics, pitch, reeds, instrument
        bore, size of tone holes, and pads--upon clarinet tone
        quality.

517.   ———. "Die Richtcharakteristiken von Klarinetten."
        Das Musikinstrument 14, no. 1 (January 1965): 21-25.

        Reports an investigation of the directional character-
        istics of clarinet tone, including the role played by
        sound reflection from the floor. The placement of the
        instrument's axis has a significant effect upon what
        is heard.

518.   ———. "Über die Stimmungen von Holzblasinstrumenten."
        Akustik der Holzblasinstrumente in Einzeldarstellungen.
        Frankfurt: Das Musikinstrument, 1966, pp. 7-21.

        An introduction to the question of the intonation of
        woodwind instruments, contemporary and historical. In-
        cludes graphs showing the tuning of several.

519.   ———. "Über die Stimmung von Klarinetten." *Akustik
        der Holzblasinstrumente in Einzeldarstellungen.*

Frankfurt: Das Musikinstrument, 1966, pp. 23-31.

A careful discussion, based on experimental investigation, of the influence exerted upon intonation by different reeds and barrel joints, and by the size and location of the tone holes.

520. Miller, Jean R. "A Spectrum Analysis of Clarinet Tones." Ph.D. dissertation, University of Wisconsin, 1956. 230 p. UM 56-3463.

Concludes in part that the distribution and amplitude of partials cannot be fully explained by either the formant or the harmonic theory.

521. Mooney, James E. "The Effect of the Oral Cavity on the Tone Quality of the Clarinet." Ph.D. dissertation, Brigham Young University, 1968. 221 p. UM 69-2007.

Reports an experimental investigation of the effect of air pressure and tongue position upon pitch and tone.

522. Myers, Herbert Wendell. "The Practical Acoustics of Early Woodwinds." D.M.A. dissertation, Stanford University, 1981. 140 p. UM 81-9026.

Examines the acoustical behavior of tone holes, bore, and material. Also describes the effect of keywork and tone generators. Notes the excellence of early instrument designs.

523. Nederveen, Cornelius J. *Acoustical Aspects of Woodwind Instruments*. Amsterdam: Knuf, 1969. 120 p.

Attempts to find a precise method for calculating the size and placement of tone holes. Notes that the material out of which the instrument is made does not affect timbre.

524. ———. "Calculations on Location and Dimensions of Holes in a Clarinet." *Acustica* 14 (1964): 227-34.

Describes a method for calculating the location and diameter of clarinet tone holes. For a more extended discussion, see Item 523, cited above.

525. Parker, Sam E. "Analyses of the Tones of Wooden and Metal Clarinets." *Journal of the Acoustical Society of America* 19 (1947): 415-19.

Concludes that the material out of which the instrument is made has no effect on tone quality.

526. Patterson, John. "Bassoon Acoustical Research." *To the World's Bassoonists*, 2, no. 1 (Winter 1971): 2.

      Describes recent research on the acoustics of the modern Heckel system instrument.

*   Phelan, James, and Mitchell D. Brody. *The Complete Guide to the Flute from Acoustics and Construction to Repair and Maintenance.* Boston: Conservatory Publications, 1980. 109 p.

      Cited above as Item 201.

527. Russell, Myron E. "The Oboe: A Comparison Study of Specifications with Musical Effectiveness." Ph.D. dissertation, University of Michigan, 1953. 321 p. UM 5723.

      Investigates the relationship between tone quality and bore, the thickness of the body of the instrument, and the size and placement of the tone holes. Concludes that the bore should conform to a specific pattern of deviations from a true cone.

528. Saunders, F.A. "Analyses of the Tones of a Few Wind Instruments." *Journal of the Acoustical Society of America* 18 (1946-47): 395-401.

      Describes the relative strength of the various harmonics in the oboe, English horn, flute, and clarinet. Finds no evidence of formants.

529. Shreffler, Anne Chatoney. "Baroque Flutes and Modern: Sound Spectra and Performance Results." *Galpin Society Journal* 36 (1983): 88-96.

      Compares the sound of Baroque and modern flutes. Analyzes a Bach sarabande for flute in regard to sound color.

530. Sirker, Udo. "Methoden der Klangfarbenforschung, darge-stellt an quasistationären Klängen von Doppelrohrblattin-strumenten." *Musicae scientiae collectanea. Festschrift Karl Gustav Fellerer zum siebzigsten Geburtstag am 7. Juli 1972*, edited by Heinrich Hüschen. Cologne: Arno Volk, 1973, pp. 561-76.

      Describes the investigations by others of the tone quality of double reed instruments and reports the results of the author's studies of shawms. Stresses the importance, especially for future investigations, of

employing not only the physical but physiological and
psychological perspectives as well.

531. Stauffer, Donald W. *Intonation Deficiencies of Wind
Instruments*. Washington, D.C.: Catholic University
of America Press, 1954. 191 p.

Describes in detail the characteristics of intonation
of wind instruments and offers suggestions for the
improvement of intonation in performance. Suggests that
the shape of the oral cavity has a significant effect
on tone quality. Also see Items 490, 503, and 521,
cited above.

*   Stubbins, William H. *The Art of Clarinetistry: The
Acoustical Mechanics of the Clarinet as a Basis for
the Art of Music Performance*. 3rd ed. Ann Arbor:
Guillaume Press, 1974. 329 p.

Cited below as Item 847.

532. Stumpf, Carl. "Trompete und Flöte." *Festschrift
Hermann Kretzschmar zum 70. Geburtstage überreicht
von Kollegen, Schülern und Freunden*. Leipzig: C.F.
Peters, 1918; reprint ed., Hildesheim: Olms, 1973,
pp. 155-57.

Describes the relative prominence of overtones in the
sound of the flute and the trumpet. Refers to the "old
question" of the influence of the material out of which
the instrument is made.

533. Syrový, Václav. "Tranzient tónu klarinetu." *Hudebni nástroje* 14, no. 1 (February 1977): 14-17.

Defines the quality of clarinet tone in terms of its
physical properties and through subjective perceptions
as well. Offers data obtained by scientific measurement.

534. Todenhoft, Charles N. "The Effect of Humidity upon the
Intonation and Response of Wood Clarinets." Mus.Ed.D.
dissertation, Indiana University, 1966. 123 p. UM
67-351.

Determines that increased humidity results in a slight
increase in the size of the bore of the instrument and
a slight rise in pitch.

*   Vaucanson, Jacques de. *An Account of the Mechanism of
an Automaton or Image Playing on the German-Flute/Le*

mécanisme du fluteur automate. London: Parker, 1742; facsimile reprint, Buren: Knuf, 1979. 46 p.

Cited above as Item 213.

535. Voigt, Wolfgang. *Untersuchungen zur Formantbildung in Klangen von Fagott und Dulzianen.* Regensburg: Bosse, 1975. 275 p.

Reports the results of a thorough experimental study. Includes a review of previous research.

536. Vorreiter, Leopold. "Der Unterschied zwischen Flöten und Pfeifen, historisch wie physikalisch." *Instrumentenbau* 30 (1976): 550-53.

Explains the differences between flutes and fifes in terms of nine criteria and discusses, with the aid of graphs, experimental results concerning the pitch of open and closed pipes of various lengths and widths.

537. Weber, Gottfried. "Praktische Resultate aus der Akustik der Blasinstrumente." *Allgemeine musikalische Zeitung* 19 (1817): 809-14, 825-32.

Describes the effects of various flute fingerings. Includes a fingering chart for the three-key flute. Supplements his lengthy discussion from the previous year, cited below as Item 538.

538. ————. "Versuch einer praktischen Akustik der Blasinstrumente." *Allgemeine musikalische Zeitung* 18 (1816): 33-44, 49-61, 65-74.

A pioneering investigation of the acoustics of wind instruments. Focuses on the overtone series. Also discusses flutes fingerings. Supplemented by the article cited above as Item 537.

*   Worman, Walton E. "Boehm's Design of the Flute: A Comparison with that of Rockstro." *Galpin Society Journal* 28 (1975): 107-20.

Cited above as Item 219.

539. ————. "Self-Sustained Nonlinear Oscillations of Medium Amplitude in Clarinet-Like Systems." Ph.D dissertation, Case Western Reserve University, 1971. 167 p. UM 71-22,869.

Develops the theory of oscillations outlined by Benade and Gans. See above, Item 453.

540. Wyman, Frederick S. "An Acoustical Study of Alto
     Saxophone Mouthpiece Chamber Design." Ph.D. disser-
     tation, University of Rochester, 1972. 196 p. UM
     72-24,995.

     Indentifies the design factors responsible for relative
     brightness and evenness of tone quality. Points out
     that the undamped and "accessory" harmonics noted in the
     investigation are not accounted for in the generally
     accepted theories.

2. Brass Instruments

541. Aebi, Willi. "Stopped Horn." *The Horn Call* 6, no. 2
     (May 1976): 46-49.

     Comments on Merewether's article below as Item 559.
     Illustrated with diagrams that show the various positions
     of the sound pressure curve in the bell.

542. ————. "The Inner Acoustics of the Horn." *The Horn
     Call* 4 (1973-74): 50-57.

     Also published, on the pages preceding, in French
     and German. Describes sound pressure within the horn
     and offers an acoustical explanation for the effect of
     hand stopping. Includes diagrams and graphs that also
     appear in the article cited above as Item 541.

543. Backus, John. "Input Impedance Curves for the Brass
     Instruments." *Journal of the Acoustical Society of
     America* 60 (1976): 470-80.

     Points out the importance of the bell and the mouth-
     piece in relation to the resonance frequencies of the
     instrument. Examines the matter of hand stopping in
     horn playing and concludes that the effect is to lower
     the frequencies of all the nodes.

544. Backus, John, and T.C. Hundley. "Harmonic Generation in
     the Trumpet." *Journal of the Acoustical Society of
     America* 49 (1970): 509-19.

     Concludes that the mechanism primarily responsible
     for the generation of harmonics is the relationship
     between the input impedance of the trumpet and the
     time-varying impedance of the player's lip opening.

545. Bahnert, Heinz, Theodor Herzberg, and Herbert Schramm.
      Metallblasinstrumente. Leipzig: Fachbuchverlag
      Leipzig, 1958. 254 p.

      A comprehensive, detailed explanation of the acoustics
      of brass instruments. Includes a survey of the history
      of brass instruments, their construction, and their
      use. Briefly describes percussion instruments as well.
      Copiously illustrated with diagrams and drawings.

546. Benade, Arthur H. "The Physics of Brasses." *Scientific
      American* 229, no. 1 (July 1973): 24-35.

      Clear and precise. An excellent introduction to the
      subject. Reprinted in Kent, Item 462, cited above.

547. Benade, Arthur H., and Erik V. Jansson. "On Plane and
      Spherical Waves in Horns with Nonuniform Flare."
      Acoustica 31 (1974): 79-98, 185-202.

      A detailed, highly technical study of sound waves in
      horns of varying taper. Compares the two forms of
      horn theory (plane wave and spherical wave) and concludes
      that for design purposes, either form is satisfactory
      for calculating resonance frequencies. Reprinted in
      Kent, Item 462, cited above.

548. Blaikley, D.J. "Communication Respecting a Point in
      the Theory of Brass Instruments." *Proceedings of
      the Musical Association* 4 (1877-78): 56-67.

      A pioneering investigation of the acoustics of brass
      instruments made by one of the most eminent acousticians
      of his day. Blaikley was technical adviser to Boosey
      and Hawkes for approximately sixty years.

*   ————. "On Quality of Tone in Wind Instruments."
      Proceedings of the Musical Association 6 (1879-80):
      79-90.

      Cited above as Item 455.

549. Blandford, W.F.H. "The Intonation of Brass Instruments."
      The Musical Times 77 (1936): 19-21, 118-21.

      Reviews the acoustic principles of the brass instru-
      ments and describes briefly the tuning problems
      encountered.

550. Cardwell, William T. "Cup-Mouthpiece Wind Instruments."
      U.S. Patent No. 3, 507, 181 (April 21, 1970).

Describes a mathematical method for determining the optimum shape of the air column in brass instruments. The method has proved of practical value in designing trumpets. Reprinted in Kent, Item 462, cited above.

* Draper, F.C. *Notes on the Boosey & Hawkes System of Automatic Compensation of Valved Brass Wind Instruments.* [Rev. ed.] London: Boosey and Hawkes, 1954. 36 p.

Cited above as Item 386.

551. Earnest, Christopher. "The Horn: Stopped, Muted, and Open." *The Horn Call* 7, no. 2 (May 1977): 34-36.

A detailed explanation of the physics of the instrument, especially in regard to hand stopping.

552. Eisner, Edward. "Complete Solutions of the 'Webster' Horn Equation." *Journal of the Acoustical Society of America* 41 (1967): 1126-46.

Reviews the theory of horns and sets forth solutions of the Webster equation. Includes an annotated bibliography of approximately 200 items.

553. Hallquist, Robert Eugene. "A Comparative Study of the Effect of Various Mouthpieces on the Harmonic Content of Trumpet Tones." Ph.D. dissertation, University of Minnesota, 1979. 130 p. UM 79-8339.

Concludes that as the dynamic level increases, the differences among the mouthpieces seem smaller. There appears to be a greater difference on lower pitches than on higher.

* Horvath, Helmuth. "Die physikalischen Aspekte der Blasinstrumente." *Oesterreichische Musikzeitschrift* 27 (1972): 649-57.

Cited above as Item 461.

* Jaeger, Jürgen. "Zu Grundfragen des Blechbläseransatzes am Beispiel der Posaune." *Beiträge zur Musikwissenschaft* 13 (1971): 56-73.

Cited below as Item 823.

* Kirby, Percival R. "Horn Chords: An Acoustical Problem." *The Musical Times* 66 (1925): 811-13.

Cited above as Item 411.

554. Knauss, H.P., and W.J. Yeager. "Vibration of the Walls
      of a Cornet." *Journal of the Acoustical Society of
      America* 13 (1941-42): 160-62.

      Suggests that the vibration of the walls of the instru-
      ment makes at most an insignificant contribution to the
      sound.

555. Kurka, Martin J. "A Study of the Acoustical Effects of
      Mutes on Wind Instrument." M.Mus. thesis, University
      of South Dakota, 1958. 102 p.

      Reports the results of an extensive experimental
      investigation. Concludes in part that mutes tend to
      project sound along the axis of the bell and that they
      affect the sound field of the instrument more in the
      medium and high registers than in the low register.

556. Long, T.H. "On the Performance of Cup Mouthpiece Instru-
      ments." *Journal of the Acoustical Society of America*
      20 (1948): 875-76.

      An answer to Young's letter, cited below as Item
      557. Reprinted in Kent, Item 462, cited above.

557. ————. "The Performance of Cup-Mouthpiece Instruments."
      Journal of the Acoustical Society of America 19 (1947):
      892-901.

      Demonstrates that in the playing of brass instruments
      there must be a pressure antinode created at or near
      the mouthpiece. Explains the harmonic content of the
      sound as being based on the overloading of the air
      column and advances theoretical reasons for several
      well-known characteristics of the instruments. Also
      see Young, cited below as Item 574, as well as Long's
      letter cited above as Item 556. Reprinted in Kent,
      Item 462, cited above.

558. Martin, Daniel W. "Lip Vibrations in Cornet Mouthpiece."
      Journal of the Acoustical Society of America 13 (1941-
      42): 305-08.

      Describes an experimental study of lip action. Re-
      printed in Kent, Item 462, cited above. Also reprinted
      in *Brass World* 4 (1968): 392-95.

*   Merewether, Richard. *The Horn, the Horn*. London:
      Pasman, 1978. 54 p.

      Cited above as Item 417.

559. ————. "The Question of Hand-Stopping." *The Horn Call*, 5, no. 2 (Spring 1975): 45-59.

A summary of the acoustical theory.

560. Meyer, Jürgen. "Akustische Untersuchungen über den Klang des Hornes." *Das Musikinstrument* 16, no. 1 (January 1967): 32-37; no. 2 (February 1967): 199-203.

An investigation of horn tone. Demonstrates that modern horns and horns from the nineteenth century exhibit their most characteristic tone color at the frequency of about 340 Hz. Notes that the tone quality of horns from the Classic period was brighter than the tone quality of later horns.

561. ————. "Die Richtcharakteristiken des Hornes." *Das Musikinstrument* 18, no. 6 (June 1969): 1-10.

Notes that horn sound is not always emitted in the direction that is best for all frequencies—parallel to the axis of the instrument. Observes that deflection of the sound off the back wall of a stage can increase the intensity by as much as fifteen decibels. Discusses the placement of the horn section in the orchestra.

562. Meyer, Jürgen, and Klaus Wogram. "Die Richtcharakteristiken von Trompete, Posaune und Tuba." *Das Musikinstrument* 19, no. 2 (February 1970): 171-80.

Investigates the extent to which directionality of sound is dependent on the frequency of the tone. Explains the effects on sound of various seating arrangements and of reverberations from walls and ceilings.

563. Müller, Ulrich R. *Untersuchungen zu den Strukturen von Klängen der Clarin- und Ventiltrompete.* Regensburg: Bosse, 1971. 165 p.

Analyzes the timbre of clarino and valve trumpets and notes the difference in resonance intensity between the two types. Also points out the difference in oscillation patterns.

564. Payne, Ian W. "Observations on the Stopped Notes of the French Horn." *Music and Letters* 49 (1968): 145-54.

Offers an acoustical explanation of hand stopping. Discusses the mode of vibration of the air column in the horn and suggests that there is a node at the bell end of the column.

565. Pyle, Robert W., Jr. "Effective Length of Horns."
     Journal of the Acoustical Society of America 57 (1975):
     1309-17.

     Redefines effective length as a continuous function
     of frequency. Notes that the effective length is
     influenced by the environment in which the instrument is
     played, owing to the presence of reflected sound.

566. Redfield, John. "Minimizing Discrepancies of Intonation
     in Valve Instruments." *Journal of the Acoustical
     Society of America* 3 (1931-32): 292-96.

     Points out the difficulty of tuning valve instruments
     and offers tuning suggestions.

567. Roberts, B. Lee. "Some Comments on the Physics of the
     Horn and Right-Hand Technique." *The Horn Call* 6, no.
     2 (May 1976): 41-45.

     Discusses the pressure waves in a horn. Points out
     that the wave length is increased when the bell is
     stopped and that the increase is greatest for the lower
     harmonics.

*   Saunders, F.A. "Analyses of the Tones of a Few Wind
     Instruments." *Journal of the Acoustical Society
     of America* 18 (1946): 395-401.

     Cited above as Item 528.

*   Smith, Nicholas Edward. "The Horn Mute: An Acoustical
     and Historical Study." D.M.A. dissertation, Univer-
     sity of Rochester, 1980. 91 p. UM 80-19,070.

     Cited above as Item 422.

*   Stumpf, Carl. "Trompete und Flöte." *Festschrift Hermann
     Kretzschmar zum 70. Geburtstage überreicht von
     Kollegen, Schülern und Freunden.* Leipzig: C.F.
     Peters, 1918; reprint ed., Hildesheim: Olms, 1973,
     pp. 155-57.

     Cited above as Item 532.

568. Webster, John. "An Electrical Method of Measuring the
     Intonation of Cup-Mouthpiece Instruments." *Journal
     of the Acoustical Society of America* 19 (1947): 902-06.

     Describes an early system employed in the study of
     the acoustics of brass instruments. Reprinted in Kent,
     Item 462, cited above.

569. ————. "Internal Differences Due to Players and the Taper of Trumpet Bells." *Journal of the Acoustical Society of America* 21 (1949): 208-14.

Describes the variations in intonation that result from changes in bell taper and also from the differences in players.

570. Wogram, Klaus. "The Acoustical Properties of Brass Instruments." *The Horn Call* 13, No. 2 (April 1983): 19-31.

Reports the results of experimental studies that show, in part, that timbre is influenced by the composition of the material out of which brass instruments are made but not by wall thickness or surface. Also describes the influence of mouthpieces, instrument taper, and hand hold, as well as the effect of directed sound radiation upon musical performance.

571. ————. "Die Beeinflussung von Klang und Ansprache durch das 'Summenprinzip' bei Blechblasinstrumenten." *International Musicological Society. Report of the Eleventh Congress, Copenhagen 1972*, edited by Henrik Glahn, Søren Sørensen, and Peter Ryom. Copenhagen: Hansen, 1974, pp. 715-20.

Discusses the acoustical result of humming into a brass instrument while producing a tone.

572. ————. "Einfluss von Material and Oberflachen aus den Klang von Blechinstrumenten." *Instrumentenbau* 30 (1976): 414-18.

Reports an experiment employing eight tenor trombones that were essentially identical to each other except for the metal and the surface coatings. Subjective and objective measurements show that the effect of material and coating upon tone was slight.

573. Woodward, J.G. "Resonance Characteristics of a Cornet." *Journal of the Acoustical Society of America* 13 (1941-42): 156-59.

Includes a chart showing the resonance curve of the instrument. Notes that the regions of resonance all lie below 2500 Hz.

574. Young, F.J. "The Natural Frequencies of Musical Horns." *Acustica* 10 (1960): 91-97.

Presents a method for calculating the natural frequencies of horns. Applies the method to a flugelhorn
and to a trombone. Offers a theoretical explanation
for the fact that the fundamental of the flugelhorn
is A flat rather than B flat, as often thought.

575. Young, Robert W. "On the Performance of Cup Mouthpiece
      Instruments." *Journal of the Acoustical Society of
      America* 20 (1948): 345-46.

Questions some of Long's conclusions (see above, Item
557) and calls attention to Blaikley's pioneering work
(see above, Items 454-455). Reprinted in Kent, Item
462, cited above.

4. Percussion Instruments

576. Bassett, Irvin G. "Vibration and Sound of the Bass
      Drum." *Percussionist* 19, no. 3 (Fall 1982): 50-58.

Compares and contrasts the properties of timpani and
the bass drum. Describes the complex vibration of the
bass drum heads, points out how the sound of the drum
can be varied by the player, and notes the relationship
between perceived pitch and the distance of the listener
from the instrument.

577. Moore, James L. "Acoustics of Bar Percussion Instruments."
      Ph.D. dissertation, Ohio State University, 1970. 188 p.
      UM 71-7522.

Reports the results of experiments testing the acoustics
of tuned bars. Includes a critical review of the literature.

578. Pomp, Anton, and Burghard Zapp. "Gongs." *The Metallur-
      gist* 9 (1933/34): 105-08, 120-22.

Examines the effect of material and manufacturing pro-
cess upon the sound of gongs.

579. Rossing, Thomas D. "Acoustics of Bar Percussion Instru-
      ments." *Percussionist* 19, no. 3 (Fall 1982): 6-17.

Describes the vibration modes of bar percussion instru-
ments--xylophone, vibraphone, triangle, marimba, and
glockenspiel. Includes a description of how bars are
tuned and discusses the function of resonators.

580. ————. "Acoustics of Percussion Instruments." *The Physics Teacher* 14 (1976): 546-55; 15 (1977): 278-88.

A thorough survey of the basic principles.

581. ————. "Chimes and Bells." *Percussionist* 19, no. 3 (Fall 1982): 42-50.

Describes the vibration modes of the instruments, pointing out that chimes have vibration modes similar to those of a vibrating bar but that bells vibrate more like plates. Points out that chimes and bells both have tuned partials and that chimes of high or low pitch could perhaps be improved by a design that takes into full account the timbre of each chime.

582. ————. "Nonlinear Effects in Percussion Instruments." *Percussionist* 19, no. 3 (Fall 1982): 68-72.

Describes the changes in frequency that can result when percussion instruments are struck with a loud blow. Also notes that in other cases nonlinear effects can result in an aftersound or shimmer.

583. Rossing, Thoms D., Craig A. Anderson, and Ronald I. Mills. "Acoustics of Timpani." *Percussionist* 19, no. 3 (Fall 1982): 18-31.

A discussion of fundamental importance. Includes a detailed description of vibration frequencies and an analysis of timpani sound.

584. Rossing, Thomas D., and Garry Kvistad. "Acoustics of Timpani: Preliminary Studies." *Percussionist* 13 (1974-75): 90-98.

Reports the procedures used and the results of experiments to determine the sound spectra and modes of vibration of the timpani.

585. Rossing, Thomas D., and Richard W. Peterson. "Vibrations of Plates, Gongs, and Cymbals." *Percussionist* 19, no. 3 (Fall 1982): 31-41.

Describes in detail the vibration modes and sound spectra of gongs and cymbals.

586. Rossing, Thomas D., and H. John Sathoff. "Modes of Vibration and Sound Radiation from Tuned Handbells." *Journal of the Acoustical Society of America* 68 (1980): 1600-07.

Thoroughly describes the vibration modes of handbells, their tuning, and the complex way in which they radiate sound. Notes the factors determining handbell tone quality.

X

INSTRUMENT MAKERS AND PERFORMERS

1. Makers

587. *Adolphe Sax.* Brochure programme de l'institut national
      belge de radiodiffusion, 26. Brussels: Institut
      national belge de radiodiffusion, 1939. 36 p.

      Consists of the two essays that are cited below as
      Items 605 and 631.

588. Altenburg, Detlef. "Musikinstrumentenbau in Köln."
      Studien zur Musikgeschichte des Rheinlandes, vol. 4,
      edited by K.W. Niemöller (Cologne: Arno Volk, 1975),
      pp. 89-99.

      Surveys instrument building in Cologne and describes
      the extant instruments and inventions. Also discusses
      the business relations of instrument makers in Cologne.

589. Ayars, Christine Merrick. *Contributions to the Art of
      Music in America by the Music Industries of Boston,
      1640-1936*. New York: Wilson, 1937. 326 p.

      Surveys the activities of Boston publishers and
      instrument makers, especially the makers of pianos and
      organs. Includes an annotated list of intruments in
      various museums and collections.

*   Birsak, Kurt. *Die Holzblasinstrumente im Salzburger
      Museum Carolino Augusteum. Verzeichnis und entwick-
      lungsgeschichtliche Untersuchungen*. Salzburger
      Museum Carolino Augusteum Jahreschriften, vol. 18.
      Salzburger Museum Carolino Augusteum, 1973. 211 p.

      Cited below as Item 715.

*   Bowers, Jane M. "The French Flute School from 1700 to
        1760." Ph.D. dissertation, University of California,
        Berkeley, 1971. 491 p.

        Cited above as Item 173.

*   ———. "New Light on the Development of the Transverse
        Flute between about 1650 and about 1770." *Journal
        of the American Musical Instrument Society* 3 (1977):
        5-56.

        Cited above as Item 174.

590.   Brenta, Gaston. "Adolphe Sax et la facture instrumentale."
        *Bulletin de classe des beaux-arts de Académie Royale
        de Belgique* 49 (1967): 54-88.

        Thoroughly reviews the career and achievements of
        Adolphe Sax. Also surveys the career of his father,
        Charles-Joseph Sax. Includes caricatures from Sax's
        day that point to the astonishment with which some
        of his instruments were greeted.

*   Brunswick. Städtisches Museum. *Verzeichnis der Sammlung
        alter Musikinstrumente im Städtischen Museum Braun-
        schweig. Instrumente, Instrumentenmacher und Instrumen-
        tisten in Braunschweig.* Brunswick: Appelhans, 1928.
        124 p.

        Cited below as Item 719.

*   Byrne, Maurice. "The Church Band at Swalcliffe."
        Galpin Society Journal 17 (1964): 89-98.

        Cited above as Item 127.

591.   ———. "The Goldsmith-Trumpet-makers of the British
        Isles." *Galpin Society Journal* 19 (1966): 71-83.

        Summarizes information about members of the Goldsmith
        Company from the sixteenth century to the mid-eighteenth
        century.

*   ———. "Schuchart and the Extended Foot-Joint."
        Galpin Society Journal 18 (1965): 7-13.

        Cited above as Item 176.

592.   ———. "Pierre Jaillard, Peter Bressan." *Galpin
        Society Journal* 36 (1983): 2-28.

        An account of the life of the instrument maker Peter

Bressan (1663-1731), who was born Pierre Jaillard. He was known for his flutes and recorders.

* Caba, G. Craig. *United States Military Drums, 1745-1865.* Harrisburg, Penn.: Civil War Antiquities and Americana, 1977. 147 p.

  Cited above as Item 435.

593. Closson, Ernest. *La facture des instruments de musique en Belgique.* Brussels: Degrace & Huy, [1935]. 108 p.

   An overview rather than a detailed survey. Includes photographs.

594. Cooper, Albert. *The Flute.* London: Cooper, 1980. 47 p.

   An account of the author's experiences as a maker of flutes. He played a major role in the development of the Murray flute.

* Crouch, Rebekah E. "The Contributions of Adolphe Sax to the Wind Band." Ph.D. dissertation, Florida State University, 1968. 134 p. UM 69-587.

  Cited above as Item 132.

* Dudgeon, Ralph Thomas. "The Keyed Bugle, Its History, Literature and Technique." Ph.D. dissertation, University of California, San Diego, 1980. 262 p. UM 80-23,094.

  Cited above as Item 331.

595. Duttenhöfer, Eva-Maria. *Gebrüder Alexander: 200 Jahre Musikinstrumentenbau in Mainz.* Mainz: Schott, 1982. 99 p.

   Traces, in considerable detail, the history of one of the most distinguished manufacturers of brass instruments. Describes the role of the firm in the improvement of brass instruments, the development of the Wagner tuba, and the reconstruction of Baroque trumpets and trombones.

596. "An Eighteenth-Century Directory of London Musicians." *Galpin Society Journal* 2 (1949): 27-31.

   A presumably comprehensive list drawn from Mortimer's *London Universal Directory* of 1763. Instrument makers are listed separately.

597. Eliason, Robert E. *Early American Brass Makers.*
Nashville: Brass Press, 1979. 56 p.

Discusses the inventions and achievements of five
prominent 19th-century American makers: Groves, Paine,
Allen, Wright, and Fiske. Includes a generous selection
of photographs.

*   ————. "Early American Valves for Brass Instruments."
Galpin Society Journal 23 (1970): 86-96.

Cited above as Item 336.

598. ————. "Flute Makers of Early America." *Woodwind
World, Brass and Percussion* 15, no. 1 (January 1976):
28-19, 49; no. 2 (March 1976): 24, 26; no. 3 (May
1976): 25-26; no. 4 (July 1976): 20-22; no. 5
(September 1976): 22-25, 36; 16, no. 1 (January
1977): 12, 14, 19, 23.

A detailed survey that concludes with the first
American manufacture of Boehm flutes.

599. ————. *Graves & Company, Musical Instrument Makers.*
Dearborn, Mich.: Edison Institute, 1975. 20 p.

Traces the history of the company, the first large
maker of wind instruments in the United States. Lists
extant instruments.

600. ————. "Oboe[s], Bassoons, and Bass Clarinets, made
by Hartford[,] Connecticut, Makers before 1815."
Galpin Society Journal 30 (1977): 43-51.

Describes the output of George Catlin, John Meacham, Jr.,
and Uzal Minor, who were active between 1799 and 1815.
Included among the instruments are bassoon-shaped bass
clarinets, which are otherwise completely unknown.

601. Ernst, Friedrich. "Die Blechblasinstrumentenbauer-Familie
Moritz in Berlin (Beitrag zur Geschichte des Berliner
Instrumentenbaues)." *Das Musikinstrument* 18, no. 4
(April 1969): 624-26.

Recounts the history of a Berlin family of instrument
makers who pioneered in the development of valve mechanisms
for trumpets and horns as well as in the manufacture of
tubas.

*   Fairley, Andrew. *Flutes, Flautists and Makers*. London:
        Pan Educational Music, 1982. 140 p.

        Cited above as Item 180.

602.   Farrell, Susan Caust. *Directory of Contemporary*
        American Musical Instrument Makers. Columbia, Mo.:
        University of Missouri Press, 1981. 216 p.

        An alphabetical list of more than 2,500 makers.
        Provides addresses, information about the instruments,
        and details about each shop. Includes a list of books
        about instrument making.

603.   Fitzpatrick, Horace. "An Eighteenth-Century Bohemian
        School of Horn-Makers." *Galpin Society Journal* 17
        (1964): 77-88.

        Includes a list of makers and their instruments.

604.   ————. "Jacob Denner's Woodwinds for Gottweig Abbey."
        Galpin Society Journal 21 (1968): 81-87.

        Describes an invoice and a cost estimate in Denner's
        hand from *ca.* 1720. The estimate lists twenty instruments,
        including a bass clarinet.

605.   Gilson, Paul. "Les géniales inventions d'Adolphe Sax."
        Adolphe Sax. Brochure programme de l'Institut national
        belge de radiodiffusion, 26. Brussels: Institut
        national belge de radiodiffusion, 1939, pp. 5-21.

        Surveys the instruments created by Sax, noting instances
        of their use in orchestral music.

606.   Groce, Nancy Jane. "Musical Instrument Making in New
        York City During the Eighteenth and Nineteenth Centuries."
        Ph.D. dissertation, The University of Michigan, 1982.
        561 p. UM 82-24,957.

        Primarily a biographical dictionary of more than 700
        makers during the period 1690-1890. Preceded by a
        general history of the musical instrument trade in New
        York.

*   Groffy, Franz. *Musikhistorisches Museum Heckel-Biebrich*.
        Abteilung Fagotte. Wiesbaden-Biebrich: Heckel, 1968.
        108 p.

        Cited below as Item 741.

*   The Hague. Gemeentemuseum. *Historische Blaasinstrumenten.*
       The Hague: Gemeentemuseum, 1974. 80 p.
       Cited below as Item 745.

607.   Haine, Malou. *Adolphe Sax (1814-1894): Sa vie, son
       oeuvre, ses instruments de musique.* Brussels: Éditions
       de l'Université de Bruxelles, 1980. 283 p.

       The definitive account. Thorough, well documented, and
       copiously illustrated.

*   Haine, Malou, and Ignace de Keyser. *Catalogue des instru-
       ments Sax au Musée instrumental de Bruxelles.* Buren:
       Knuf, 1980. 280 p.

       Cited below as Item 746.

608.   Halfpenny, Eric. "Biographical Notices of the Early
       English Woodwind-Making School, *c.* 1650-1750."
       Galpin Society Journal 12 (1959): 44-52.

       Summarizes the lives of John Ashbury, Joseph Bradbury,
       Peter Bressan, Samuel Drumbleby, and the Stanesbys.

609.   ————. "Further Light on the Stanesby Family." *Galpin
       Society Journal* 13 (1960): 59-69.

       Enlarges upon the biographical information given by
       Halfpenny in the article cited above as Item 608.

610.   ————. "Smith, London." *Galpin Society Journal* 21
       (1968): 105-07.

       Provides biographical information about an English
       maker of instruments. Dates two natural horns made by
       Smith.

611.   Hellyer, Roger. "Some Documents Relating to Viennese
       Wind-Instrument Purchases, 1779-1837." *Galpin Society
       Journal* 28 (1975): 50-59.

       Transcribes the entries concerning wind instruments in
       the records of the Viennese Hoftheater. The records
       supplement the information found in Langwill (see below,
       Item 623) and in some cases appear to contradict it.

612.   Heyde, Herbert. "Die Blasinstrumentenbauer, Jehring
       (Adolf) und Heckel (Adorf, Dresden, Biebrich)."
       Beiträge zur Musikwissenschaft 19 (1977): 121-24.

       Traces the histories of the Jehring and Heckel families

from the eighteenth century to the twentieth. Describes the significance of both families to the history of wind instruments.

613. ————. "Eine Geschäftskorrespondenz von Johann Wilhelm Haas aus dem Jahre 1719." *Aufsätze und Jahresbericht 1976 für die Freunde des Musikinstrumenten-Museums der Karl-Marx-Universität*, edited by Helmut Zeraschi. Leipzig: Direktorat für Forschung der Karl-Marx-Universität, 1977, pp. 32-38.

Reviews the correspondence of a trumpet maker that sheds light on aspects of the instrument's construction.

614. Hoza, Václav. "Václav František Červený (1819-1896)." *Brass Bulletin*, no. 23 (1978): 25-29.

Sketches the life of an important Czech designer and maker of brass instruments. Well illustrated. Parallel texts in German, French, and English. Also see Item 619, cited below.

615. Huene, Friedrich von. "Makers' Marks from Renaissance and Baroque Woodwinds." *Galpin Society Journal* 27 (1974): 31-47.

An annotated list of marks.

616. Jahn, Fritz. "Die Nürnberger Trompeten- und Posaunenmacher im 16. Jahrhundert." *Archiv für Musikwissenschaft* 7 (1925): 23-52.

Surveys the careers and achievements of the Schnitzers and other Nuremberg instrument makers. Also describes the use of brass instruments during the period.

617. Jarcho, Saul. "Two Kinds of Trumpet." *Bulletin of the New York Academy of Medicine* 47, no. 4 (April 1971): 5428-30.

Reports that the London Museum preserves the visiting card of William Bull, a well-known seventeenth-century maker of musical instruments. The card states that Bull made "All Sorts of Trumpetts and Kettle Drums, ffrench Hornes, Speaking Trumpets, hearing Hornes for Deafe People."

618. Jenkins, David. "Woodwind Instruments in France, 1690-1750: Their Makers, Theoreticians and Music." Ph.D. dissertation, University of Edinburgh, 1973. 2 vols. 250, 147 p.

Traces the history of the beginnings of the woodwind industry in France and describes French achievements in instrument design and manufacture. Includes a translation and discussion of Louis Bergeron's *Manuel du tourneur*, a manual for instrument makers. Also describes the musical organization of the French court as well as French woodwind music during the period.

619. Keller, Jindřich. "Nástrojářské dilo Františka Václava Červeneho." *Hudebni nástroje* 3 (1967): 73-78.

Surveys the achievements of the Czech instrument maker Václav František Červený (1819-1896), who, in addition to making conventional instruments, invented a number of brass instruments and a new type of rotary valve. Also see Item 614, cited above.

*   ————. "Pištelnici a trubari. Pojednáni o výrobě dechových hudebnich nástroju v Cechách před rokem 1800." *Sbornik Národniho muzea v Praze. Acta musei nationalis pragae* 29 (1975): 161-243.

Cited above as Item 146.

620. Kirvin, Martin. "A Century of Wind Instrument Manufacturing in the United States: 1860-1960." Ph.D. dissertation, University of Iowa, 1961. 282 p. UM 61-5584.

Traces the growth of the industry, focusing on approximately fifty firms still doing business in 1960.

*   Körner, Friedrich. "Ein Horn von Michael Nagel in Graz." *Historisches Jahrbuch der Stadt Graz* 2 (1969): 87-96.

Cited above as Item 413.

621. Langwill, Lyndesay G. "Brustgrün of Flensburg." *Galpin Society Journal* 15 (1962: 95-96.

Offers biographical information about a family of instrument makers from the early nineteenth century.

622. ————. "F. Boie of Göttingen (1762-1809)." *Galpin Society Journal* 14 (1961): 72-73.

Contributes to the biography of a maker of woodwinds.

623. ————. *An Index of Musical Wind-Instrument Makers*. 4th ed. Edinburgh: Langwill, 1974. 272 p.

An enlarged and revised edition of the basic source of information on the subject. Invaluable to students of the history of wind instruments.

* ————. "Two Rare Eighteenth-Century London Directories." *Music and Letters* 30 (1949): 37-43.

Cited below as Item 661.

624. Luke, James W., Jr. "The Clarinets of Thomas Key of London." D.M.A. dissertation, University of Missouri, Kansas City, 1969. 90 p. UM 71-3694.

Sketches Key's career, which lasted from *ca.* 1800 to *ca.* 1850, inventories his clarinets and describes those that are extant.

625. Meer, John Henry van der. "More about Denner." *Galpin Society Journal* 36 (1983): 127-28.

Comments upon the article by Phillip Young, cited below as Item 641.

* ————. "Musikinstrumentenbau in Bayern bis 1800." *Musik in Bayern*, edited by Robert Münster and Hans Schmidt. Tutzing: Schneider, 1972. Vol. 2, pp. 17-38.

Cited above as Item 153.

626. Montagu, Jeremy. "A Query on the Habits of Instrument Makers." *Galpin Society Journal* 27 (1974): 135-37.

Includes a description of the markings on a flute from 1836.

* Morley Pegge, Reginald. "Callcott's Radius French Horn." *Galpin Society Journal* 3 (1950): 49-51.

Cited above as Item 418.

627. Nichols, William. "The Denner Family of Nuremberg." *NACWPI Journal* 23, no. 2 (Winter 1974-75Z): 39-48.

Traces the history of the family and discusses Jacob Denner's contributions to the development of the clarinet.

628. Nickel, Ekkehart. *Der Holzblasinstrumentenbau in der freien Reichstadt Nürnberg*. Munich: Katzbichler, 1971. 496 p.

Includes a survey of the use of woodwind instruments in

the sixteenth and early seventeenth centuries. Notable
partly for its discussion of the contributions of the
Denner family.

629. Ottner, Helmut. *Der Wiener Musikinstrumentenbau 1815-
1833*. Tutzing: Schneider, 1977. 172 p.

A comprehensive biographical dictionary of Viennese
instrument makers during the period.

630. Pechstein, Klaus. "Die Merkzeichentafel der Nürnberger
Trompeten- und Posaunenmacher von 1640." *Mitteilungen
des Vereins für Geschichte der Stadt Nürnberg* 59 (1972):
198-202.

Identifies and illustrates the maker's marks on Nuremberg
trumpets and trombones.

631. Remy, Albert. "La vie tourmentée d'Adolphe Sax." *Adolphe
Sax*. Brochure programme de l'Institut national belge
de radiodiffusion, 26. Brussels: Institut national
belge de radiodiffusion, 1939, pp. 23-36.

A somewhat breathless biographical sketch. Stresses the
difficulties of Sax's life and career.

632. Rindlisbacher, Hilde. "Musikinstrumentenmacher auf Indus-
trie- und Gewerbeausstellungen in der Schweiz im 19.
Jahrhundert (ohne Klavier- und Orgelbauer)." *Glareana*
18, no. 2 (June 1969): 2-19.

Lists the manufacturers and the instruments they showed
at Swiss industrial and trade exhibitions in the nineteenth
century.

*   Roquet, Antoine E. *Les Hotteterre et les Chédeville,
célèbres joueurs et facteurs de flûtes, hautbois, bassons
et musettes des xviie et xviiie siècles*. Paris: Sagot,
1894. 54 p.

Cited below as Item 676.

*   Schmid, Manfred Hermann. *Theobald Boehm 1794-1881: Die
Revolution der Flöte. Katalog der Ausstellung zum 100.
Geburtstag von Boehm*. Tutzing: Schneider, 1981. 192 p.

Cited below as Item 790.

633. Smithers, Don L. "The Trumpets of J.W. Haas: A Survey of
Four Generations of Nuremberg Brass Instrument Makers."
Galpin Society Journal 18 (1965): 23-41.

Describes the work of a little-known family of makers from the seventeenth and eighteenth centuries.

*   Sterl, Raimund Walter. "Regensburgs Musikinstrumentenbauer von der Mitte des 15. Jahrhunderts bis zur Neuzeit." *Verhandlungen des Historischen Verein für Oberpfalz und Regensburg* 113 (1973): 145-60.

Cited above as Item 161.

634. Teahan, John. "A List of Irish Instrument Makers." *Galpin Society Journal* 16 (1983): 28-32.

Lists makers through the nineteenth century.

635. Ventzke, Karl, and Dietrich Hilkenbach. *Boehm-Instrumente/Boehm Woodwinds.* Vol. 1: *Theobald Boehm 1794-1881.* Frankfurt: Das Musikinstrument, 1982. 71 p.

Traces Boehm's life, lists his works, and surveys his achievements. Parallel texts in German and English.

636. White, Jack Okey. "Renold Otto Schilke: His Contributions to the Development of the Trumpet." D.A. dissertation, New York University, 1980. 176 p. UM 80-17,545.

Surveys Schilke's life and career and describes the changes he made in trumpet design.

637. "Woodwind Instruments by P-I Bressan." *Galpin Society Journal* 17 (1964): 106-07.

A checklist of thirty-five instruments from the late seventeenth and early eighteenth centuries.

*   Wörthmüller, Willi. "Die Instrumente der Nürnberger Trompeten- u. Posaunenmacher." *Mitteilungen des Vereins für Geschichte der Stadt Nürnberg* 46 (1955): 372-480.

Cited above as Item 382.

638. ————. "Die Nürnberger Trompeten- und Posaunenmacher des 17. und 18. Jahrh." *Mitteilungen des Vereins für Geschichte der Stadt Nürnberg* 45 (1954): 208-325.

A comprehensive account and chronology of Nuremberg makers of brass instruments. For a description of the instruments themselves, see above, item 382.

639. Wright, Michael. "Bergeron on Flute-Making." *Galpin Society Journal* 29 (1976): 26-34.

Translates the section "Flûtes et flageolet" from L.-E. Bergeron's *Manuel du tourneur* (1792-96; ed., 1816). A translation of the entire manual appears in Item 618, cited above.

640. Young, Phillip T. "Inventory of Instruments: J.H. Eichentopf, Poerschman, Sattler, A. and H. Grenser, Grundmann." *Galpin Society Journal* 31 (1978): 100-34.

Includes an annotated list of known instruments. Observes that probably no such maker as Grundmann Grenser ever existed, despite references by other writers.

641. ———. "Some Further Instruments by the Denners." *Galpin Society Journal* 35 (1982): 78-85.

Reports additions to the inventory published earlier (see below, Item 642). Notes evidence for adding five bassoons to the inventory and describes the contents of two previously unreported collections.

642. ———. "Woodwind Instruments by the Denners of Nürnberg." *Galpin Society Journal* 20 (1967): 9-16.

An inventory of the extant instruments. Supplemented by the article cited above as Item 641.

2. Performers

*   Arfinengo, Carlo. *La tromba e il trombone*. Ancona, Milan: Bèrben, 1973. 48 p.

Cited above as Item 99.

*   Baker, Nicholson. "Playing Trombone." *Atlantic*, March 1982, pp. 39-58.

Cited below as Item 1165.

*   Bate, Philip. *The Oboe: An Outline of Its History, Development, and Construction*. 3rd ed. New York: Norton, 1975. 236 p.

Cited above as Item 77.

*   Bechler, Leo, and Bernhardt, Rahm. *Die Oboe und die ihr verwandten Instrumente nebst biographischen Skizzen der bedeutendsten ihrer Meister.* Leipzig: Merseburger, 1914; reprint eds., Wiesbaden: Sändig, 1972; Buren: Knuf, 1978. 98 p.

Cited above as Item 78.

643.   Bednař, Jaroslav. "Česká Fagotová Škola." *Hudebni nástroje* 4 (1967): 136-39.

Traces the history of the Czech bassoon school, which originated with the founding of the Prague Conservatory. Stresses the importance of three players particularly: Josef Füger, Karel Pivoňka, and Karel Bidlo.

*   Beyer, Werner. "The Classical Solo Concerto for Trombone and Its Interpreters in the 19th Century." *Brass Bulletin* 25 (1979): 51-55.

Cited below as Item 1000.

*   Bigotti, Giovanni. *Storia dell'oboe e sua letteratura.* Padua: Zanibon, 1974. 77 p.

Cited above as Item 79.

*   Blandford, W.F.H. "The 'Bach Trumpet'." *Monthly Musical Record* 65 (1935): 49-51, 73-76, 97-100.

Cited above as Item 326.

*   ————. "Some Observations on 'Horn Chords: An Acoustical Problem'." *The Musical Times* 67 (1926): 128-31.

Cited above as Item 401.

644.   Bridges, Glenn. *Pioneers in Brass.* Detroit: Sherwood, 1965. 113 p.

A collection of mostly brief biographical sketches of prominent solo performers of the past, from Arban to Pryor. Illustrated with photographs. Includes lists of recordings, which, unfortunately, are lacking in detail. Excerpts reprinted in *Journal of Band Research* 6, No. 2 (Spring 1970): 13-18; 7, No. 1 (Fall 1970): 28-32.

*   Brunswick, Städtisches Museum. *Verzeichnis der Sammlung alter Musikinstrumente im Städtischen Museum Braunschweig. Instrumente, Instrumentenmacher und Instrumentisten in Braunschweig.* Brunswick: Appelhans, 1928. 124 p.

Cited below as Item 719.

645. Bryan, Paul. "Haydn's Hornists." *Haydn-Studien* 3 (1973):
      52-58.

      Identifies and traces the careers of the horn players
      who served the Esterházy family from 1761 to 1790. Dis-
      cusses the marching repertory and some aspects of horn
      performance practice.

*   Burkart, Richard E. "The Trumpet in the Seventeenth
      Century with Emphasis on its Treatment in the Works of
      Henry Purcell and a Biography of the Shore Family of
      Trumpeters." Ph.D. dissertation, University of Wisconsin,
      1972. 153 p. UM 72-9111.

      Cited above as Item 328.

646. Clarke, Herbert L. *How I Became a Cornetist: The Autobiog-
      raphy of a Cornet-Playing Pilgrim's Progress.* St. Louis:
      Huber, 1934; reprint ed., Kenosha, Wis.: Leblanc, n.d.
      74 p.

      Originally published as a series of articles in *Fillmore's
      Musical Messenger.* Reprint edition includes a biographical
      sketch of Frank Holton, a well-known trombonist and manu-
      facturer of brass instruments with whom Clarke was asso-
      ciated.

647. Coar, Birchard. *A Critical Study of the Nineteenth-Century
      Horn Virtuosi in France.* DeKalb, Ill.: Coar, 1952.
      168 p.

      A thorough survey. The bibliography includes a good list
      of French tutors from the nineteenth century. Includes
      biographical sketches of important players, together with
      lists of all the prize winners on horn at the Paris
      Conservatory during the eighteenth and nineteenth centuries.

*   Dahlqvist, Reine. *The Keyed Trumpet and Its Greatest
      Virtuoso, Anton Weidinger.* Nashville: Brass Press,
      1975. 25 p.

      Cited above as Item 329.

648. Eichborn, Hermann. "Girolamo Fantini, ein Virtuos des
      siebzehnten Jahrhunderts, und seine Trompeten-Schule."
      Monatshefte für Musikgeschichte 22 (1890): 112-38.

      Sketches Fantini's biography and describes his achieve-
      ment. The pioneering discussion.

*   "An Eighteenth-Century Directory of London Musicians."
      Galpin Society Journal 2 (1949): 27-31.

Cited above as Item 596.

649. Estock, Joseph. "A Biographical Dictionary of Clarinetists
      Born before 1800." Ph.D. dissertation, University of
      Iowa, 1972. 405 p. UM 73-13,528.

      Includes a brief history of the clarinet to *ca.* 1825.

*   Fairley, Andrew. *Flutes, Flautists and Makers.* London:
      Pan Educational Music, 1982. 140 p.

      Cited above as Item 180.

*   Frei-Rauber, Herbert. *Trompete und Trompeter.* Mellingen:
      Herbert Frei, 1976. 48 p.

      Cited above as Item 101.

650. Gade, Per. "Anton Hansen (1877-1947), Father of Trombone
      Playing in Scandinavia." *Brass Bulletin*, no. 27 (1979):
      27-40; no. 28 (1979): 13-28; no. 29 (1980): 81-94.

      A biographical account based largely on Hansen's memoirs.
      Parallel texts in German, French, and English.

*   Galleras, Rober. *Histoire de la flûte.* Pau: Moderne,
      1977. 89 p.

      Cited above as Item 68.

*   Giraud, Adrien. *Histoire et richesses de la flûte.*
      Paris: Gründ, 1953. 143 p.

      Cited above as Item 69.

651. Greene, Grady J., Jr. "Louis François Dauprat: His Life
      and Works." Ed.D. dissertation, University of Northern
      Colorado, 1971. 294 p. UM 71-14,526.

      Traces the life of the famous horn player and teacher
      of the nineteenth century.

652. Griswold, Harold Eugene. "Étienne Ozi (1754-1813):
      Bassoonist, Teacher, and Composer." D.M.A. dissertation,
      Peabody Conservatory, 1979. 658 p. UM 80-2561.

      Traces Ozi's biography and discusses his tutors.

*   Haensel, Robert. "Die Stadtpfeifer und die Stadtkapelle
      in Lobenstein." *Festschrift zur Ehrung von Heinrich
      Albert (1604-1651)*, edited by Günther Kraft. Weimar:
      Uschmann, 1954, pp. 36-38.

Cited above as Item 141.

*   Halfpenny, Eric. "The Boehm Clarinet in England."
         Galpin Society Journal 30 (1977): 2-7.

         Cited above as Item 282.

653.   Hickman, David B. "Herbert Lincoln Clarke (1867-1945)."
         Brass Bulletin, no. 18 (1977): 13-18; no. 19 (1977):
         19-27; no. 21 (1978): 27-32; no. 22 (1978): 27-32.

         Summarizes the life and career of one of the most eminent
         cornet players of the past. Well illustrated.

654.   Hodges, Woodrow Joe. "A Biographical Dictionary of
         Bassoonists Born before 1825." Ph.D. dissertation,
         University of Iowa, 1980." 699 p. UM 80-22,036.

         Includes information on approximately 800 bassoonists.
         Also includes a short history of the bassoon up to 1825.

655.   Hoover, Cynthia Adams. "The Trumpet Battle At Niblo's
         Pleasure Garden." *The Musical Quarterly* 55 (1969):
         384-95.

         A fascinating account of the musical competition in
         New York in 1834 between the trumpeters John Thompson
         Norton and Alessandro Gambati. Both players performed on
         natural trumpets. Norton was declared the winner.

656.   Kingdon Ward, Martha. "Mozart's Clarinettist." *Monthly
         Musical Record* 85 (1955); 8-14.

         Sketches Anton Stadler's biography and notes the
         strength of his influence upon Mozart's music.

657.   Kling, Henri. "Giovanni Punto, célèbre corniste (1748-
         1803)." *Bulletin français de la S.I.M.* [*La revue
         musicale de la S.I.M.*] 4 (1908): 1066-82.

         Surveys his life and describes his works, giving
         particular attention to his horn method. Stresses
         Punto's importance as a composer for horn.

658.   Köchel, Ludwig Ritter von. *Die kaiserliche Hof-Musik-
         kapelle in Wien von 1543 bis 1867*. Vienna: Beck,
         1869. 160 p.

         Lists chronologically the musicians employed by the
         court, identifying them by name and instrument or voice
         type. Gives the dates of their service and, in many
         cases, their salaries.

*   Kölbel, Herbert. *Von der Flöte: Brevier für Flötenspieler.*
       2nd ed. Kassel: Bärenreiter, 1966. 249 p.

       Cited above as Item 70.

659.   Krause, Robert James. "A Biographical Dictionary of
       European Oboists before 1900." D.M.A. dissertation,
       University of Miami, 1981. 119 p. UM 82-01427.

       Includes citations of sources of information for
       the entries.

660.   Kroll, Oskar. "Weber und Baermann." *Neue Zeitschrift
       für Musik* 103 (1936): 1439-43.

       Traces the career of the clarinet virtuoso Heinrich
       Josef Baermann (1784-1847), describes his relationship
       to Weber, and points out the high quality of Weber's
       music for clarinet.

661.   Langwill, Lyndesay G. "Two Rare Eighteenth-Century
       London Directories." *Music and Letters* 30 (1949):
       37-43.

       Reports information found in two directories, from
       1763 and 1794, relating to composers, performers, and
       instrument makers.

662.   Laplace, Michel. "The Founders of the French Trumpet
       School: Merri Franquin, Eugene Foveau and Raymond
       Sabarich." *Brass Bulletin*, no. 29 (1980): 67-80.

       Brief biographical sketches accompanied by photographs.

663.   LaRue, Jan, and Howard Brofsky. "Parisian Brass Players,
       1751-1793." *Brass Quarterly* 3 (1959-60): 133-40.

       Describes the composition of the brass sections of
       Parisian orchestras, discusses various employment practices
       and outlines the employment histories of all the known
       brass players.

*   Lorenzo, Leonardo de. *My Complete Story of the Flute.*
       New York: Citadel Press, 1951. 493 p.

       Cited above as Item 196.

*   ————. *To the Nine Muses.* Santa Barbara, Calif.:
       De Lorenzo, 1957. 25 p.

       Cited above as Item 197.

664. Mathez, Jean-Pierre. *Joseph Jean-Baptiste Laurent Arban
      1825-1889: Portrait d'un musicien français du xix^e
      siècle.* Moudon: Éditions BIM, 1977. 69 p.

      A biographical sketch accompanied by an attractive
      sampling of illustrations. Distinguished by the generous
      quotation of letters and additional contemporaneous
      material that would otherwise not be readily available.
      Also appears in several installments in *Brass Bulletin*,
      nos. 9-15 (1974-76).

665. Mayer, Richard. "Klarinet a ceské zeme." *Opus musicum*
      5 (1973): 66-71, 108-12.

      An overview of important Bohemian clarinetists and
      composers for the clarinet during the period from 1750
      to 1850.

666. Metcalf, Owen Wells. "The New York Brass Quintet: Its
      History and Influence on Brass Literature and Pedagogy."
      D.M.A. dissertation, Indiana University, 1978. 103 p.

      An account of the group from its founding in 1954 to
      1978. Includes biographical information about its members.

667. "Mikhail Innokentievitch Tabakov (1877-1956), Founder of
      the Soviet Trumpet School." *Brass Bulletin*, no. 22
      (1978): 61-70.

      Outlines his achievements and sets forth the principles
      of his teaching. Drawn from articles by G. Orvid and
      S. Riaouzov. Parallel texts in German, French, and
      English.

668. Miller, James E. "The Life and Works of Jan Václav Stich
      (Giovanni Punto)--A Checklist of 18th Century Horn
      Concertos and Players." Ph.D. dissertation, University
      of Iowa, 1962. 2 vols. 259 p. UM 62-4986.

      Offers an account of Stich's life together with an
      annotated list of forty-six horn concertos from the
      eighteenth century and a checklist of horn players from
      the period.

*   Morley Pegge, Reginald. *The French Horn: Some Notes on
      the Evolution of the Instrument and Its Technique.*
      2nd ed. New York: Norton, 1973. 222 p.

      Cited above as Item 114.

* Müller, Georg. *Friedrich der Grosse, seine Flöten und sein Flötenspiel.* Berlin: Parrhysius, [1932]. 20 p.

Cited above as Item 199.

669. "Orchestras: Psychic Symphony." *Time*, February 17, 1967, pp. 69-70.

Describes with humor and some insight the personalities of orchestral musicians typed according to their instruments.

670. Pettitt, Stephen. *Dennis Brain.* London: Robert Hale, 1976. 192 p.

A biography of the legendary British horn player. Includes a preface by Benjamin Britten and a list of Brain's recordings.

671. Phelan, Jack. "Walter Guetter--Bassoonist." *Woodwind Anthology.* Evanston, Ill.: Instrumentalist, 1976, p. 599.

Reviews the achievements of the former principal bassoonist of the Philadelphia Orchestra, called by Stokowski "the Heifetz of the bassoon."

672. Rascher, Sigurd. "Sigurd Rascher Discusses the Saxophone." *Woodwind Anthology.* Evanston, Ill.: Instrumentalist, 1976, pp. 669-70.

Describes Rascher's impact upon various composers.

673. Rasmussen, Mary. "Gottfried Reiche and His 'Vier und zwanzig Neue Quatricinia' (Leipzig 1696)." *Brass Quarterly* 4 (1960-61): 3-17.

Sketches the biography of Bach's legendary trumpeter and describes his own surviving collection of works.

674. ————. "Two Early Nineteenth-Century Trombone Virtuosi: Carl Traugott Queisser and Friedrich August Belcke." *Brass Quarterly* 5 (1961-62): 3-17.

An account of the lives and remarkable careers of two contemporaries of Thalberg and Paganini.

675. Rhodes, David J. "Franz Anton Pfeiffer and the Bassoon." *Galpin Society Journal* 36 (1983): 97-103.

Discusses the playing of one of the finest bassoonists of the eighteenth century and describes his instrument.

*   Rhodes, Emile. *Les trompettes du roi.* Paris: Picard,
        1909. 71 p.

        Cited above as Item 364.

*   Rockstro, Richard S. *A Treatise on the Construction, the
        History, and the Practice of the Flute.* 2nd ed.
        London: Musica Rara, 1928; reprint ed., London: Musica
        Rara, 1967.

        Cited above as Item 71.

676.   Roquet, Antoine E. *Les Hotteterre et les Chédeville,
        célèbres joueurs et facteurs de flûtes, hautbois,
        bassons et musettes des xviie et xviiie siècles.* Paris:
        Sagot, 1894. 54 p.

        Provides biographical sketches of twenty-two players
        and makers of woodwind instruments from the seventeenth
        and eighteenth centuries. Focuses primarily on the large
        and especially important Hotteterre family. Written under
        the pseudonym Ernest Thoinan.

677.   Savo, Gaetano. *Cenni storici sull' origine del clarinetto.*
        Salerno: Lamberti, 1939. 11 p.

        Includes a list of prominent players, foreign and Italian.

*   Sconzo, Fortunato. *Il flauto e i flautisti.* Milan:
        Hoepli, 1930. 180 p.

        Cited above as Item 73.

678.   Selfridge-Field, Eleanor. "Annotated Membership Lists of
        the Venetian Instrumentalists' Guild, 1672-1727."
        B.M.A. Research Chronicle 9 (1971): 1-52.

679.   Sélianine, Anatoly. "Vassily Guergnievitch Brandt (1869-
        1923)." *Brass Bulletin*, no. 26 (1979): 59-68.

        Includes approximately 550 names appearing on five
        membership surveys.

*   Štědroň, Bohumir. "Die Landshafts-Trompeter und -Tympanist-
        en im alten Brünn." *Die Musikforschung* 21 (1968):
        438-58.

        Cited above as Item 371.

680.   Storch, Laila. "Joseph Fiala--18th Century Oboist Redis-
        covered." *Woodwind Anthology.* Evanston, Ill.: Instru-
        mentalist, 1976, pp. 305-06.

Recounts the life of the virtuoso oboist and composer, who was a friend of Mozart.

681. Taylor, Laurence. "The Fabulous Mr. Nicholson." *Woodwind Anthology*. Evanston, Ill.: Instrumentalist, 1976, pp. 112-15.

An account of the life and achievements of the flutist and composer Charles Nicholson (1795-1837).

* Titus, Robert A. "The Solo Music for the Clarinet in the Eighteenth Century." Ph.D. dissertation, University of Iowa, 1962. 619 p. UM 62-2412.

Cited below as Item 989.

682. Werner, Arno. "Johann Ernst Altenburg, der letzte Vertreter der heroischen Trompeter- und Paukerkunst." *Zeitschrift für Musikwissenschaft* 15 (1932-33): 258-74.

Traces Altenburg's life in considerable detail.

683. Weston, Pamela. "Beethoven's Clarinettists." *The Musical Times* 111 (1970): 1212-13.

Recounts the relationship between Beethoven and Josef Bahr (1770-1819), for whom Beethoven undoubtedly wrote his works for clarinet. Credit for inspiring these works is sometimes given erroneously to Joseph Beer, the Berlin virtuoso.

684. ————. *Clarinet Virtuosi of the Past*. London: Hale, 1971. 292 p.

Fourteen essays on the most important European players from the eighteenth through the early twentieth century.

685. ————. *More Clarinet Virtuosi of the Past*. London: Weston, 1977. 392 p.

A biographical dictionary of players, many from the twentieth century. Includes some Americans. Cites recordings.

XI

DISCUSSIONS OF INSTRUMENT CLASSIFICATION AND
DESCRIPTIONS OF INSTRUMENT COLLECTIONS

1. Instrument Classification

686. Bessaraboff, Nicholas. *Ancient European Musical Instruments: An Organological Study of the Musical Instruments in the Leslie Lindsey Mason Collection at the Museum of Fine Arts, Boston*. Cambridge, Mass.: Harvard University Press, 1941. 503 p.

A landmark in the classification of musical instruments. Contains general discussions as well as detailed descriptions of the individual instruments, 213 in all. Well illustrated. For a discussion of the book and of its author, see the article cited below as Item 1170.

687. Buchner, Alexander. "K otázce systematiky hudebnich nástrojů." *Hudebni nastroje* 14 (1977): 79-80, 143-45, 174-79.

Reviews and compares the instrument classification systems of Gevaert, Hornbostel and Sachs, and Mahillon. Describes the Usák classification and outlines Hutter's system. Summaries printed in English, German, and Russian.

688. Dräger, Hans-Heinz. "Instrumentenkunde." *Die Musik in Geschichte und Gegenwart*, edited by Friedrich Blume. Kassel: Bärenreiter, 1949- . Vol. 6 (1957), cols. 1288-95.

A thoughtful systematic discussion together with a brief history of organology. Includes a good bibliography.

689. Elschek, Oskar. "Historische Quellentypen der Instrumentenkunde und die ihnen angemessenen quellenkritischen Methoden." *Studia instrumentorum musicae popularis*, vol. 4: *Bericht uber die 4. Internationale Arbeitstag-*

ung der *Study Group on Folk Musical Instruments des International Folk Music Council in Balatonalmádi 1973*, edited by Erich Stockmann. Stockholm: Musikhistoriska museet, 1976, pp. 10-30.

Discusses the terminology, function, and morphology of folk and art instruments.

690. Heyde, Herbert. *Grundlagen des natürlichen Systems der Musikinstrumente.* Leipzig: Deutscher Verlag für Musik, 1975. 148 p.

A complex study in classification embracing all instruments, from primitive to electronic.

691. Hornbostel, Erich M. von, and Curt Sachs. "Classification of Musical Instruments." *Galpin Society Journal* 14 (1961): 3-29.

A translation by Anthony Baines and Klaus P. Wachsmann of "Systematik der Musikinstrumente. Ein Versuch," *Zeitschrift für Ethnologie* 4-5 (1914). A pioneering and influential essay. The translation is reprinted in *The New Grove Dictionary of Music and Musicians*, ed. Stanley Sadie (London: Macmillan, 1980), vol. 9, pp. 241-45.

692. Jenkins, Jean L. "A New System of Classifying Musical Instruments Used in the U.S.S.R." *Galpin Society Journal* 13 (1960): 95-97.

Describes the system devised by I.Z. Ahlender, which is based on Mahillon (see below, Item 720).

693. Nixdorff, Heide. *Zur Typologie und Geschichte der Rahmentrommeln. Kritische Betrachtung zur traditionellen Instrumententerminologie.* Berlin: Reimer, 1971. 286 p.

Primarily a discussion of instrument classification. Concerned almost entirely with folk instruments but including several--such as the tambourine--that have found their way into art music.

694. Reinecke, Hans-Peter. "Einige Bemerkungen zur methodologischen Basis instrumentaler Forschung." *Studia instrumentorum musicae popularis, vol. 3: Festschrift to Ernst Emsheimer on the Occasion of His 70th Birthday January 15th 1974*, edited by Gustaf Hilleström. Stockholm: Nordiska musikforlaget, 1974, pp. 176-79.

Stresses the need for classifying instruments in their broad sociological and morphological context.

695. Sachs, Curt. *Geist und Werden der Musikinstrumente.*
     Berlin: Reimer, 1929, reprint ed., Buren: Knuf, 1975.
     282 p.

     Presents a comprehensive classification of instruments.
     Of fundamental importance to the systematic study of
     instruments.

696. ————. *Handbuch der Musikinstrumentenkunde.* 2nd ed.
     Leipzig: Breitkopf und Härtel, 1930; reprint eds.,
     Leipzig: Breitkopf und Härtel, 1966; Hildesheim:
     Olms, 1967; Wiesbaden: Breitkopf und Härtel, 1967.
     419 p.

     A pioneering description and categorization that focuses
     largely on non-European instruments.

697. Stauder, Wilhelm. *Einführung in die Instrumentenkunde.*
     Wilhelmshaven: Heinrichshofen, 1974. 191 p.

     A general introduction to the study of musical instru-
     ments. Includes a list of collections, brief descriptions
     of instruments according to type, a good basic bibliog-
     raphy, and a short history of organology.

698. Stockmann, Erich, et al. "Discussion." *Report of the
     Eleventh Congress of the International Musicological
     Society Copenhagen 1972.* Copenhagen: Wilhelm Hansen,
     1974. Vol. 1, pp. 152-65.

     Focuses on the question of the classification of musical
     instruments and of the role of acoustical research in
     their study.

699. Veenstra, Adolf. "The Classification of the Flute."
     Galpin Society Journal 17 (1964): 54-63.

     Outlines a new system.

                    2. Instrument Collections

700. Albrecht, Theodore, et al. *An Annotated Catalogue of
     Musical Instruments in the Collections of the Western
     Reserve Historical Society.* Cleveland: Case Western
     Reserve University, 1978. 65 p.

     A preliminary catalog of 102 instruments. Includes an
     index of makers.

701. Antwerp, Museum Vleeshuis. *Musiekinstrumenten van het*
      Koninklijk Vlaams Muziekconservatorium to Antwerpen:
      Catalogus. Antwerp: Govaerts, 1967. 47 p.

      A catalog--by Jeanine M. Lambrechts-Douillez, M. Castel-
      lani-Jamar, and Jan Gerarts--listing and describing 176
      items, most of which are illustrated at the end of the
      book. The collection, from the Royal Flemish Conservatory
      of Music, has been loaned to the Vleeshuis Museum in
      Antwerp.

702. Ardács, A.M., and István Lakatos. "Musikinstrumente im
      Historischen Museum Klausenburg (Cluj, Kolozsvar)."
      Studia musicologica 15 (1973): 335-54.

      Provides detailed descriptions of the instruments in
      the museum. Notes that the city of Cluj enjoyed an active
      musical life during the late eighteenth century, the
      period from which the most valuable instruments in the
      collection come.

703. Arundel Society, London. *Musical Instruments in the*
      South Kensington Museum. 2nd ed. London: Chapman
      and Hall, 1875. 402 p.

      Lists and describes 380 instruments. Preceded by a
      history of musical instruments. Illustrated with drawings
      and plates. Prepared by Carl Engel.

*   Ayars, Christine Merrick. *Contributions to the Art of*
      Music in America by the Music Industries of Boston,
      1640-1936. New York: Wilson, 1937. 326 p.

      Cited above as Item 589.

*   Baltimore Museum of Art. *Musical Instruments and Their*
      Portrayal in Art. Baltimore: Museum of Art, 1946.
      48 p.

      Cited below as Item 1166.

704. Basel. Universität. Historische Museum. *Alte Musik-*
      instrumente in Basel. Basel: Historische Museum, 1978.
      48 p.

      An introduction to the collection. Includes twenty
      photographs together with descriptions. The German text,
      by Walter Nef, is accompanied by summaries in French and
      English. The photographs are by Peter Herman.

705. Basel. Universität. Historisches Museum. *Katalog der Musikinstrumente im historischen Museum zu Basel.* Basel: Birkhauser, 1906. 74 p.

    A descriptive catalog, by Karl Nef, of 294 items. Illustrated by twelve pages of photographs. Bound together with *Festschrift zum Zweiten Kongress der Internationalen Musikgesellschaft* (Basel: Reinhardt, 1906).

706. Bate, Philip. "Bernard Hague (1893-1960)." *Galpin Society Journal* 15 (1962): 92-94.

    An obituary together with a list of the wind instruments in Hague's collection at the University of Glasgow.

707. Berlin. Staatliche Akademische Hochschule für Musik. *Sammlung alter Musikinstrumente bei der Staatlichen Hochschule für Musik zu Berlin. Beschreibender Katalog.* Berlin: Bard, 1922. 384 cols.

    A descriptive catalog by Curt Sachs. Includes more than 3,100 items. Illustrated with drawings and photographs.

708. Berlin. Staatliches Institut für Musikforschung. *Die Berliner Musikinstrumenten Sammlung.* Berlin: Institut für Musikforschung, 1952. 58 p.

    A descriptive introduction, by Alfred Berner, to the principal types of instruments found in the collection. Illustrated.

709. Berlin. Staatliches Institut für Musikforschung. *Führer durch das Musikinstrumenten-Museum.* Berlin: Staatliches Institut für Musikforschung, 1939. 144 p.

    A non-technical guide to the display. Illustrated.

710. Berlin. Staatliches Institut für Musikforschung. *Katalog der Blechblasinstrumente: Polsterzungeninstrumente.* Berlin: Staatliches Institut für Musikforschung, 1976. 199 p.

    A well-illustrated, well-annotated classified catalog, by Dieter Krickeberg and Wolfgang Rauch, of 217 brass instruments in the collection of Karl-Marx-Universität. Includes excellent indexes.

711. Berlin. Staatliches Institut für Musikforschung. *Musikinstrumenten-Museum Berlin. Ausstellungsverzeichnis.* Berlin: Staatliches Institut für Musikforschung, 1965. 144 p.

A guide to the instruments on display, listing but not describing them. Includes a small selection of photographs.

712. Berlin. Staatliches Institut für Musikforschung. *Das Musikinstrumenten-Museum Berlin: Eine Einführung in Wort und Bild.* Berlin: Staatliches Institut für Musikforschung, 1968. 70 p.

A collection of fifty-six plates together with brief descriptions of the instruments shown. Prefaced by a history of the collection by Irmgard Otto.

713. Berner, Alfred. "Instrumentensammlungen." *Die Musik in Geschichte und Gegenwart,* edited by Friedrich Blume. Kassel: Bärenreiter, 1949- . Vol. 6 (1957), cols. 1295-1310.

Traces the history of instrument collections generally and lists the collections of the present day.

714. Bernoulli, Wilhelm. "My Collection of Historical Brass Instruments and Drums." *Brass Bulletin* 5, no. 6 (1973): 90-92.

Briefly describes a Swiss collection of 684 instruments. Illustrated with twenty plates.

* Bessaraboff, Nicholas. *Ancient European Musical Instruments: An Organological Study of the Musical Instruments in the Leslie Lindsey Mason Collection at the Museum of Fine Arts, Boston.* Cambridge, Mass.: Harvard University Press, 1941. 503 p.

Cited above as Item 686.

715. Birsak, Kurt. *Die Holzblasinstrumente im Salzburger Museum Carolino Augusteum. Verzeichnis und Entwicklungsgeschichtliche Untersuchungen.* Salzburger: Salzburger Museum Carolino Augusteum, 1973. 211 p.

A catalog of 128 items together with an index of instrument makers. Includes discussion of tuning problems of the Baroque transverse flute, the double-bass shawm, a contra-bassoon from 1732, the German chalumeau, and the early clarinet.

716. ————. "Die Sammlung alter Musikinstrumente im Salzburger Museum Carolino Augusteum." *Oesterreichische Musikzeitschrift* 7 (1970): 399-403.

Briefly describes the collection and its early history.

717. Blagodatov, Georgil Ivanovich. *Katalog Sobranija Muzikal-nykh Instrumentov.* Leningrad: Muzyka, 1972. 127 p.

A catalog of the musical instrument collection of the Leningrad Institute of Theatre, Music, and Cinematography. The collection consists mostly of folk and non-European instruments. It includes, however, rather extensive holdings of orchestral wind instruments.

*   Boyden, David. "Nicholas Bessaraboff's *Ancient European Musical Instruments. Notes* 28 (1971): 21-27.

Cited below as Item 1170.

718. Boyden, David, ed. *Catalogue of the Collection of Musical Instruments in the Department of Music, University of California, Berkeley.* Part I. Berkeley: University of California, 1972. 104 p.

A carefully annotated list of eighty-eight instruments, chiefly of European origin or design.

719. Brunswick. Städtisches Museum. *Verzeichnis der Sammlung alter Musikinstrumente im Städtischen Museum Braun-schweig. Instrumente, Instrumentenmacher und Instrumen-tisten in Braunschweig.* Brunswick: Appelhans, 1928. 124 p.

A catalog, by Hans Schröder, of 113 items, together with an extensive compilation of references from documents relating to instruments, performers, and instrument makers from the fifteenth to the eighteenth century.

720. Brussels. Conservatoire royale de musique. *Catalogue de-scriptif et analytique du musée instrumental du Conserva-toire royale de musique de Bruxelles.* 2nd ed. 5 vols. Ghent: Hoste, 1893-1922.

Prepared by Victor-Charles Mahillon. Arranged according to his system of classification. Includes an essay explain-ing the system. Lists and describes more than 3,000 instruments in what is one of the finest collections in the world.

721. Carse, Adam. "The 'Adam Carse' Collection of Wind Instru-ments." *Galpin Society Journal* 2 (1949): 3-9.

A personal account of the collection now in the Horniman Museum, London.

722. Cincinnati. Art Museum. *Musical Instruments, A Guide to the Permanent Collection*. Cincinnati: Cincinnati Art Museum, 1949. 23 p.

    Lists 110 instruments. Preceded by a brief introduction by Emanuel Winternitz.

723. Cole, Robert M. "Historical Flute Exhibit." *Woodwind World, Brass and Percussion* 16, no. 6 (1977): 8-10.

    Describes nineteen items from the collection of the University of Wisconsin.

724. Coover, James. *Musical Instrument Collections: Catalogues and Cognate Literature*. Detroit: Information Coordinators, 1981. 464 p.

    A comprehensive list of altogether 2,418 items. Partly annotated. An indispensable reference tool.

725. Copenhagen. Carl Claudius Collection. *Carl Claudius' samling af gamle musikinstrumenter*. Copenhagen: Levin og Munskgaard, 1931. 423 p.

    Contains descriptions of 799 items, including more than 700 instruments. Prepared by Godtfred Skjerne.

726. Copenhagen. Musikhistorisk Museum. *Das Musikhistorische Museum zu Kopenhagen: Beschreibender Katalog*. Copenhagen: Gad; Leipzig: Breitkopf und Härtel, 1911. 172 p.

    Lists and describes the 631 items in the collection. Prepared by Angul Hammerich.

727. Darmstadt. Hessiches Landesmuseum. *Musikinstrumente aus dem Hessischen Landesmuseum, 16.-19. Jahrhundert*. Darmstadt: Hessisches Landesmuseum, 1980. 63 p.

    An illustrated catalog of the exhibition held in 1980. Includes pictures and descriptions of twenty wind instruments. Describes the collection and provides an account of the musical life of Darmstadt from 1600 to 1900.

728. Day, Charles Russell. *A Descriptive Catalogue of Musical Instruments Recently Exhibited at the Royal Military Exhibition, London, 1890*. London: Eyre and Spottiswoode, 1891. 253 p.

    Lists and describes more than 450 items. Includes general discussions of the various types of instruments.

Also includes a chapter on musical pitch. Illustrated.

729. Edinburgh. Edinburgh International Festival of Music and
      Dance. *The Galpin Society Twenty-First Anniversary
      Exhibition of European Musical Instruments: Illustrated
      Catalogue*. Edinburgh: Lorimer and Chalmers; London:
      Galpin Society, 1968. 99 p.

      A descriptive catalog of 716 items, including 649 instru-
      ments, on exhibit at the 1968 Edinburgh Festival. Includes
      40 plates of photographs. Edited by Graham Melville-Mason.

730. Eisenach. Bachmuseum. *Historische Musikinstrumente im
      Bachhaus Eisenach*. Eisenach: Bachhaus, 1976. 296 p.

      Lists and describes in considerable detail a collection
      of 207 instruments, including many wind instruments.
      Extremely well illustrated. Prepared by Herbert Heyde.

731. Eisenach. Bachmuseum. *Verzeichnis der Sammlung alter
      Musikinstrumente im Bachhaus zu Eisenach*. 4th ed.
      Leipzig: Breitkopf und Härtel, 1964. 97 p.

      Lists and describes 320 items. Illustrated. Compiled
      by Friedrich Breidert and Conrad Freyse.

732. Emerson, John A. *Musical Instruments--East and West:
      A Catalog of an Exhibition on the Occasion of the
      Twelfth Congress of the International Musicological
      Society (Berkeley, California, August 21-22, 1977)*.
      Berkeley: Music Library, University of California,
      1977. 61 p.

      An annotated list of 139 instruments, chiefly primitive
      and non-western.

733. Emsheimer, Ernst. "Musikmuseets instrumentsamlingar."
      *Svenska musikperspektiv: Minnesskrift vid kungl.
      musikaliska akademiens 100-arsjubileum 1971*, edited by
      Gustaf Hilleström. Stockholm: Nordiska Musikforlaget,
      1971, pp. 115-56.

      Describes the origin and growth of the instrument collec-
      tion at the music museum. Includes a detailed inventory
      of the holdings, including 2,426 European art instruments.

734. Eschler, Thomas J. "A Collection of Historical Musical
      Instruments of the University of Erlangen: A Checklist."
      Galpin Society Journal 36 (1983): 115-24.

      Lists seventy-seven instruments.

735. Fesperman, John. "Report from Washington: Music and Instruments at the Smithsonian Institution." *Current Musicology* 6 (1968): 63-65.

    Describes the instrument collection at the Smithsonian as well as the general program of its Division of Musical Instruments.

736. Florence. Conservatorio de musica "Luigi Cherubini." Museo. *Gli strumenti musicali e il Museo del Conservatorio "Luigi Cherubini" di Firenze.* Florence: LICOSA, 1969. 286 p.

    A well-annotated catalog of 221 items, prepared by Vinicio Gai. Includes inventories from the past and other documents significant to the history of the collection. Illustrated.

* Florence. Galleria degli Uffizi. *Mostra di strumenti musicali in disegni degli Uffizi.* Florence: Olschki, 1952. 47 p.

    Cited below as Item 1175.

* Florence. Galleria degli Uffizi. *I disegni musicali del Gabinetto degli "Uffizi" e delle minore collezioni publiche a Firenze.* Florence: Olschki, 1951. 233 p.

    Cited below as Item 1176.

737. Gábry, György. *Old Musical Instruments.* Translated by Éva Rácz. Budapest: Corvina, 1969. 42 p.

    Describes the most interesting instruments in Hungary, particularly those in the Hungarian National Museum. Includes a catalog and forty-eight plates.

738. Galpin Society. *British Musical Instruments: An Exhibition, August 7-30, 1951.* London: Galpin Society, 1951. 35 p.

    A brief guide to an exhibition of more than 600 items held in 1951. The instruments were mostly of British origin or provenance.

739. Galpin, Brian. "Canon Galpin's Check Lists." *Galpin Society Journal* 25 (1972): 4-21.

    An annotated edition of Francis W. Galpin's check list of his instrument collection, which was made in 1890. Notes the subsequent history and present location of each traceable item.

740. Garden, Greer. "Models of Perfection--Woodwind Instruments
      from the Museum of the Paris Conservatoire." *Recorder
      and Music Magazine* 4, no. 4 (1971): 116-17.

      Touches upon a number of remarkable instruments, includ-
      ing N. Winnen's bassonore (said to have four times the
      power of a bassoon), crystal flutes, a bassoon by Sax
      with twenty-three keys, a contrabass oboe, and a walking-
      stick clarinet.

741. Groffy, Franz. *Musikhistorisches Museum Heckel-Biebrich.
      Abteilung Fagotte.* Wiesbaden-Biebrich: Heckel, 1968.
      108 p.

      A catalog and brief description of the collection.
      Includes an index of makers. Illustrated with many line
      drawings.

742. Haefer, J. Richard. *A Catalogue and History of the
      Musical Instrument Collection of the Arizona Pioneers'
      Historical Society, Tucson, Arizona.* Sells, Ariz.:
      Haefer, 1971.

      Describes a collection of forty-two instruments, dating
      from *ca.* 1750 to the 1920s. Also lists musical instruments
      in other Arizona museums.

743. The Hague. Gemeentemuseum. *Catalogus van de muziekinstru-
      menten.* Vol. 1: *Hoorn- en trompetachtige blaasinstru-
      menten.* Amsterdam: Knuf; New York: Da Capo, 1970.
      85 p.

      A descriptive catalog of 136 instruments prepared by
      Leo J. Plenckers. Includes photographs of twenty-eight
      instruments, including an example of the tuba-Dupré, a
      soprano ophicleide of peculiar appearance. Introduction
      in English and Dutch.

744. The Hague. Gemeentemuseum. *Exotic and Ancient Musical
      Instruments in the Department of Musical History of the
      Municipal Museum at The Hague.* The Hague: Nijgh &
      Van Ditmar, 1955. 51 p.

      A general description, by A.W. Ligtvoet, accompanied by
      photographs. Text in Dutch and English.

745. The Hague. Gemeentemuseum. *Historische Blaasinstrumenten.*
      The Hague: Gemeentemuseum, 1974. 80 p.

      Catalog of an exhibition of 224 items--including
      paintings and lithographs--that was held in 1974. Contains

descriptions of the individual instruments, general essays
on instruments, and an account of instrument manufacture
in Amsterdam during the seventeenth and eighteenth centuries. Text in Dutch only.

746. Haine, Malou, and Ignace de Keyser. *Catalogue des instru-*
      ments Sax au Musée instrumental de Bruxelles. Buren:
      Knuf, 1980. 280 p.

      An exemplary catalog of sixty-nine instruments. Fully
      annotated and profusely illustrated. Includes biographical
      sketches of Charles-Joseph, Adolphe, Alphonse, Adolphe
      Edouard, and Henri Sax. Also includes a brief discussion
      of types of keys and pistons and a comprehensive list of
      extant instruments.

747. Hamburg. Museum für Hamburgische Geschichte. *Verzeichnis*
      der Sammlung alter Musikinstrumente. Hamburg: Alster,
      1930. 95 p.

      A descriptive catalog by Hans Schröder. Well illus-
      trated.

748. Heyde, Herbert. *Flöten*. Musikinstrumenten-Museum der
      Karl-Marx Universität Leipzig, Katalog, vol. 1. Leipzig:
      Deutscher Verlag für Musik, 1978. 160 p.

      A well-annotated descriptive catalog. Includes sixteen
      pages of photographs of instruments and makers' marks.

749. ————. *Trompeten, Posaunen, Tuben*. Musikinstrumenten-
      Museum der Karl-Marx-Universität Leipzig, Katalog, vol.
      3. Leipzig: Deutscher Verlag für Musik, 1980. 264 p.

      An extremely well-documented catalog. Includes biograph-
      ical sketches of instrument makers, mouthpiece measure-
      ments, valve diagrams, drawings of makers' marks, and
      forty-eight plates.

750. Heyer, Wilhelm. Musikhistorisches Museum von Wilhelm
      Heyer in Köln. *Kleiner Katalog der Sammlung alter*
      Musikinstrumente. Cologne: Heyer, 1913. 250 p.

      A catalog by Georg Kinsky of more than 2,500 items.
      Includes wind instruments, which were to have been des-
      cribed more fully in the third volume of the full
      catalog. The volume was never published.

751. Hill, Jackson. *The Harold E. Cook Collection of Musical*
      Instruments, An Illustrated Catalog. Lewisburg, Penn.:

Bucknell University Press, 1975. 67 p.

Valuable especially for its illustrations. The
collection includes approximately 150 instruments.

752. Jenkins, Jean L., ed. *International Directory of Musical
      Instrument Collections.* Buren: Knuf, 1977. 166 p.

      An indispensable guide. For each museum notes the
      number of instruments in each category, lists publications
      dealing with instruments, and describes the specialties
      of each collection.

753. Karp, Cary. "Baroque Woodwind in the Musikhistoriska
      Museet, Stockholm." *Galpin Society Journal* 25 (1972):
      80-86.

      A descriptive list. Includes photographs.

*   Keller, Jindřich. "Pištelníci a trubaři. Pojednáni o
      vyrobě dechových hudebnich nástroju v Čechách před
      rokem 1800." *Sborník Národního muzea v Praze. Acta
      musei nationalis pragae* 29 (1975): 161-243.

      Cited above as Item 146.

754. Krickeberg, Dieter. "Die alte Musikinstrumentensammlung
      der Naumburger St. Wenzelskirche im Spiegel ihrer
      Verzeichnisse." *Jahrbuch des Staatlichen Instituts
      für Musikforschung 1977*, pp. 7-30.

      Discusses the seventeenth-century wind instruments
      preserved in the collection and compares them with those
      listed in old catalogs.

755. Lambertini, Michel Angelo. *Primeiro nucleo de um museu
      instrumental em Lisboa: Catalogi sommario.* Lisbon:
      n.p., 1914. 147 p.

      Lists and briefly describes the collection of Alfredo
      Keil, which serves as the basis for the collection now
      part of the museum of the National Conservatory in Lisbon.

756. Larson, André P. "Catalogue of the Nineteenth-Century
      British Brass Instruments in the Arne B. Larson Collec-
      tion of Musical Instruments." Ph.D. dissertation,
      University of West Virginia, 1974. 165 p. UM 75-12,399.

      A detailed examination of 43 instruments. The collec-
      tion, containing approximately 2,500 instruments, is
      housed at the University of South Dakota at Vermillion.

757. ————. "A Catalog of the Double Reed Instruments in
      Arne B. Larson Collection of Musical Instruments."
      M. Mus. thesis, University of South Dakota, 1968. 102 p.

      Lists and describes fifty-three instruments. Includes
      a brief history of double reed instruments, emphasizing
      the period from 1700 to 1950.

758. Leeuwen, Boomkamp, Carel van, and John Henry van der Meer.
      *The Carel van Leeuwen Boomkamp Collection of Musical
      Instruments*. Amsterdam: Knuf, 1971. 190 p.

      A descriptive catalog of a collection of 112 items,
      including nineteen wind instruments. Notable primarily
      for its string instruments and bows. Each instrument is
      illustrated in a full-page photograph.

759. Leipzig, Karl-Marx-Universität. Musikinstrumentenmuseum.
      Musikinstrumente. Leipzig: Prisma, 1970. 60 p.

      Lists and describes forty-two historical instruments.
      Includes thirty-two plates. By Winfried Schrammek.
      Photographs by Rolf Langematz.

760. Leipzig. Karl-Marx-Universität. *Musikinstrumente aus
      dem Musikinstrumenten-Museum der Karl Marx-Universität
      Leipzig*. Leipzig: Prisma, 1970. 42 p.

      A selection of thirty-two photographs together with
      descriptions by Winfried Schrammek of the instruments
      depicted.

761. Library of Congress. *Musical Instruments in the Dayton
      C. Miller Flute Collection at the Library of Congress,
      a Catalog*, vol. 1: *Recorders, Fifes, and Simple System
      Transverse Flutes of One Key*. Washington, D.C.:
      Library of Congress, 1982. 351 p.

      Compiled by Michael Seyfrit. The first of a projected
      seven-volume catalog. Includes illustrations of 273 instru-
      ments as well as x-rays, bore graphs, and line drawings.

762. Library of Congress. *The Dayton C. Miller Flute Collec-
      tions, a Checklist of the Instruments*. Washington, D.C.:
      Library of Congress, 1961. 115 p.

      Compiled by Laura E. Gilliam and William Lichtenwanger.
      A preliminary list of the 1,593 instruments in the collec-
      tion.

763. Linz. Oberösterreichisches Landesmuseum. *Die Musikinstru-*
     menten-Sammlung des Oberösterreichischen Landesmuseums.
     Linz: Demokratische Druck- und Verlags-Gesellschaft,
     1952. 47 p.

     A catalog by Othmar Wessely. Briefly describes 188
     items.

764. London. Horniman Museum. *The Adam Carse Collection of*
     Musical Wind Instruments. London: London County
     Council, 1951. 88 p.

     Lists and briefly describes a collection of 320 items.
     Includes an introduction by Carse.

765. London. Horniman Museum. *Wind Instruments of European*
     Art Music. London: Inner London Education Authority,
     1974. 107 p.

     A descriptive catalog, by E.A.K. Ridley, of the wind
     instruments in the Horniman Museum, including the Adam
     Carse Collection. Also includes a history of wind instru-
     ments and of valves. Well illustrated with photographs.

766. London. Royal College of Music. *Catalogue of Historical*
     Musical Instruments, Paintings, Sculpture, and Drawings.
     London: Royal College of Music, 1952. 16 p.

     Lists 293 instruments.

767. Lübeck. St. Annen Museum. *Die Sammlung alter Musikinstru-*
     mente im St. Annen-Museum. Lübeck: St. Annen Museum,
     1959. 10 p.

     Prepared by Georg Karstädt. Describes the collection
     and lists its contents. Illustrated with six plates.

768. Lucerne. Richard-Wagner Museum. *Katalog der städtischen*
     Sammlung alter Musikinstrumente im Richard-Wagner-Museum
     Tribschen/Luzern. Lucerne: Richard Wagner Museum,
     1956.

     Lists the 217 instruments in the collection. Illustrated
     with sixteen plates. Prepared under the direction of
     René Vannes.

769. Luton. Museum and Art Gallery. *The Ridley Collection*
     of Musical Wind Instruments in the Luton Museum.
     Luton: Museum and Art Gallery, 1957. 32 p.

     An annotated, illustrated catalog of seventy-five items,

mostly woodwind instruments. Prefaced by a brief general
description of the instruments.

770. Marvin, Bob. "Recorders and English Flutes in European
Collections." *Galpin Society Journal* 25 (1972):   30-57.

Primarily a list. Includes measurements of two flutes.

771. Meer, John Henry van der. "Germanisches Nationalmuseum
Nürnberg: Geschichte seiner Musikinstrumentensammlung."
*Jahrbuch des Staatlichen Instituts für Musikforschung
Preussischer Kulturbesitz 1979/80*. Berlin: Merseberger,
1981, pp. 9-78.

Sketches the history of the collection and details the
acquisitions made during each administration. Includes a
good bibliography.

772. Milan. Conservatorio di musica Giuseppe Verdi. Museo.
*Gli strumenti musicali nel Museo del conservatorio di
Milano*. Milan: Hoepli, 1908. 109 p.

A classified descriptive catalog by Eugenio de Guarinoni.
Includes 278 items, 177 of which are of European origin.
Illustrated with thirty-two plates.

773. Milan. Museo di antichi strumenti musicali. *Museo degli
strumenti musicali: Catalogo*. Milan: Castello
Storzesco, 1963. 448 p.

A well-annotated catalog, by Natale and Franco Gallini,
of 641 items. Generously illustrated with 141 plates,
some in color. Earlier catalogs were published in 1953
and 1958. The basis for the collection is the private
collection of Natale Gallini.

774. Mount Holyoke College. *The Belle Skinner Collection of
Old Musical Instruments, Holyoke, Massachusetts*.
Philadelphia: Beck, 1933. 210 p.

An illustrated catalog, by William Skinner, of eighty-
nine instruments, now on loan to Yale University.

775. Munich. Bayerisches Nationalmuseum. *Ausstellung alte
Musik, Instrumente, Noten und Dokumente aus drei Jahr-
hunderten. Katalog*. Munich: Hieber, 1951. 71 p.

A catalog, by Alfons Ott, of an exhibition of 636
items. Includes brief descriptions of the instruments
as well as twenty-three plates.

776. Munich. Deutsches Museum von Meisterwerken der Naturwissenschaft und Technik. *Die Blasinstrumente im Deutschen Museum. Beschriebender Katalog.* Munich: Oldenbourg, 1976. 108 p.

An annotated catalog, by Heinrich Seifers, of approximately 450 instruments, including two flutes by Boehm and a saxophone from the workshop of Adolphe Sax.

777. Music Library Association. *A Survey of Musical Instrument Collections in the United States and Canada.* Ann Arbor: Music Library Association, 1974. 137 p.

Briefly describes collections of all kinds. Includes information on the availability of the collections to the public. Prepared by William Lichtenwanger with the assistance of Dale Higbee, Cynthia Adams Hoover, and Phillip T. Young.

778. Nef, Walter. *Alte Musikinstrumente in Basel.* Schriften der Historischen Museums Basel, 2. Basel: Stiftung für das Historische Museum Basel, 1974. 47 p.

Describes and illustrates thirty-two instruments, including a crystal flute. The photographs, many in color, are by Peter Herman.

779. New York. Metropolitan Museum of Art. *Catalogue of the Crosby Brown Collection of Musical Instruments of All Nations,* vol. 1: *Europe.* New York: Metropolitan Museum of Art, 1902. 296 p.

An annotated guide to the collection, arranged according to the plan of its display. Includes a large number of wind instruments.

780. Nuremberg. Germanisches Nationalmuseum. *Verzeichnis der europäischen Musikinstrumente im Germanischen Nationalmuseum Nürnberg,* vol. 1: *Hörner und Trompeten, Membranophone. Idiophone.* Wilhelmshaven: Heinrichshofen, 1979. 137 p.

A fully annotated catalog, by John Henry van der Meer, of one of the world's greatest collections. Includes 195 illustrations. Prefaced by a history of the collection.

* Oromszegi, Otto. "Bassoons at the Narodni Museum, Prague." *Galpin Society Journal* 24 (1971): 96-101.

Cited above as Item 260.

781. Oxford. University. Faculty of Music. Bate Collection.
      The Bate Collection of Historical Wind Instruments:
      Catalogue of the Instruments. Oxford: Faculty of
      Music, 1976. 64 p.

      Prepared by Anthony Baines. Omits folk and exotic
      instruments. Otherwise a complete list of the collection.
      Includes detailed measurements of eighty-nine woodwind
      instruments.

782. Paris. Conservatoire national de musique. *Le musée du*
      Conservatoire national de musique. Catalogue raisonné
      des instruments de cette collection. Paris: Didot,
      1875. 145 p.

      Lists and briefly describes a collection of 630 items.
      Prepared by Gustave Chouquet, the curator of the collection.
      Important partly for its system of classification of
      musical instruments, which influenced subsequent cata-
      logers. A revised and expanded edition, cited below as
      Item 783, was published in 1884, with supplements--by
      Léon Pillaut--in 1894, 1899, and 1903.

783. Paris. Conservatoire national de musique. *Le musée du*
      Conservatoire national de musique. Catalogue descriptif
      et raisonné. 2nd ed. Paris: Didot, 1884. 276 p.

      Like its predecessor (item 782), prepared by Gustave
      Chouquet. Lists and briefly describes 1,006 items,
      most of them instruments employed in European art music.

784. Paris. Exposition universelle internationale, 1900.
      Musée retrospectif de la classe 17. Rapport du comité
      d'installation. Paris: Eyméoud, [1900]. 119 p.

      Provides a general description of the musical instruments
      and accessories on exhibit. Includes a complete list of
      the 349 items. Represents a summary of the state of
      instrument making, especially in France, at the end of
      the nineteenth century. Well illustrated with drawings
      and photographs. Prepared under the direction of Albert
      Jacquot.

785. Pass, Walter. "Die Instrumentensammlung des Tiroler
      Landesmuseums Ferdinandeum." *Oesterreichische*
      Musikzeitschrift 26 (1970): 693-98.

      Briefly summarizes the history and contents of the
      collection in Innsbruck, expecially the string instruments.
      Also mentions a few notable wind instruments.

786. Pierre, Constant. *La facture instrumentale à l'Exposition
     universelle de 1889; notes d'un musicien sur les instru-
     ments à souffle nouveaux et perfectionnés.* Paris:
     Libraire de l'art indépendant, 1890. 316 p.

     Describes the many kinds of modern wind instruments on
     display at the exhibition, including such rarities as the
     baroxyton, lyrophone, and an Evette-Schaeffer system
     clarinet. Illustrated with drawings. An excellent survey
     of the state of wind instrument manufacture in Europe at
     the time.

787. Pressley, E. Wayne. "Musical Wind Instruments in the
     Moravian Musical Archives, Salem, N.C.: A Descriptive
     Catalogue." D.M.A. dissertation, University of Kentucky,
     1975. 163 p. UM 76-16,594.

     Provides detailed descriptions of the instruments.
     Includes thirty-five photographs.

788. Roos, Wilhelm. "The Musical Instrument Collection at
     Meran." *Galpin Society Journal* 32 (1979): 10-23.

     Includes descriptions of a Renaissance transverse flute,
     a tenor oboe (by W. Kress), and three trumpets (two by
     Friedrich and one by Paulus Schmidt).

789. Salzburg. Museum Carolino-Augusteum. *Alte Musikinstrumente
     im Museum Carolino Augusteum Salzburg.* Leipzig: Breit-
     kopf und Härtel, 1932. 46 p.

     An annotated catalog, by Karl Geiringer, of 288 items.
     Includes an index of makers.

*   Schlosser, Julius. *Unsere Musikinstrumente: Eine
     Einführung in ihre Geschichte.* Vienna: Schroll, 1922.
     80 p.

     Cited above as Item 31.

790. Schmid, Manfred Hermann. *Theobald Boehm 1794-1881: Die
     Revolution der Flöte. Katalog der Ausstellung zum 100.
     Geburtstag von Boehm.* Tutzing: Schneider, 1981. 192 p.

     A well-annotated illustrated catalog of 235 instruments
     in the collection of the Munich Stadtmuseum. Includes a
     number of brief essays on aspects of Boehm's life and
     career, on the manufacture of woodwind instruments in
     Munich during Boehm's lifetime, on the flute in England
     and France, on other Boehm-system woodwinds, and on the
     contemporary flute.

791. Smithsonian Institution. *Handbook of the Collection of Musical Instruments in the United States National Museum.* Washington, D.C.: Smithsonian Institution, 1927; reprint ed., New York: Da Capo, 1971. 164 p.

 Prepared by Frances Densmore. A general description of the instruments that form the basis for the collection.

792. Thibault, Geneviève, Jean Jenkins, and Josiane Bran-Ricci. *Eighteenth-Century Musical Instruments: France and Britain/Les instruments de musique au xviii siècle: France et Grande Bretagne.* London: Victoria and Albert Museum, 1973. 225 p.

 A well-illustrated and well-annotated catalog of an exhibition of more than 100 instruments from the collections of the Conservatoire National Supérieur de Musique in Paris, the Victoria and Albert Museum, and the Horniman Museum.

793. Tokyo. Musashino Ongaku Daigaku. Gakki Hakubutsukan. *Catalogue. Museum of Musical Instruments. Musashino Academiae Musicae, on the Fortieth Anniversary of the Institute.* 2 vols. Tokyo: Musashino Academia Musicae, 1969, 1974. 108, 58 p.

 By Shun'ichi Kikuchi and Osamu Yamaguchi. Text in Japanese and English. Illustrated.

794. Toronto. Royal Ontario Museum. *Musical Instruments in the Royal Ontario Museum.* Edited by Ladislav Cseleny. [Toronto]: Royal Ontario Museum, 1971. 96 p.

 A catalog of more than 100 items.

795. University of Michigan. *Catalogue of the Stearns Collection of Musical Instruments.* 2nd ed. Ann Arbor: The University of Michigan, 1921. 276 p.

 Lists and briefly describes the collection, which contained at the time approximately 1,400 items, including many wind instruments. Illustrated with photographs. Prepared by Albert A. Stanley.

796. University of South Dakota. *Keyed Brass Instruments in the Arne B. Larson Collection.* Vermillion, S.D.: The Shrine to Music Foundation, 1980. 34 p.

 A selection of photographs of thirty-one instruments in the collection of the University of South Dakota. Includes brief descriptions. Prepared by Gary M. Stewart.

797.   Ventzke, Karl. *Saxophonisches seit 1842*. Düren:
       Leopold-Hoesch-Museum, 1981. 38 p.

       Catalog of an exhibition of saxophones, music, pictures,
       and various publications from Ventzke's collection. Well
       illustrated.

798.   Victoria and Albert Museum, South Kensington. *Catalogue
       of Musical Instruments*, vol. 2: *Non-Keyboard Instruments*.
       London: Her Majesty's Stationery Office, 1968. 121 p.

       A classified, well-annotated catalog by Anthony Baines.
       Illustrated with 138 plates. The collection includes
       approximately fifty wind instruments.

799.   Vienna. Kunsthistorisches Museum. *Die Sammlung alter
       Musikinstrumente. Beschreibendes Verzeichnis*. Vienna:
       Schroll, 1920. 143 p.

       Prepared by Julius Schlosser. Lists and describes in
       detail a collection of 361 instruments. Most are illus-
       trated by photographs. Includes essays on the various
       types of instruments as well as on the evolution of
       instruments generally.

800.   Warner, Robert A. *The Stearns Collection of Musical
       Instruments--1965*. Ann Arbor: School of Music, The
       University of Michigan, [1965]. 11 p.

       An account of the origin of the collection together
       with an overview of its contents.

801.   Webb, John. "A Collection in Graslitz." *Galpin Society
       Journal* 36 (1983): 131-32.

       Briefly describes a collection of 500 instruments in
       Bohemia.

802.   Willms, Wolfgang. "Die Flötensammlung von Dr. med.
       Wolfgang Willms in Aachen-Laurensberg." *Glareana* 16,
       nos. 3-4 (December 1967).

       A descriptive catalog of 247 instruments, mostly from
       the nineteenth and twentieth centuries. Includes a few
       woodwind instruments other than flute. Illustrated.

803.   Winternitz, Emanual. "The Crosby Brown Collection of
       Musical Instruments: Its Origin and Development."
       Metropolitan Museum Journal 3 (1970): 337-56.

       A rather informal account. Well illustrated with
       photographs. Also published separately.

804. Woodward, Bonnie Blaszczyk. "The Dayton C. Miller Flute Collection." *Woodwind Anthology*. Evanston, Ill.: Instrumentalist, 1976, pp. 244-47.

     Reviews some of the most important features of the instruments in the collection.

805. Yale University. *A Catalogue of the Pedro Traversari Collection of Musical Instruments*. [Washington, D.C., New Haven, Conn.]: Organization of American States and Yale University, 1978. 138 p.

     A descriptive catalog, by Richard Rephann, of the collection once owned by Pedro Traversari Salazar of Quito and now owned by Yale University. The collection, comprising 5,008 items, consists mostly of folk instruments, but it includes a significant number of nineteenth-century wind instruments. Catalog published with facing Spanish translations by Lola Ordiaga.

806. Yale University. *Checklist, Yale Collection of Musical Instruments*. New Haven, Conn.: Yale University, 1968. 43 p.

     Lists 444 items, including 310 instruments.

807. Yale University. *Musical Instruments at Yale*. New Haven, Conn.: Yale University Art Gallery, [1960], 32 p.

     A fully illustrated and well-documented catalog, by Sibyl Marcuse, of an exhibition held in 1960. Included among the twenty-six instruments described are an oboe and three matched clarinets from the eighteenth century as well as a fifteenth-century bugle.

XII

DISCUSSIONS OF PERFORMANCE, HISTORICAL AND CONTEMPORARY

1. General

*   Anfinson, Roland E. "A Cinefluorographic Investigation of Selected Clarinet Playing Techniques." *Journal of Research in Music Education* 17 (1969): 227-39.

      Cited below as Item 1163.

*   Battipaglia, Victor A. "The Double-Lip Embouchure in Clarinet Playing." D.M.A. dissertation, University of Rochester, 1975. 103 p. UM 75-29,845.

      Cited below as Item 1167.

808.   Biggers, Cornelia Anderson. *Contra-Bassoon: A Guide to Performance.* Bryn Mawr, Penn.: Elkan-Vogel, 1977. 48 p.

      Deals only with the problems peculiar to the contra-bassoon and not to the bassoon. Discusses posture, equipment, fingering, tone production, reeds, and performance problems. Includes a fingering chart for the German-system instrument.

809.   Blades, James. *Orchestral Percussion Technique.* 2nd ed. London: Oxford University Press, 1973. 87 p.

      A guide for percussion students. Useful also to conductors and composers for its explanations of notation.

*   Boehm, Theobald. *The Flute and Flute-Playing in Acoustical Technical, and Artistic Aspects.* Translated by Dayton C. Miller. New York: Dover, 1964. 197 p.

      Cited above at Item 66.

810. Camden, Archie. *Bassoon Technique.* London: Oxford University Press, 1961. 74 p.

    Focuses on orchestral playing. Includes a bibliography of music for the bassoon prepared by William Waterhouse.

811. Chapman, Frederick B. *Flute Technique.* 4th ed. London: Oxford University Press, 1973. 89 p.

    A guide for students. Includes a lengthy list of flute music.

812. Cooper, Lewis Hugh, and Howard Toplansky. *Essentials of Bassoon Technique.* Union, N.J.: Toplansky, 1968. 372 p.

    An exhaustive compendium of fingering charts. Well annotated.

813. Dunbar, Rudolph. *Treatise on the Clarinet (Boehm System).* London: Dallas, 1939. 141 p.

    Contains exercises, a few original etudes, and discussions of a variety of matters--including performance technique, reed selection, musical style, and the history of the clarinet. A native of British Guiana, the author headed the School of Modern Clarinet Playing in London and also distinguished himself as the first black conductor of the London Philharmonic Orchestra.

* Eichborn, Hermann. *Der Dämpfung beim Horn oder Die musikalische Natur des Horns.* Leipzig: Breitkopf und Härtel, 1897. 39 p.

    Cited above at Item 405.

814. Farkas, Philip. *The Art of Brass Playing.* Bloomington, Ind.: Brass Publications, 1962. 65 p.

    A detailed discussion of embouchure, articulation, and breath control.

815. ————. *The Art of French Horn Playing.* Evanston, Ill.: Summy-Birchard, 1956. 95 p.

    A relatively comprehensive guide for horn players. Includes a selection of exercises and etudes.

* ————. *A Photographic Study of 40 Virtuoso Horn Players' Embouchures.* Bloomington, Ind.: Wind Music, 1970. 41 p.

    Cited below as Item 1174.

816. Fink, Reginald H. *The Trombonist's Handbook: A Complete*
      Guide to Playing and Teaching the Trombone. Athens,
      Ohio: Accura, 1977. 145 p.

      Useful particularly for its annotated lists of trombone
      music and the annotated bibliography of textbooks dealing
      with the trombone and with brass instruments generally.

817. Gärtner, Jochen. *The Vibrato, with Particular Considera-*
      tion Given to the Situation of the Flutist. Translated
      by Einar W. Anderson. Regensburg: Bosse, 1981. 172 p.

      Reviews past discussions of vibrato--including those
      by Ganassi, Praetorius, Leopold Mozart, and Spohr--and
      surveys the research of the twentieth century. Describes
      in detail the physiological/anatomical basis of flute
      vibrato and offers suggestions and exercises for the
      development of both laryngeal and thoracic/abdominal
      vibratos.

818. Hadamowsky, Hans. "Der Wiener Bläserstil." *Oesterreich-*
      ische Musikzeitschrift 24 (1969): 691-97.

      Evaluates and compares the Viennese and French styles
      of wind playing.

*   Hall, Jody C. "A Radiographic, Spectrographic, and
      Photographic Study of the Non-Labial Physical Changes
      which Occur in the Transition from Middle to Low and
      Middle to High Registers during Trumpet Performance."
      Ph.D. dissertation, Indiana University, 1954. 313 p.
      UM 10,146.

      Cited below as Item 1178.

819. Hanson, Shelley J. "A Systematic Approach to the
      Making and Adjusting of Single Reeds." Ph.D. disser-
      tation, Michigan State University, 1979. 119 p.
      UM 79-7339.

      A detailed discussion of a non-traditional method.

820. Hasan, Muhamed Ahmed Hasan. "K voprosu o razvitii
      ispolnitel'skogo apparata trombnista." Ph.D.
      dissertation, Moscow Conservatory, 1974. 172 p.

      A guide to trombone performance. Includes a descrip-
      tion of the physiology of breathing, tonguing, and the
      embouchure.

821. Henderson, Hayward. "An Experimental Study of Trumpet
     Embouchure." *Journal of the Acoustical Society of
     America* 14 (1942-43): 58-64.

     Describes the embouchure requirements for the produc-
     tion of good tone.

822. Hofmann, Heinrich. *Über den Ansatz der Blechbläser.*
     Kassel: Bärenreiter, 1956. 77 p.

     A comprehensive discussion of the anatomy and physiology
     of brass playing. Distinguished partly by its careful
     attention to the evidence provided by writers from the
     sixteenth through the nineteenth century.

*   Hyatt, Jack H. "The Soprano and Piccolo Trumpets:
     Their History, Literature, and a Tutor." D.M.A.
     dissertation, Boston University, 1974. 238 p.
     UM 74-20,473.

     Cited above as Item 349.

823. Jaeger, Jürgen. "Zu Grundfragen des Blechbläseransatzes
     am Beispiel der Posaune." *Beiträge zur Musikwissenschaft*
     13 (1971): 56-73.

     Discusses sound production in brass instruments,
     expecially the trombone, in regard to embouchures in
     which little pressure is applied. Describes the
     acoustical factors and the physical process.

824. Johnson, Keith. *The Art of Trumpet Playing.* Ames,
     Iowa: Iowa State University Press, 1981. 50 p.

     A comprehensive discussion of playing technique.
     Includes a general chapter on instruments and mouth-
     pieces. Presented without benefit of musical examples
     or more than passing mention of specific compositions.

825. Kirby, Percival R. *The Kettle-Drums: A Book for Composers,
     Conductors and Kettle-Drummers.* London: Oxford Univ-
     ersity Press, 1930. 73 p.

     Mainly a discussion of performance technique. Intro-
     duced by a brief but useful survey of the use of timpani
     in orchestral music.

826. Kleinhammer, Edward. *The Art of Trombone Playing.*
     Evanston, Ill.: Summy-Birchard, 1963. 107 p.

A guide for performers. Includes many exercises and
a selective list of music and method books for trombone
and bass trombone.

827. Ledet, David A. *Oboe Reed Styles: Theory and Practice*.
      Bloomington, Ind.: Indiana University Press, 1981.
      212 p.

      A careful analysis based on an examination of the reeds
      of eighty-one oboists from Europe and the United States.
      Includes photographs and detailed descriptions of the
      reeds (168 in all). Also includes biographical infor-
      mation on the oboists. Introduced by an extended dis-
      cussion of tone production.

828. Leno, Lloyd. "Lip Vibration Characteristics of the
      Trombone Embouchure in Performance." *Brass Anthology*.
      Evanston, Ill.: Instrumentalist, 1976, pp. 572-77.

      Concludes that there are at least two types of embouch-
      ures as classified according to the direction of the air
      stream and that lip action, a complex phenomenon, varies
      according to this direction. Also see Item 851, cited
      below.

829. Le Roy, René. *Traité de la flûte, historique, technique
      et pédagogique*. Paris: Éditions musicales translan-
      tiques, 1966. 103 p.

      Also published in a German translation by Christiane
      Nicolet-Gerhard (Kassel: Bärenreiter, 1970). Primarily
      a discussion of the principles of flute playing. Includes
      technical exercises, a brief history of the instrument,
      and an overview of its acoustics.

830. Lotsch, Hans. *Das grosse Rohrbuch. Systematischer
      Lehrgang für den Bau von Fagottrohren*. Frankfurt:
      Das Musikinstrument, 1974. 74 p.

      Thorough and detailed. Well illustrated with photo-
      graphs and drawings. Includes instructions for making
      contra-bassoon reeds. The first book of its kind in
      German.

831. Mason, J. Kent. *The Tuba Handbook*. Toronto: Sonante
      Publications, 1977. 107 p.

      Mostly a discussion of performances problems. Includes
      a brief history of the instrument and a bibliography.

832. Maxted, George. *Talking About the Trombone*. London: Baker, 1970. 63 p.

    A guide for performers. Includes a brief history of the instrument, a description of its acoustics, and remarks on orchestral playing based on the author's experiences.

833. Popkin, Mark, and Loren Glickman. *Bassoon Reed Making*. Evanston, Ill.: Instrumentalist, 1969. 30 p.

    A thorough, well-illustrated manual. Includes a section on bassoon repair, maintenance, and adjustment.

834. Porter, Maurice M. *The Embouchure*. London: Boosey and Hawkes, 1967. 144 p.

    Describes in detail the functions of various parts of the body that are important to wind playing, including the diaphragm, lungs, chest muscles, throat, and mouth. Also discusses embouchure comfort, discomfort, and fatigue.

835. Putnik, Edwin. *The Art of Flute Playing*. Evanston, Ill.: Summy-Birchard, 1973. 87 p.

    A manual for performers and teachers. Includes exercises.

* Richmond, Stanley. *Clarinet and Saxophone Experience*. New York: St. Martin's Press, 1972. 137 p.

    Cited above as Item 93.

836. Roos, J. "The Physiology of Playing the Flute." *Archives néerlandises de phonétique expérimentale* 12 (1936): 1-26; 14 (1938): 4-17.

    Carefully investigates the questions of air pressure velocity, and breathing. Describes the changes that occur during the production of flageolet tones and suggests that the most important factor in their production might be the distance between lips and instrument.

837. Rothwell, Evelyn. *Oboe Technique*. London: Oxford University Press, 1953. 106 p.

    A manual for students. Includes a list of music for oboe and English horn.

838. Russell, Myron E. *Oboe Reed Making and Problems of
      the Oboe Player.* 3rd ed. Stamford, Conn.: Jack
      Spratt, 1960. 56 p.

      Provides detailed instructions for reed making, des-
      cribes the correct oboe embouchure and comments upon
      oboe fingering. Includes a short graded list of oboe
      methods and music.

839. Schleiffer, J. Eric. *The Art of Bassoon Reed Making.*
      Oneonta, N.Y.: Swift-Dorr, 1974. 22p.

      A succinct, well-illustrated manual.

840. Schmitz, Hans-Peter. *Flötenlehre.* 2 vols. Kassel:
      Bärenreiter, 1955. 121, 116 p.

      Treats every aspect of flute playing. Includes many
      exercises. An English translation of the text appears
      as *School of Flute-Playing,* translated by Evelyn Frank
      and John Hays (Kassel: Bärenreiter, 1966; 2 vols., 24 p.).

841. Schuller, Gunther. *Horn Technique.* London: Oxford
      University Press, 1962. 118 p.

      Primarily a manual for performers. Includes a chapter
      for composers on scoring for the horn. Also offers
      suggestions for conductors and provides an extensive
      list of repertory.

842. Sherman, Roger. *The Trumpeter's Handbook.* Athens, Ohio:
      Accura, 1979. 147 p.

      A comprehensive guide to performance. Includes a
      discussion of the specific characteristics of trumpets
      in various keys. Also includes a brief annotated
      bibliography of music and books.

843. Shivas, Andrew A. *The Art of Tympanist and Drummer.*
      London: Dobson, 1957. 72 p.

      A practical discussion of drum technique intended
      mostly for the beginning student.

*   Sidorfsky, Frank M. "A Critical Study of Books on the
      Clarinet." D.M.A. dissertation, University of
      Rochester, 1973. 195 p.

      Cited below as Item 1191.

844. Spencer, William. *The Art of Bassoon Playing.* Evanston, Ill.: Summy-Birchard, 1958. 77p.

Includes detailed instructions on reed making and advice on instrument selection, tone production, and articulations. Also includes a list of music and recordings.

845. Sprenkle, Robert, and David Ledet. *The Art of Oboe Playing.* Evanston, Ill.: Summy-Birchard, 1961. 96 p.

Notable partly for its detailed discussion of reed making.

846. Stein, Keith. *The Art of Clarinet Playing.* Evanston, Ill.: Summy-Birchard, 1958. 80 p.

A good general guide to performance.

847. Stubbins, William H. *The Art of Clarinetistry: The Acoustical Mechanics of the Clarinet as a Basis for the Art of Music Performance.* 3rd ed. Ann Arbor: Guillaume Press, 1974. 329 p.

Thoroughly examines the acoustics of the instrument, with particular emphasis upon its practical consequences for the performer. Provides a detailed description of reed making and discusses the elements essential to good clarinet playing. An invaluable book.

848. Teal, Larry. *The Art of Saxophone Playing.* Evanston, Ill.: Summy-Birchard, 1963. 112p.

A comprehensive discussion of the instrument and the manner in which it should be played. Notable particularly for its detailed treatment of embouchure and tone quality.

849. Thurston, Frederick. *Clarinet Technique.* 3rd ed. London: Oxford University Press, 1977. 94 p.

Intended for the intermediate or advanced student of the clarinet. Includes a chapter by Alan Hacker on twentieth-century music and one by John Davies on the preparation for examinations and public performances. Also includes a list of published music, prepared by Georgina Dobrée.

* Usov, Jurij, ed. *Metodika obučenija igre na duhuvyh instrumentah,* 4. Moscow: Muzyka, 1975. 225 p.

Cited above as Item 166.

850. Weait, Christopher. *Bassoon Reed-Making: A Basic Technique.*
     New York: McGinnis and Marx, 1970. 31 p.

     A practical, well-illustrated guide.

851. Weast, Robert D. "A Stroboscopic Analysis of Lip Function."
     Brass Anthology. Evanston, Ill.: Instrumentalist, 1976,
     pp. 337–39.

     Reports that the lower lip functions independently of
     the upper lip in brass playing and that the activity of
     the lower lip, which is quite erratic, is irrelevant to
     tone production. Also see the article by Leno, cited
     above as Item 828.

852. Weisberg, Arthur. *The Art of Wind Playing.* New York:
     Schirmer Books, 1975. 145 p.

     Discusses playing techniques, style, and interpretation.
     Includes chapters on dynamics and intonation, tonguing,
     vibrato, breathing, and technique. Provides a historical
     overview of style and offers guidelines for interpretation.
     Interesting partly for its strong concern with resonance.

853. Wick, Denis. *Trombone Technique.* London: Oxford Univ-
     ersity Press, 1971. 152 p.

     Focuses mainly on practical questions of performance.
     Includes a discussion of the trombone in the brass band,
     a description of the various kinds of trombone and of
     related instruments, and a brief but good list of reper-
     tory.

854. Wilkins, Frederick. *The Flutist's Guide.* Elkhart, Ind.:
     Artley, 1957. 84 p.

     A guide to performance intended for less advanced
     players.

855. Willaman, Robert. *The Clarinet and Clarinet Playing.*
     Rev. ed. New York: Carl Fischer, 1954. 316 p.

     A comprehensive guide to performance. Includes a
     fingering chart notable for its extensive annotations.
     Includes a discussion of the concert band, of perfor-
     mance in commercial orchestras, and of the clarinet
     quartet.

2. Historical Tutors and Historical Performance Practice

*   Altenburg, Johann Ernst. *Essay on an Introduction to the Heroic and Musical Trumpeters' and Kettledrummers' Art.* Translated by Edward H. Tarr. Nashville: Brass Press, 1974. 148 p.

Cited above as Item 321.

*   ————. *Versuch einer Anleitung zur heroisch-musikalischen Trompeter- und Paukerkunst.* Edited by Frieder Zschoch. Leipzig: Deutscher Verlag für Musik, 1973. 156 p.

Cited above at Item 322.

*   Bagans, Karl. "Ueber die Trompete in ihrer heutigen Anwendbarkeit im Orchester." *Berliner allgemeine musikalische Zeitung* 6 (1829): 337-41.

Cited above at Item 323.

856. Barber, Elinore. "Riemenschneider Bach Library Vault Holdings." *Bach* 7, no. 2 (April 1976): 30-31.

Discusses John Gunn's *Art of Playing the Flute* (1973).

857. Barbour, J. Murray. "Unusual Brass Notation in the Eighteenth Century." *Brass Quarterly* 2 (1958-59): 139-46.

Points out the use of various clefs in transposition.

858. Bendinelli, Cesare. *The Complete Art of Trumpet Playing, 1614.* Translated by Edward H. Tarr. Nashville: Brass Press, 1975. 19 p.

A translation of the text of Item 859, cited below. Includes a commentary upon the book and a description of Bendinelli's instrument.

859. ————. *Tutta l'arte della trombetta 1614.* Edited by Edward H. Tarr. Documenta musicologica, series 2, vol. 5. Kassel: Bärenreiter, 1975. 119 p.

Facsimile edition of Bendinelli's manuscript collection of 332 ricercari, toccatas, trumpet calls, and short sonatas.

860. Bennett, Wayne. "Methods for the Clarinet From 1698 to 1900." *NACWPI Journal* 19, no. 4 (summer 1971): 23-28.

An annotated list of historical tutors.

861. Blandford, W.F.H. "Bach's Trumpets." *Monthly Musical Record* 61 (1931): 44-45.

Argues that Bach's trumpet parts could be played more easily if the performing groups were reduced to historical size.

862. Blasius, Frédéric. *Nouvelle méthode de clarinette et raisonnement des instruments.* Paris: Porthaux, [ca. 1796]; facsimile reprint, Geneva: Minkoff, 1972. 113 p.

Consists largely of a series of gradually more demanding exercises. The first progressive tutor. For commentary and an English translation, see Item 900, cited below.

*   Brown, Thomas Martin, Jr. "Clarino Horn, Hunting Horn, and Hand Horn: Their Comparative Roles in the Classic Music of the Eighteenth Century." D.A. dissertation, Ball State University, 1978. 153 p. UM 79-18,786.

Cited below as Item 1004.

*   Caba, G. Craig. *United Stated Military Drums, 1745-1865.* Harrisburg, Penn.: Civil War Antiquities and Americana, 1977. 147 p.

Cited above as Item 435.

*   Coar, Birchard. *A Critical Study of the Nineteenth-Century Horn Virtuosi in France.* DeKalb, Ill.: Coar, 1952. 168 p.

Cited above as Item 647.

863. Corrette, Michel. *Méthode de la flûte traversière 1735.* Buren: Knuf, 1978.

A facsimile edition with a new introduction by Mirjam Nastasi. English translation cited below as Item 871. Another facsimile edition published Hildesheim: Olms, 1975.

864. ————. *Méthode raisonnée pour apprendre aisément à
      jouer de la flûte traversière.* 2nd ed. Paris: n.p.,
      1773; facsimile reprint, Geneva: Minkoff, 1977. 65 p.

      Facsimile of first edition cited above as Item 863.
      Second edition includes fingering charts for oboe and
      clarinet as well as for flute. English translation
      of the first edition cited below as Item 871.

*   Damm, Peter. "Das Horn in der ersten Hälfte des 18.
      Jahrhunderts. Versuche der Interpretation hoher
      Hornpartien." *Die Blasinstrumente und ihre Verwendung*,
      edited by Eitelfreidrich Thom. Magdeburg: Rat des
      Bezirkes; Leipzig: Zentralhaus für Kulturarbeit, 1977,
      pp. 37-41.

      Cited above as Item 403.

*   Deaton, James W. "The Eighteenth-Century Six-Keyed
      Clarinet: A Study of Its Mechanical and Acoustical
      Properties and Their Relationship to Performance of
      Selected Literature." D.M.A. dissertation, University
      of Texas at Austin, 1972. 137 p. UM 73-7683.

      Cited above as Item 275.

865. Domnich, Heinrich. *Méthode de premier et second cor.*
      Paris: LeRoy, 1807; facsimile reprint, Geneva: Minkoff,
      1974. 114 p.

      The first definitive tutor for horn. Distinguishes
      between first and second horn players, illustrates the
      appropriate mouthpieces, and presents exercises to
      develop technique and flexibility. Also discusses
      hand-stopping.

866. Douglass, Robert. "The First Trumpet Method: Girolamo
      Fantini's *Modo per imparare a sonare di tromba* (1638)."
      Journal of Band Research 7, no. 2 (Spring 1971): 18-22.

      Describes the treatise and translates the second entitled
      "Advice for Those Who Wish to Learn to Play the Trumpet."

867. Duvernoy, Frédéric. *Méthode pour le cor.* Paris: Le Roy,
      [*ca.* 1804]; facsimile reprint, Geneva: Minkoff, 1972.
      63 p.

      Exercises, duos, and trios prefaced by a brief des-
      cription of playing technique. Distinguished by excel-
      lent illustrations of mouthpieces and of the way in which
      the horn is held.

868. Ehmann, Wilhelm. "New Brass Instruments Based on Old
      Models." *Brass Quarterly* 1 (1957-58): 214-15.

      Describes the efforts of German instrument makers and
      recounts the author's experience in conducting ensembles
      employing instruments built upon Baroque models.

*   Eichborn, Hermann. *The Old Art of Clarino Playing on
      Trumpets*. Translated by Bryan A. Simms. Denver:
      Tromba Publications, 1976. 34 p.

      Cited above as Item 332.

*   ————. *Die Trompete in alte und neuer Zeit. Ein
      Beitrag zur Musikgeschichte und Instrumentationslehre*.
      Leipzig: Breitkopf und Härtel, 1881; reprint ed.,
      Wiesbaden: Sändig, 1968. 118 p.

      Cited above as Item 333.

869. Fantini, Girolamo. *A Modern Edition of Girolamo Fantini's
      Trumpet Method (1638)*. Edited by W. Ritchie Clendenin
      and William R. Clendenin. Boulder, Colo.: Empire
      Printing, 1977. 163 p.

      An edition, in modern notation, of *Modo per imparare
      a sonare di tromba*. Includes a realization of the bass
      lines. For a facsimile edition of the original, see
      Item 870, cited below.

870. ————. *Modo per imparare a sonare di tromba*. Frankfurt:
      Daniel Watsch, 1638; facsimile reprint ed., Nashville:
      Brass Press, 1972. 88 p.

      A collection of trumpet calls, exercises, dances, and
      short sonatas for the trumpet, together with technical
      suggestions. Another facsimile reprint, together with
      an English translation and commentary by Edward H. Tarr,
      was published by Brass Press in 1978.

871. Farrar, Carol Reglin. *Michel Corrette and Flute-Playing
      in the Eighteenth Century*. Musical Theorists in
      Translation, vol. 9. Brooklyn: Institute of Mediaeval
      Music, 1970. 63 p.

      A well-annotated translation of Corrette's *Méthode
      raisonnée pour apprendre aisément à jouer de la flûte
      traversière*, cited above as Item 863. Prefaced by an
      overview of flutes, flute articulation, and vibrato in
      the eighteenth century.

* Farrington, Frank. "Dissection of a Serpent." *Galpin Society Journal* 22 (1969): 81-96.

  Cited above as Item 388.

872. Freillon-Poncein, Jean-Pierre. *La véritable manière d'apprendre à jouer en perfection du hautbois, de la flute et du flageolet.* Paris: Collombat, 1700; facsimile reprint, Geneva: Minkoff, 1971. 74 p.

  Primarily a collection of short exercises, together with fingering charts, technical suggestions, and brief explanations of various dance forms. Reprint edition bound together with Vanderhagen, cited below as Item 923.

873. Gallo, F. Alberto. "Il 'Saggio per ben sonare il flautotraverso' di Antonio Lorenzoni nella cultura musicale italiana del Settecento." *La rassegna musicale* 31 (1961): 102-11.

  Described the contents of Lorenzoni's tutor (1779), paying particular attention to his remarks regarding expression.

* Goossens, Léon, and Edwin Roxburgh. *Oboe.* London: Macdonald and Jane, 1977. 236 p.

  Cited above as Item 80.

* Griswold, Harold Eugene. "Étienne Ozi (1754-1813): Bassoonist, Teacher, and Composer." D.M.A. dissertation, Peabody Conservatory, 1979. 658 p. UM 80-02561.

  Cited above as Item 652.

874. Grush, James. "A Guide to the Study of the Classical Oboe." D.M.A. dissertation, Boston University, 1972. 272 p. UM 72-25,121.

  Surveys eighteenth-century instructional material, lists instruments available for study in U.S. collections, and offers suggestions for performance. Includes fingering charts and a bibliography of music.

875. Güttler, Ludwig. "Möglichkeiten und Probleme bei der
      Wiedergabe hoher Trompetenpartien aus der ersten
      Hälfte des 18. Jahrhunderts aus der Sicht des
      heutigen Spielers." *Die Blasinstrumente und ihre
      Verwendung*, edited by Eitelfriedrich Thom. Magdeburg:
      Rat des Bezirkes; Leipzig: Zentralhaus für Kulturarbeit,
      1977, pp. 22-25.

      Reviews the problems entailed in the performance of
      Baroque trumpet parts and argues for the use of modern
      valve instruments in place of natural trumpets.

876. Hadidian, Eileen. "Johann Georg Tromlitz's Flute
      Treatise: Evidences of Late Eighteenth Century Per-
      formance Practice." D.M.A. dissertation, Stanford
      University, 1979. 44 p. UM 80-2043.

      Translates and comments upon Tromlitz's *Unterricht*
      (1971), comparing it with contemporaneous flute tutors
      and, in respect to breathing, to treatises on singing.
      A facsimile edition of the treatise is cited below
      as Item 920.

877. Halfpenny, Eric. "The Earliest English Bassoon Tutor."
      Galpin Society Journal 17 (1964): 103-05.

      Describes the *Compleat Instructions for the Bassoon
      or Fagotto*, which was published between 1776 and 1782.

878. ————. "Early English Bassoon Fingerings." *Galpin
      Society Journal* 18 (1965): 127.

      Sheds light on the source of the "Gamut or Scale for
      the Bassoon" mentioned in the article cited above as
      Item 877.

879. ————. "The French Hautboy: A Technical Survey, Part
      I." *Galpin Society Journal* 6 (1953): 23-24.

      Primarily a comparison of the instructions given in
      a number of English oboe tutors from the late seven-
      teenth and early eighteenth centuries. Supplemented
      by Item 880, cited below.

880. ————. "The French Hautboy: A Technical Survey, Part
      II." *Galpin Society Journal* 8 (1955): 50-59.

      Compares the fingerings given in the tutors examined
      in the first part of the article, cited above as Item
      879.

881. ———. "A Seventeenth-Century Tutor for the Hautboy."
Music and Letters 30 (1949): 355-63.

Reports the discovery of an English oboe tutor from
1695, the first such printed tutor known. Reproduces
the preface, signed by John Banister the Younger, which
gives reasons for the instrument's sudden popularity
in England. Describes the contents of the tutor in
detail.

882. Harris-Warrick, Rebecca. "Newest Instructions for the
German Flute: A Method Book for the One-Keyed Flute
Based on the Eighteenth-Century Tutors." D.M.A.
dissertation, Stanford University, 1977. 263 p.

A synthesis of instructions found in twenty-two tutors
from the late eighteenth century. Includes a helpful
annotated bibliography of flute tutors.

883. Hartig, Linda Bishop. "Johann George Tromlitz's *Unterricht die Flöte zu spielen:* A Translation and Comparative Study." Ph.D. dissertation, Michigan State
University, 1982. 570 p. UM 82-24,437.

For a reprint of the original treatise, see Item 920,
cited below. Also see Item 876, cited above.

884. Haynes, Bruce. "Making Reeds for the Baroque Oboe."
Early Music 4 (1976): 31-34, 173-82.

Discusses original sources and reeds surviving from
the Baroque. Compares modern and Baroque reeds and
provides instructions for making reeds.

885. Hedrick, Peter. "Henri Brod's *Méthode pour le hautbois*
Reconsidered." *Consort* 30 (1974): 53-62.

Discusses Brod's tutor, published *ca.* 1826, in regard
to its treatment of interpretation, reed making, and
oboe technique.

886. Horner, Don Arlen. "The Teaching of the Bassoon from
c. 1700 to c. 1825: A Survey of Selected Pedagogical
Material." D.M.A. dissertation, University of Oregon,
1980. 200 p. UM 80-25,861.

Based on an examination of twenty-four sources from
1697 to *ca.* 1825. Describes the instructions given
regarding playing position, embouchure, articulation,
fingering, and reed making.

887. Horsley, Imogene. "Wind Techniques in the Sixteenth and
     Early Seventeenth Centuries." *Brass Quarterly* 4 (1960):
     49-63.

     Points out the emphasis placed upon improvisation as
     an element of virtuosity. Also describes the patterns
     of articulation employed during the period, as shown in
     treatises from Ganassi to Mersenne.

888. Hotteterre, Jacques. *L'Art de préluder sur la flûte
     traversière, sur la flûte à bec, sur le hautbois et
     autres instruments de dessus.* Paris: Hotteterre,
     1719; facsimile reprint, Geneva: Minkoff, 1978. 65 p.

     A manual for improvising. Consists mainly of examples.

889. ————. *Principes de la flûte traversière, ou flûte
     d'allemagne; de la flûte à bec, ou flûte douce; et
     du haut bois.*

     First edition published in 1707. The earliest tutor
     for transverse flute. Discusses the recorder but says
     very little about the oboe. Describes flute and recorder
     playing position, embouchure, ornaments, and tonguing.
     Facsimile reprint bound together with De Lusse, cited
     below as Item 894. Facsimile reprint of the 1728
     edition published with German translation, Kassel:
     Bärenreiter, 1941/1958. For an English translation of
     the first edition, see below, Item 890.

890. ————. *Principles of the Flute, Recorder, and Oboe.*
     Translated by David Lasocki. New York: Praeger,
     1968. 88 p.

     A translation of the first edition (1707). A primary
     source of information regarding Baroque performance
     practice and flute playing. A facsimile reprint of the
     third edition is cited above as Item 889.

891. Hugot, A., and J.G. Wunderlich. *Méthode de flûte.*
     Paris: Le Roy [1804]; facsimile reprint, Geneva:
     Minkoff, 1974, and Buren: Knuf, 1975. 152 p.

     Served as the fundamental tutor for nineteenth-century
     flutists. Adopted as a teaching manual at the Paris
     Conservatory. Consists primarily of exercises but also
     includes brief discussions of embouchure, articulation,
     and ornamentation. Knuf reprint preceded by an extensive
     introduction by David Jenkins.

892. Kennedy, Dale Edwin. "The Clarinet Sonata in France before 1800 with a Modern Performance Edition of Two Works." Ph.D. dissertation, University of Oklahoma, 1979. 247 p. UM 80-12,284.

Discusses performance practice in regard to clarinet music of the late eighteenth century.

* Kling, Henri. "Giovanni Punto, célèbre corniste (1748-1803)." *Bulletin français de la S.I.M.* [*La revue musicale de la S.I.M.*] 4 (1908): 1066-82.

Cited above as Item 657.

893. Lefèvre, Xavier. *Méthode de clarinette*. Paris: Le Roy, 1802; facsimile reprint, Geneva: Minkoff, 1974. 144 p.

Primarily a collection of etudes. Includes a discussion of ornaments, articulation, breath production, and style.

894. Lichtmann, Margaret Stevens. "A Translation with Commentary of August Eberhardt Müller's *Elementarbuch fuer Floetenspieler*." D.M.A. dissertation, Boston University, 1982. 321 p. UM 82-22,724.

The tutor, which was originally published *ca.* 1815, helps to shed light on the argument between the advocates of the older one-key flute and the newer flutes with larger bore.

895. Lusse, Charles de. *L'art de la flûte traversière*. Paris: De Lusse [*ca.* 1761]; facsimile reprint, Geneva: Minkoff, 1973; facsimile reprint, with an introduction by Greta Moens-Haenen, Buren: Knuf, 1980. 41 p.

Mostly a collection of duets and etudes. Preceded by fingering charts for the one-key flute and a brief explanation of ornaments and playing technique. The Minkoff reprint is bound together with Hotteterre, *Principes de la flûte*, cited above as Item 889.

896. Lyle, Andrew. "John Mahon's Clarinet Preceptor." *Galpin Society Journal* 30 (1977): 52-55.

Reports the location of a copy of the *New and Complete Preceptor for the Clarinet* in an edition from 1811-16. Outlines its contents and concludes that it provides very little information about clarinet playing during the period or about performance practice generally.

897. Mahaut, Antoine. *Nouvelle méthode pour apprendre en*
      peu de temps à jouer de la flûte traversière. Paris:
      Legoux, 1759; facsimile reprint, Geneva: Minkoff,
      1972. 63 p.

      Valuable for the information it provides in regard
      to performance practice, especially the playing of
      trills. The second half of the manual consists of
      flute duets.

*   Marsh, John. "Hints to Young Composers of Instrumental
      Music." *Galpin Society Journal* 18 (1965): 57-71.

      Cited above as Item 152.

898. Mather, Betty Bang. *Interpretation of French Music*
      from 1675 to 1775 for Woodwind and Other Performers.
      New York: McGinnis and Marx, 1973. 104 p.

      Useful especially for its discussion of articulation.
      Includes an excellent bibliography. Supplemented by
      the anthology cited below as Item 899.

899. Mather, Betty Bang, and David Lasocki. *Free Ornamenta-*
      tion in Woodwind Music, 1700-1775: An Anthology with
      Introduction. New York: McGinnis and Marx, 1976.
      158 p.

      Presents sixty-six musical examples. Supplements
      Mather's *Interpretation*, cited above as Item 898.

*   Menke, Werner. *History of the Trumpet of Bach and*
      Handel. Translated by Gerald Abraham. London:
      Reeves, [1934]. 128 p.

      Cited above as Item 358.

900. Menkin, William. "Frédéric Blasius: *Nouvelle méthode*
      de clarinette et raisonnement des instruments. A
      Complete Translation with an Historical and Biograph-
      ical Background of the Composer and His Compositions
      for the Clarinet." D.M.A. dissertation, Stanford
      University, 1980. 100 p.

      Useful primarily for the translation. For a facsimile
      reprint of the treatise, see above Item 862.

901. *Méthode de serpent pour le service du culte et le service*
      militaire. Paris: Magasin de musique du Conservatoire
      Imperial, [*ca.* 1813]; facsimile reprint, Geneva:
      Minkoff, 1974. 33 p.

Attributed to Abbé Nicolas Roze. Primarily a series of exercises of graduated difficulty followed by a collection of duets of varied musical character. Prefaced by a thumbnail sketch of the history of the instrument and brief instructions for playing it.

902. Moens-Haenen, Greta. "The Italian Sonata for Transverse Flute." *Galpin Society Journal* 30 (1977): 156-57.

Argues against the use of any kind of breath vibrato, except as a tremolo, in the performance of eighteenth-century flute music.

903. Ozi, Étienne. *Méthode de basson*. Paris: Le Roy, 1803; facsimile reprint, Geneva: Minkoff, 1974. 145 p.

A collection of etudes together with instructions for making reeds, forming the embouchure, tonguing, and playing ornaments.

904. Peeples, Georgia Kay. "The Bassoon in America, 1800-1840, as Depicted in Contemporary Pedagogic Sources." D.M.A. dissertation, University of Maryland, 1981. 87 p. UM 82-14,397.

Reviews the history of American bassoon playing during the period 1775-1840. Discusses general method books that contain instructions for playing bassoon as well as the two bassoon tutors published during the time.

* Pizka, Hans. *Das Horn bei Mozart/Mozart and the Horn*. Kirchheim: Pizka, 1980. 276 p.

Cited below as Item 1186.

905. Powley, Harrison. "Some Observations on Jean Georges Kastner's *Méthode complète et raisonnée de timbales* (ca. 1845)." *Percussionist* 17 (1979-80): 63-74.

Describes and illustrates the drum strokes presented in Kastner's tutor, comparing his treatment with Altenburg's (see above, Items 321 and 322).

906. Quantz, Johann Joachim. *On Playing the Flute*. Translated by Edward R. Reilly. New York: Macmillan, 1966. 368 p.

A fine translation of the most important eighteenth-century treatise on flute playing. The treatise, first published in 1752, is invaluable for its general discussion

of performance practice. Prefaced by an excellent
introduction by Reilly. A facsimile reprint of the
1789 edition is cited below as Item 907.

907. ————. *Versuch einer Anweisung die Flöte traversiere
      zu spielen.* 3rd ed. Wroclaw: Korn, 1789; facsimile
      reprint, edited by Hans-Peter Schmitz, Kassel:
      Bärenreiter, 1953. 352 p.

      English translation cited above as Item 906.

*   Rasmussen, Mary. "Bach-Trumpet Madness; or, A Plain
      and Easy Introduction to the Attributes, Causes and
      Cure of a Most Mysterious Musicological Malady."
      Brass Quarterly 5 (1961-62): 37-40.

      Cited above as Item 361.

908. ————. "On the Modern Performance of Parts Originally
      Written for the Cornett: An Introduction to a Problem."
      Brass Quarterly 1 (1957-58): 20-28.

      Describes the characteristics and uses of the cornett
      in its heyday, offers the hope that the instrument might
      be revived, and argues that when cornetts are unavailable
      the parts should be assigned to oboes.

909. ————. "Some Notes on the Articulations in the Melodic
      Variation Tables of Johann Joachim Quantz's *Versuch
      einer Anweisung die Flöte traversiere zu spielen*
      (Berlin 1752, Breslau 1789)." *Brass and Woodwind
      Quarterly* 1 (1966-68): 3-26.

      Establishes, on the basis of a study of Quantz, a
      set of rules for phrasing and articulation in eighteenth-
      century music.

*   Reilly, Edward R. *Quantz and His "Versuch."* [Philadel-
      phia]: American Musicological Society, 1971. 178 p.

      Cited above as Item 203.

*   Remsen, Lester E. "A Study of the Natural Trumpet and
      Its Modern Counterpart." D.M.A. dissertation, Univ-
      ersity of Southern California, 1960. 183 p.

      Cited above as Item 363.

910. Rice, Albert R. "Valentin Roeser's Essay on the
     Clarinet (1764), Background and Commentary." M.A.
     thesis, Claremont Graduate School, 1977. 189 p.

     A discussion of the treatise, the first theoretical
     study of the clarinet, as compared to other treatises
     of the period. Traces the history of the chalumeau and
     the two-key clarinet, sketches Roeser's life, and offers
     a translation of the first section of the treatise.
     Includes a list of music employing the chalumeau.
     Roeser's *Essai* is cited below as Item 911.

911. Roeser, Valentin. *Essai d'instruction à l'usage de
     ceux qui composent pour la clarinette et le cor.*
     Paris: Mercier, 1764; facsimile reprint, Geneva:
     Minkoff, 1972. 24 p.

     Intended to provide composers with a guide to the
     limitations and potential of the instruments. An
     important treatise historically. For a discussion,
     see above, Item 910. Reprint edition bound together
     with Vanderhagen, cited below as Item 922.

912. Rousseau, Eugene E. "Clarinet Instructional Materials
     from 1732 to *ca.* 1825." Ph.D. dissertation, University
     of Iowa, 1962. 256 p. UM 63-961.

     A comprehensive examination. Provides detailed in-
     formation regarding reeds, mouthpieces, embouchure,
     ornamentation, and fingerings. Includes a translation
     of the section on clarinet in Frölich's *Vollständige
     theoretisch-practische Musikschule* (1810-11), which
     is also cited above in Item 278.

913. Sachs, Curt. "Eine unkritische Kritik des Klarinblasens."
     Archiv für Musikwissenschaft 2 (1919/20): 335-36.

     Points out that the trumpet of Bach's day was approx-
     imately two meters long, not four as sometimes claimed.
     States that the use of the contemporary sopranino trumpet
     violates the spirit of eighteenth-century music.

*   Scheck, Gustav. *Die Flöte und ihre Musik.* Mainz:
     Schott, 1975. 263 p.

     Cited above as Item 72.

914. Schrammek, Winfried. "Gedanken zur Restaurierung
      historischer Musikinstrumente." *Festschrift für
      Walter Wiora zum 30. Dezember 1966*, edited by
      Ludwig Finscher and Ludwig Mahling. Kassel: Bärenreiter,
      1967, pp. 62-65.

      Discusses the problems involved in restoring unused
      old instruments and notes that old instruments that
      have been in constant use are likely to be the most
      suitable for use today.

915. Schünemann, Georg. "Zur Flötentechnik des XVIII.
      Jahrhunderts." *Allgemeine Musik-Zeitung* 35 (1908):
      377-78.

      Summarized the instructions for articulation and
      phrasing given by Hotteterre, Quantz, and Lorenzoni.

916. Smith, Catherine P. "Characteristics of Transverse
      Flute Performance in Selected Flute Methods from
      the Early 18th Century to 1828." D.M.A. dissertation,
      Stanford University, 1969. 112 p.

      Thoroughly investigates matters of tone quality,
      vibrato (breath and finger-generated), and fingered
      slides.

917. Smith, David. "Trombone Technique in the Early Seven-
      teenth Century." D.M.A. dissertation, Stanford
      University, 1981. 98 p.

      Reviews the types of articulation described in
      treatises of the period, surveys ornamentation, and
      describes the instrument.

918. Sorenson, Richard A. "Tuba Pedagogy: A Study of Selected
      Method Books, 1840-1911." Ph.D. dissertation, Uni-
      versity of Colorado, 1972. 367 p. UM 73-1832.

      Analyzes twenty-five tutors. Includes a summary of
      the history of the tuba.

919. *Textes sur les instruments de musique au xviiie siècle.*
      Geveva: Minkoff, 1972. 209 p.

      A facsimile reprint of six short treatises, including
      *Découverte de l'embouchure de la flûte allemande, ou
      traversière, avec les principes pour la bien prendre*
      (Paris: LeClerc, 1956). Its author is unknown.

920. Tromlitz, Johann George. *Ausführlicher und gründlicher*
      Unterricht die Flöte zu spielen. Leipzig: Böhme, 1971;
      facsimile reprint, Amsterdam: Knuf: 1973. 376 p.

      Comprehensive. Includes an extensive treatment of
      ornamentation. Intended for the two-key flute. Reprint
      edition prefaced by a short introduction, in English,
      by Frans Vester.

921. Tulou, Jean-Louis. *Méthode de flûte progressive et raison-*
      née. Paris: Brandus, 1851; facsimile reprint, Geneva:
      Minkoff, 1973. 129 p.

      A systematic tutor for the one-key flute. Points out
      that people with thick lips or with an overshot jaw will
      have difficulty making a beautiful sound. Describes
      embouchure and playing position, provides exercises in
      various keys, and concludes with a set of progressively
      more difficult etudes.

922. Vanderhagen, Armand. *Méthode nouvelle et raisonnée pour*
      la clarinette. Paris: Boyer, 1798; facsimile reprint,
      Geneva: Minkoff, 1972. 37 p.

      Relatively comprehensive. Discusses embouchure,
      provides a fingering chart, discusses reeds, describes
      proper articulation, and explains various aspects of
      notation and performance practice. Reprint edition
      bound together with Roeser, cited above as Item 911.

923. ———. *Méthode nouvelle et raisonnée pour le hautbois.*
      Paris: Naderman, [*ca.* 1792]; facsimile reprint, Geneva:
      Minkoff, 1971. 65 p.

      A series of brief lessons illustrating a variety of
      musical problems (syncopation, dotted rhythms, articu-
      lations, etc.) together with a group of six duets. Intro-
      duced by brief discussions of embouchure, reed selection,
      tone quality, and choice of music. Facsimile reprint
      bound together with Freillon-Poncein, cited above as
      Item 872.

924. Vester, Frans. "Blazer en vibrato." *Mens en melodie*
      16 (1961): 74-78.

      Traces--very quickly--the history of woodwind vibrato
      through the eighteenth century and reviews its use during
      the first half of the twentieth century.

925. Warner, Thomas E. *An Annotated Bibliography of Woodwind Instruction Books, 1600-1830.* Detroit: Information Coordinators, 1967. 138 p.

An annotated list of more than 450 tutors, treatises, and instruction books.

926. ————. "Indications of Performance Practice in Woodwind Instruction Books of the 17th and 18th Centuries." Ph.D. dissertation, New York University, 1964. 459 p. UM 65-1678.

An authoritative account followed by an annotated list of tutors. The list provided the basis for the book cited above as Item 925.

927. ————. "Tromlitz's Flute Treatise: A Neglected Source of Eighteenth-Century Performance Practice." *A Musical Offering: Essays in Honor of Martin Bernstein*, edited by Edward H. Clinkscale and Claire Brook. New York: Pendragon Press, 1977, pp. 261-73.

Discusses the most important aspects of Tromlitz's treatment of ornaments, describes his suggestions for articulation, and summarizes his recommendations for improvements to the flute. A facsimile reprint of the treatise is cited above as Item 920.

928. ————. "Two Late Eighteenth-Century Instructions for Making Double Reeds." *Galpin Society Journal* 15 (1962): 25-33.

Discusses the instructions given in treatises by Garnier and Ozi. A facsimile edition of the latter is cited above as Item 903.

929. Youngs, Lowell V. "Jean Xavier Lefèvre: His Contributions to the Clarinet and Clarinet Playing." D.M.A. dissertation, Catholic University of America, 1970. 180 p. UM 70-20,000.

Includes a comparison of Lefèvre's *Méthode de clarinette* with tutors by Vanderhagen, Müller, Bärmann, Berr, and Klosé. Concludes in part that Lefèvre's influence was not especially great, except for his addition of a sixth key to the instrument.

3. Discussions of Contemporary Techniques and Notation

930. Baker, David. *Contemporary Techniques for the Trombone.*
      New York: Colin, 1974. 2 vols. 482 p.

      A systematic method for trombone culminating in
      excerpts from works by Baker, Donald Erb, Bernard Heiden,
      and others. Includes lists of contemporary music and
      recordings.

931. Bartolozzi, Bruno. *New Sounds for Woodwind.* Trans-
      lated and edited by Reginald Smith Brindle. 2nd ed.
      London: Oxford University Press, 1982. 113 p.

      A pioneering description of the techniques of producing
      multiphonics and other new sounds. Includes fingering
      charts and a recording.

932. Caravan, Ronald L. "Extensions of Technique for Clarinet
      and Saxophone." D.M.A. dissertation, University of
      Rochester, 1974. 275 p. UM 75-578.

      A comprehensive account of new techniques and effects,
      including multiple sonorities, vocal sounds, percussive
      effects, quarter tones, and air sounds. Includes finger-
      ing charts.

933. Dempster, Stuart. *The Modern Trombone: A Definition of
      Its Idioms.* Berkeley: University of California Press,
      1979. 110 p.

      An engagingly written discussion of what seems to be
      every conceivable trombone effect. Also discusses
      musical theatrics. Includes compositions by the author
      and by Robert Erickson. Published with two seven-inch
      recordings illustrating the text.

934. Dick, Robert. *The Other Flute: A Performance Manual of
      Contemporary Techniques.* London: Oxford University
      Press, 1975. 154 p.

      Primarily a set of instructions and fingering charts
      as aid to the production of microtones and multiple
      sonorities. Includes a chapter on the electronic modifi-
      cation of sound as well as a composition by the author
      ("Afterlight") that demonstrates the effects discussed.
      Published with a recording that illustrates the text.

935. Farmer, Gerald J. "Multiphonic Trills and Tremolos for
      Clarinet." D.M.A. dissertation, University of Oregon,
      1977. 123 p.

      Inventories possible multiphonics as drawn from existing
      charts, published and unpublished compositions, and the
      author's personal experimentation.

936. Globokar, Vinko. "Possibilities for Development of
      Brass Instruments." *Brass Bulletin*, nos. 5-6 (1973):
      15-33.

      A guide to new musical effects, including microtones,
      combinations of vocal and instrumental sounds, and
      various types of articulation. Parallel texts in German,
      French, and English.

*   Heine, Alois. *Akustische Phänomene: Untersuchungen und
      Experimente mit der Klarinette und Einführung in die
      Ausatztechniken zur Erzeugung von Überblasetönen,
      Untertönen und Akkordklängen.* Munich: Katzbichler,
      1978. 87 p.

      Cited above as Item 498.

937. Heiss, John. "The Flute: New Sounds." *Perspectives of
      New Music* 10 (1971-72): 153-58.

      Supplements Heiss's earlier articles, cited below as
      Items 938 and 939. Provides fingerings for low register
      harmonics, discusses the introduction of vocal sounds,
      and lists additional multiple sonorities.

938. ————. "For the Flute: A List of Double-Stops, Triple-
      Stops, Quadruple-Stops, and Shakes." *Perspectives of
      New Music* 5 (1966-67): 139-41.

      Discusses and provides fingerings for new musical
      effects. Supplemented by the articles cited here as
      Items 937 and 939.

939. ————. "Some Multiple-Sonorities for Flute, Oboe,
      Clarinet and Bassoon." *Perspectives of New Music*
      7 (1968-69): 136-42.

      Lists, explains, and offers instructions for perform-
      ing multiple sonorities. Supplemented by the articles
      cited above as Items 937 and 938.

940. Howell, Thomas. *The Avant-Garde Flute: A Handbook for Composers and Flutists.* Berkeley: University of California Press, 1974. 290 p.

A comprehensive guide to modern flute techniques. Includes a discussion of special effects such as key percussion, whistle tones, noise sounds, and amplification. Provides an extensive list of fingerings for multiphonics.

941. Lapina, Theodore. "Multitone Fingerings on the Heckel System Bassoon and the Multitone Fingering Chart." *NACWPI Journal* 25, no. 3 (February 1977): 19-38.

Includes a discussion of the production, value, and uses of multiphonics. The chart contains 336 fingerings.

942. McNerney Famera, Karen. "Mutes, Flutters, and Trills: A Guide to Composers for the Horn." M.Mus. thesis, Yale University, 1967. 200 p.

Describes the execution and notation of a variety of effects, including flutter tonguing, hand stopping, muting, and trills.

943. Papastefan, John J. "Contemporary Timpani Techniques." *Percussionist* 17 (1979-80): 75-87.

Describes and illustrates a variety of new techniques and effects.

944. Petrulis, Stanley D. "A Stylistic and Performance Analysis of Three Contemporary Compositions for the Bassoon Which Use New Performance Techniques." D.M.A. dissertation, Indiana University, 1977. 138 p.

Includes a survey of recent performance techniques.

945. Post, Nora. "The Development of Contemporary Oboe Technique." Ph.D. dissertation, New York University, 1979. 217 p. UM 79-18,862.

A comprehensive analysis of monophonic and multiphonic sounds together with a discussion of the electronic modification of sound. Includes fingering charts and a bibliography of music. Also describes the early development of contemporary oboe technique, with particular emphasis on the music of Varèse and Stefan Wolpe.

946. ————. "Multiphonics for the Oboe." *Interface* 10
      (1981): 113-36; reprinted in *Journal of the Inter-
      national Double Reed Society* 10 (1982): 12-35.

      An intelligent discussion of the use of oboe multi-
      phonics and their notation. Includes a fingering chart.

947. Randolph, David Mark. "New Techniques in the Avant-Garde
      Repertoire for Solo Tuba." D.M.A. dissertation,
      University of Rochester, 1978. 161 p. UM 78-11,493.

      Examines avant-garde techniques found in nine works
      for solo tuba in regard to notation, methods of sound
      production, and musical context.

948. Read, Gardner. *Contemporary Instrumental Techniques.*
      New York: Schirmer Books, 1976. 259 p.

      Valuable as a survey of techniques and effects found
      in contemporary music.

949. Rehfeldt, Phillip. *New Directions for Clarinet.*
      Berkeley: University of California Press, 1977.
      135 p.

      An invaluable guide to the requirements placed on
      clarinetists by contemporary composers. Includes multi-
      phonics charts by Rehfeldt and by William O. Smith as
      well as a good bibliography of new music. Published
      with a recording by Rehfeldt that illustrates the text.

950. Smoker, Paul A. "A Comprehensive Performance Project
      in Trumpet Literature with a Survey of Some Recently
      Developed Trumpet Techniques and Effects Appearing
      in Contemporary Music." D.M.A. dissertation, Uni-
      versity of Iowa, 1974. 222 p. UM 74-21,961.

      Includes a discussion of mutes, jazz effects, glis-
      sandos, microtones, multiphonics, vocal sounds, mouth-
      piece sounds, and percussive noises.

951. Szalonek, Lucjan. "O nie wykorzystanych walorach
      sonorystycznych instrumentow detych." *Res facta* 7
      (1973): 110-19.

      Points out the possibility of woodwind instruments
      producing multiphonics with as many as four sounds.
      Also notes the possibility of trills with multiple
      notes.

952. Whaley, David R. "The Microtonal Capability of the Horn." D.M.A. dissertation, University of Illinois, 1975. 154 p. UM 76-7010.

   Describes a new system of producing microtones.

953. Willis, Morya Elaine. "Notation and Performance of Avant-Garde Literature for the Solo Flute." Ph.D. dissertation, University of Florida, 1982. 198 p. UM 82-26,445.

   Surveys contemporary notational practice and examines the acoustical basis of avant-garde techniques.

XIII

DISCUSSIONS OF MUSIC FOR WIND AND PERCUSSION INSTRUMENTS

1. Wind and Percussion Instruments in General

954. Becker, Heinz. *History of Instrumentation.* Translated
by Robert Kolben. Anthology of Music, edited by
Karl G. Fellerer, vol. 24. Cologne: Arno Volk, 1964.
125 p.

A collection of seventy-six examples preceded by an
excellent short account of the historical development
of orchestration. Includes a short list of relevant
treatises.

955. Biber, Walter. "Aus der Geschichte der Balsmusik in der
Schweiz." *Bericht über die erste internationale
Fachtagung zur Erforschung der Blasmusik,* edited by
Wolfgang Suppan and Eugen Brixel. Tutzing: Schneider,
1976, pp. 127-43.

Surveys wind music in Switzerland from the Middle
Ages to the present day.

956. Bolen, Charles W. "Open-Air Music of the Baroque: A
Study of Selected Examples of Wind Music." Ph.D.
dissertation, University of Indiana, 1954. 276 p.
UM 8778.

Describes the music written for French equestrian
ballets and other open-air activities, as well as the
music played by tower musicians in Germany. Also see
Item 375, cited above.

957. Brenet, Michel. "French Military Music in the Reign of Louis XIV." *The Musical Quarterly* 3 (1917): 340-57.

A useful survey. Focuses on marches.

958. Broder, Nathan. "The Wind Instruments in Mozart's Symphonies." *The Musical Quarterly* 19 (1933): 238-59.

Traces the development of Mozart's orchstration, carefully describing--in full detail--Mozart's use of wind instruments in representative works.

* Brown, Howard Mayer. *Sixteenth-Century Instrumentation: The Music for the Florentine Intermedii.* N.p.: American Institute of Musicology, 1973. 229 p.

Cited above as Item 122.

959. Cucuel, Georges. *Études sur un orchestre au xviiie siècle.* Paris: Fischbacher, 1913. 65 p.

Comprises two essays, one on eighteenth-century instrumentation and one on the music of Gossec, Schencker, and Procksch. The essay on instrumentation provides an excellent survey of the use of wind instruments and the harp in French orchestral music of the period, especially the music performed at the concerts presented by the lawyer and music patron La Pouplinière.

* *Die Blasinstrumente und ihre Verwendung sowie zu Fragen des Tempos in der ersten Hälfte des 18. Jahrhunderts: Konferenzbericht der 4. Wissenschaftlichen Arbeitstagung Blankenburg/Harz, 16./27. Juni 1976.* Edited by Eitelfriedrich Thom. Magdeburg: Rat des Bezirkes; Leipzig: Zentralhaus für Kulturarbeit, 1977. 92 p.

Cited above as Item 121.

960. Engel, Carl. "Mozarts Instrumentation." *Mozart Jahrbuch 1956.* pp. 51-74.

Discusses Mozart's choice of instruments and his treatment of them. Includes a comparison with the practices of his contemporaries.

961. Hasse, Karl. "Die Instrumentation J.S. Bachs." *Bach Jahrbuch* 26 (1929): 90-141.

A comprehensive survey. Includes a discussion of Bach's use of wind instruments.

962. Deleted.

*   Kastner, Georges. *Manuel général de musique militaire
        à l'usage des armées français.* Paris: Didot, 1848;
        facsimile reprint, Geneva: Minkoff, 1973. 410 p.

        Cited above as Item 145.

*   Kurtz, Saul James. "A Study and Catalog of Ensemble
        Music for Woodwinds Alone or with Brass from *ca.* 1700
        to *ca.* 1825." Ph.D. dissertation, University of Iowa,
        1971. 250 p. UM 72-8273.

        Cited below as Item 1067.

963. Schlenger, Kurt. "Über Verwendung und Notation Holz-
        blasinstrumente in den frühen Kantaten Joh. Seb.
        Bachs." *Bach Jahrbuch* 28 (1931): 88-106.

        Discusses the transpositions, general musical treat-
        ment, and the expressive significance of the woodwind
        instruments employed in the cantatas written before
        1727.

964. Veit, Gottfried. *Die Blasmusik: Studie über die geschicht-
        liche Entwicklung geblasenen Musik.* Bozen: Verband
        Südtiroler Musikkapellen, 1972. 97 p.

        Surveys the history of concerted music for winds.

965. Whitwell, David. *A New History of Wind Music.* Evanston,
        Ill.: Instrumentalist, 1972. 80 p.

        A collection of the author's articles published in
        The Instrumentalist, 1965-69. Consists of superficial
        descriptions of wind music by a large number of composers.

2. Woodwind Instruments

966. Anderson, Marcia Hilden. "A Survey of Twentieth-Century
        Finnish Clarinet Music and an Analysis of Selected
        Works." Ph.D. dissertation, Michigan State University,
        1975. 172 p. UM 75-20,808.

        Examines the role of the clarinet in Finnish music of
        the twentieth century, touches upon twenty-two works for
        clarinet, and analyzes three of them (by Erik Bergman,
        Pentti Raitio, and Aare Merikanto).

967. Boese, Helmut. *Die Klarinette als Soloinstrument in der Musik der Mannheimer Schule.* Dresden: Dittert, 1940. 126 p.

     Describes and discusses the clarinet concertos by Karl Stamitz, Franz Tausch, Peter von Winter, Franz Danzi, and others. Overlooks the concerto by Johann Stamitz discovered by Gradenwitz (see below, Item 975). Includes a thematic catalog of nineteen concertos.

*   Bowers, Jane M. "The French Flute School from 1700 to 1760." Ph.D. dissertation, University of California, Berkeley, 1971. 491 p.

     Cited above as Item 173.

968. Brenet, Michel. "Rameau, Gossec et les clarinettes." *Le guide musicale* 49 (1903): 183-85, 203-05, 227-28.

     Notes Rameau's use of clarinets in *Acante et Céphise* (1751) and suggests that Gossec's subsequent claim that in 1757 he was the first to use them might simply reflect his ignorance of Rameau's work.

969. Castellani, Marcello. "The Italian Sonata for Transverse Flute and Basso Continuo." *Galpin Society Journal* 29 (1976): 2-10.

     Focuses on music for the first one-key transverse flutes with conical bore, which were created by French craftsmen at the court of Louis XIV. The first known compositions for the instrument in Italy appeared in the early eighteenth century.

970. Chatwin, R.B. "Handel and the Clarinet." *Galpin Society Journal* 3 (1950): 3-8.

     Notes that Handel employed the clarinet in an overture (Cambridge, Fitzwilliam Museum, MS 30.H.14) and in the opera *Tamerlane.* Also notes that he used the chalumeau in the opera *Riccardo Primo.*

*   Croll, Gerhard, and Kurt Birsak. "Anton Stadlers 'Bassett-klarinette' und das 'Stadler-Quintett' KV 581. Versuch einer Anwendung." *Oesterreichische Musikzeitung* 24, No. 1 (January 1969): 3-11.

     Cited above as Item 272.

*   Cucuel, Georges. "La question des clarinettes dans
       l'instrumentation du xviiie siècle." *Zeitschrift
       der Internationalen Musikgesellschaft* 12 (1910-11):
       280-84.

       Cited above as Item 273.

*   Dahlqvist, Reine. "Taille, Oboe da Caccia and Corno
       Inglese." *Galpin Society Journal* 26 (1973): 58-71.

       Cited above as Item 224.

971.   Dart, Thurston. "The Earliest Collections of Clarinet
       Music." *Galpin Society Journal* 4 (1951): 39-41.

       Notes and briefly describes Roger's *Airs à deux
       chalumeaux, deux trompettes, deux violons, deux flutes,
       deux clarinelles, ou cors de chasse,* which was published
       between 1707 and 1716. The key of the pieces, seventy-
       eight altogether, is invariably D major. Two of the
       pieces are provided with bass parts; the others are
       unaccompanied.

*   ————. "The Mock Trumpet." *Galpin Society Journal* 6
       (1953): 35-40.

       Cited above as Item 274.

972.   Dazeley, George. "The Original Text of Mozart's Clarinet
       Concerto." *The Music Review* 9 (1948): 166-72.

       Argues persuasively that the concerto, and the quintet
       K. 581, were originally intended for an A clarinet with
       an extension down to low C. Offers a number of suggested
       emendations to restore the original form of the concerto.
       Also see Item 272, cited above, and Item 976, cited
       below.

973.   Dobrinski, Ingeborg. *Das Solostuck für Querflöte in
       der ersten Hälfte des 20. Jahrhunderts.* Regensburg:
       Bosse, 1981. 278 p.

       A comprehensive examination of the repertory, together
       with analyses of several works and an index of works
       published between 1900 and 1975.

*   Du Bois, Elizabeth Ann. *A Comparison of Georg Philipp
       Telemann's Use of the Recorder and the Transverse
       Flute as Seen in His Chamber Works.* Emporia, Kansas:
       Emporia State University, 1982. 72 p.

       Cited above as Item 178.

* Farup-Madsen, Inge. "Vivaldis anvendelse af fløjteinstrumenter." *Musik & Forskning* 3 (1977): 182.

Cited above as Item 181.

974. Fleury, Louis. "Music for Two Flutes without Bass."
Music and Letters 6 (1925): 110-18.

Calls attention to flute duets by Kuhlau and by various
French composers of the eighteenth century.

975. Gradenwitz, Peter. "The Beginnings of Clarinet Literature." *Music and Letters* 17 (1936): 145-50.

Reports the author's discovery of the earliest concerto for clarinet. Argues persuasively that the work,
preserved in manuscript with only the last name of the
composer identified, was written by Johann Stamitz and
not by Karl.

* Hacker, Alan. "Mozart and the Basset Clarinet." *The
Musical Times* 110 (1969): 359-62.

Cited above as Item 281.

976. Hess, Ernst. "Die ursprüngliche Gestalt des Klarinet-
tenkonzertes KV 622." *Mozart Jahrbuch 1967*, pp. 18-30.

Reviews Dazeley's arguments (see above, Item 972) and
those of others regarding the original form of Mozart's
clarinet concerto and the quintet, K.581. Agrees that
both works were intended for basset clarinet. Provides
and discusses revisions for a large number of passages
in the concerto.

* Hunt, Edgar. "Some Light on the Chalumeau." *Galpin
Society Journal* 14 (1961): 41-44.

Cited above as Item 289.

977. Jerome, Wilbert D. "The Oboe Concerto Before 1775."
Ph.D. dissertation, Bryn Mawr College, 1973. 175 p.
UM 74-8951.

Observes that many of the stylistic features of the
oboe concerto after 1730 show the influence of the
virtuosos of the period, among them the brothers Besozzi.

978. Kingdon Ward, Martha. "Mozart and the Bassoon." *Music and Letters* 30 (1949): 8-25.

     An appreciative survey of Mozart's use of the instrument, pointing out the high quality of the writing for bassoon in the music of his maturity.

*   Kolneder, Walter. "Die Klarinette als Concertino-Instrument bei Vivaldi." *Die Musikforschung* 4 (1951): 185-91.

     Cited above as Item 293.

*   ————. "Noch einmal: Vivaldi und die Klarinette." *Die Musikforschung* 8 (1955): 209-11.

     Cited above as Item 294.

*   Lanning, Edward F. "The Clarinet as the Intended Solo Instrument in Johann Melchior Molter's Concerto 34." D.M.A. dissertation, University of Missouri, Kansas City, 1969. 62 p. UM 69-19,452.

     Cited above as Item 296.

979. Lasocki, David. "Flute and Recorder in Combination: Recent Additions to the Baroque Repertoire." *Recorder & Music* 4 (1974): 391-95.

     Discusses newly discovered works by Johann Samuel Endler, Johann Christoph Pepusch, and Pierre Prowo. Mentions three modern works for flute and recorder.

980. Laurencie, Lionel de la. "Rameau et les clarinettes." *La revue musicale de la S.I.M.* 9, no. 2 (February 1913): 27-28.

     Points out documents that demonstrate Rameau's use of clarinets in performances of the opera *Zoroastre* (1749). Clarinets are not indicated in the score.

981. Lawson, Colin. "Graupner and the Chalumeau." *Early Music* 11 (1983): 209-16.

     Discusses Johann Christoph Graupner's use of the chalumeau and also of the clarinet.

982. ————. "Telemann and the Chalumeau." *Early Music* 9 (1981): 312-19.

     An overview of Telemann's use of the instrument. Notes the use also by a number of contemporaneous German and Austrian composers.

*   Lebermann, Walter. "Zur Besetzungsfrage der Concerti
       grossi von A. Vivaldi." *Die Musikforschung* 7 (1954):
       337-39.

       Cited above as Item 298.

983.   McGowan, Richard A. "Italian Baroque Solo Sonatas for
       the Recorder and the Flute." Ph.D. dissertation, The
       University of Michigan, 1974. 530 p. UM 75-756.

       Observes that the repertory relfects the improvements
       in flute making and flute playing that took place in
       France during the late seventeenth and early eighteenth
       centuries.

*   Merriman, Lyle C. "Solos for Unaccompanied Woodwind
       Instruments: A Checklist of Published Works and Study
       of Representative Examples." Ph.D. dissertation,
       University of Iowa, 1963. 181 p. UM 64-3398.

       Cited below as Item 1095.

984.   Münster, Robert. "München oder Mannheim? Ein Beitrag
       zum Thema: Mozart und die Klarinette." *Acta Mozartiana*
       18 (1971): 10-13.

       Describes the role of the clarinet in Mannheim and
       in Munich, reviews Mozart's use of the instrument prior
       to 1778, and suggests that Mannheim exerted a stronger
       influence upon Mozart--in regard to the clarinet--than
       Munich.

*   Pound, Gomer J. "A Study of Clarinet Solo Concerto
       Literature Before 1850: With Selected Items Edited
       and Arranged for Contemporary Use." Ph.D. dissertation,
       Florida State University, 1965. 355 p. UM 65-9410.

       Cited below as Item 1103.

985.   Reich, Willi. "Bemerkungen zu Mozarts Klarinetten-
       Konzert." *Zeitschrift für Musikwissenschaft* 15
       (1933): 276-78.

       Discusses the differences between the reading given
       in the Mozart *Gesamtaufgabe* and that given in a manu-
       script copy from the collection of Aloys Fuchs (1799-
       1853).

986. Riemenschneider, Albert. *The Use of Flutes in the Works of J.S. Bach.* Washington, D.C.: Music Division, Library of Congress, 1950. 23 p.

    Surveys Bach's use in vocal music. Discusses recorder as well as transverse flute.

987. Sandner, Wolfgang. *Die Klarinette bei Carl Maria von Weber.* Wiesbaden: Breitkopf und Härtel, 1971. 257 p.

    Reviews the use of the clarinet in the music of the eighteenth and early nineteenth centuries and describes Weber's treatment of the instrument. Includes a comprehensive list of Weber's works employing clarinet.

 * Selfridge-Field, Eleanor. "Vivaldi's Esoteric Instruments." *Early Music* 6 (1978): 332-38.

    Cited above as Item 310.

988. Sidorfsky, Joyce Ann. "The Oboe in the Nineteenth Century: A Study of the Instrument and Selected Published Solo Literature." Ph.D. dissertation, University of Southern Mississippi, 1974. 376 p. UM 75-9604.

    Discusses representative compositions, partly in regard to the technical requirements they make, and surveys the mechanical development of the oboe in the nineteenth century.

 * Street, Oscar W. "The Clarinet and Its Music." *Proceedings of the Musical Association* 42 (1915-16): 89-115.

    Cited above as Item 95.

 * Sumrall, Joel N. "The Literature for Clarinet and Voice and Its Historical Antecedents." D.M.A. dissertation, University of Illinois, 1974. 192 p. UM 75-11,883.

    Cited below as Item 1110.

 * Thalheimer, Peter. "Der Flauto piccolo bei Johann Sebastian Bach." *Bach Jahrbuch* 52 (1966): 138-46.

    Cited above as Item 210.

989. Titus, Robert A. "The Solo Music for the Clarinet in
      the Eighteenth Century." Ph.D. dissertation, Univer-
      sity of Iowa, 1962. 619 p. UM 62-2412.

      Carefully traces the history of the clarinet concerto
      in the period. Lists known concertos and performers.

990. Valasek, Marion Louise. "Flute Quartets from the
      Second Half of the Eighteenth Century." Mus.A.D.
      dissertation, Boston University, 1977. 171 p.
      UM 77-21,694.

      Places the flute quartet in the context of the
      Viennese Classical style. Discusses in detail works
      by Adam Kroll, Franz Anton Schubert, Giovanni Battista
      Viotti, Joseph Haydn, and Charles Henri Kunze.

*   Waln, Ronald L. "A Comprehensive Performance Project
      in Flute Literature with an Essay on Chamber Music for
      Solo Voices, Flute, and Keyboard or Continuo, and Includ-
      ing an Annotated Bibliography of Selected Literature."
      Ph.D. dissertation, University of Iowa, 1971. 182 p.
      UM 71-22,105.

      Cited below as Item 118.

991. Warren, Charles S. "A Study of Selected Eighteenth-
      Century Clarinet Concerti." 2 vols. Ph.D. dissertation,
      Brigham Young University, 1963. 844 p. UM 64-3475.

      Analyzes twenty concertos. Notes the importance of
      the *concerts spirituel* in encouraging solo performances
      by clarinet virtuosos and thereby in the development
      of the clarinet concerto.

992. Weber, Gottfried. "Ueber Instrumentalbasse bey vollstim-
      migen Tonstücken." *Allgemeine musikalische Zeitung*
      18 (1816): 693-702, 709-14, 725-29, 749-53, 765-69.

      Includes a discussion of the use of bass wind instruments.

*   West, Charles W. "A Comprehensive Performance Project
      in Clarinet Literature with an Essay on Music for
      Woodwinds and Strings Five to Thirteen Players, Com-
      posed between *ca*. 1900 and *ca*. 1973; A Catalogue of
      Compositions, and Analyses of Selected Works by
      Composers Active in the United States after 1945."
      D.M.A. dissertation, University of Iowa, 1975. 275 p.
      UM 76-2204.

      Cited below as Item 1120.

993.   Wlach, Hans. "Die Oboe bei Beethoven." *Studien zur*
       Musikwissenschaft 14 (1927): 107-24.

       Reviews the characteristics of the oboe of Beethoven's
       day and describes in detail his treatment of the instrument.
       Asserts that in most of Beethoven's works, the oboe sym-
       bolizes peace, the rural, and the pastoral.

                        3. Brass Instruments

994.   Altenburg, Detlef. "Zum Repertoire der Hoftrompeter
       im 17. und 18. Jahrhundert." *Bericht über die*
       erste internationale Fachtagung zur Erforschung der
       Blasmusik, Graz 1974, edited by Wolfgang Suppan and
       Eugen Brixel. Tutzing: Schneider, 1976, pp. 47-60.

       Categorizes and discusses the contents of collections
       of trumpet music by Magnus Thomsen (1598), Hendrich
       Lübeck (*ca.* 1600), and Cesare Bendinelli (1614). A
       facsimile edition of Bendinelli's collection is cited
       above as Item 859.

995.   Baines, Anthony. "The Evolution of Trumpet Music up
       to Fantini." *Proceedings of the Royal Musical Associa-*
       tion 101 (1974-75): 1-9.

       Examines indications of early forms of cavalry calls
       found in manuscripts from *ca.* 1600. Discusses their
       use in 15th-century vocal works and in the toccata
       from *Orfeo*. Also discusses the origins of the clarino
       style.

996.   Barbour, J. Murray. "Franz Krommer and His Writing for
       Brass." *Brass Quarterly* 1 (1957-58): 1-9.

       Describes the forward-looking treatment of brass
       instruments, especially the horns, given in the orchestral
       works of Krommer (1759-1831).

997.   ―――. *Trumpets, Horns, and Music.* East Lansing, Mich.:
       Michigan State University Press, 1964. 170 p.

       Deals with the use of natural brass instruments in
       ensemble music from *ca.* 1600 to 1830. Does not discuss
       playing techniques or the design of instruments. Valuable
       as a survey of compositional practice.

* ———. "Unusual Brass Notation in the Eighteenth
  Century." *Brass Quarterly* 2 (1958-59): 139-46.

  Cited above as Item 857.

998. ———. "The Use of Brass Instruments in Early Scores."
  Bulletin of the American Musicological Society, No. 4
  (1940): 16-17.

  Surveys eighteenth-century music and points to the
  acceptance of harmonic clashes in works by Bach, Handel,
  and Steffani.

999. Besseler, Heinrich. "Die Enstehung der Posaune." *Acta
  musicologica* 22 (1950): 8-35.

  Describes in careful detail the use of the trombone
  in the polyphony of the early fifteenth century.

1000. Beyer, Werner. "The Classical Solo Concerto for Trombone and Its Interpreters in the 19th Century."
  Brass Bulletin 25 (1979): 51-55.

  A brief sketch of a slight history. Parallel texts
  in German, French, and English.

1001. Blandford, W.F.H. "Bach's Horn Parts." *The Musical
  Times* 77 (1936): 748-50.

  Survey's Bach's use of brass instruments, points out
  the difficulty of performing Bach's horn parts, and
  suggests that players might employ small horns in
  C and D alto or possible F and G instead of the horns
  they normally use.

1002. ———. "Handel's Horn and Trombone Parts" *The Musical
  Times* 80 (1939): 697-99, 746-47, 794.

  Centers on Handel's use of horns. Points out the
  keys he employed and describes his melodic treatment
  of the instrument. Notes that he must have expected
  the use of horns with detachable crooks. Describes
  the effectiveness of Handel's writing for trombone.

* ———. "Studies on the Horn." *The Musical Times* 63
  (1922): 544-47, 622-24, 693-97; 66 (1925): 29-32,
  124-29, 221-23.

  Cited above as Item 402.

1003. Blankenburg, Walter. "Von der Verwendung von Blechblasin-
       strumenten in Bachs kirchenmusikalischen Werken und
       ihrer Bedeutung." *Musik und Kirche* 20 (1950): 65-71.

       Surveys Bach's use of brass instruments. Describes
       the musical purposes to which the instruments are put.

1004. Brown, Thomas Martin, Jr. "Clarino Horn, Hunting Horn,
       and Hand Horn: Their Comparative Roles in the Classic
       Music of the Eighteenth Century." D.A. dissertation,
       Ball State University, 1978. 153 p. UM 79-18,786.

       Indentifies and describes three styles of playing
       current during the period. Notes the relative scarcity
       of horn parts in orchestral music of the late eighteenth
       century that require hand stopping and suggests that
       the reason might lie in a change in the concept of the
       tone quality desired.

1005. Brüchle, Bernhard. "An Unknown Work for Horn by Richard
       Strauss." *The Horn Call* 3 (1972-73): 21.

       Describes an Andante for horn and piano written for
       Strauss's father's silver wedding anniversary (August
       1888).

1006. Bryan, Paul. "The Horn in the Works of Mozart and
       Haydn: Some Observations and Comparisons." *Haydn
       Yearbook* 9 (1975): 189-255.

       Describes and notes the difference between Mozart's
       and Haydn's writing for horn. Points out the influence
       of the hornist Leutgeb on Mozart's employment of hand-
       stopped chromatics and of Carl Franz upon Haydn's solo-
       istic horn writing.

*   Burkart, Richard E. "The Trumpet in the Seventeenth
       Century with Emphasis on its Treatment in the Works
       of Henry Purcell and a Biography of the Shore Family
       of Trumpeters." Ph.D. dissertation, University of
       Wisconsin, 1972. 153 p. UM 72-9111.

       Cited above as Item 328.

1007. Ciurczak, Peter L. "The Trumpet in Baroque Opera: Its
       Use as a Solo, Obbligato, and Ensemble Instrument."
       Ph.D. dissertation, North Texas State University, 1974.
       962 p. UM 75-13,665.

       Based on an examination of 641 operas. Defines the
       characteristics of clarino style, *principale* style, and
       filler-fanfare style and delineates the elements that

constitute Baroque trumpet style generally. Includes a chronology of operas with clarino trumpet parts.

1008. Gifford, Robert Marvin, Jr. "A Comprehensive Performance Project in Trombone Literature with an Essay Consisting of a Survey of the Use of the Trombone in Chamber Music with Mixed Instrumentation Composed since 1956." D.M.A. dissertation, University of Iowa, 1978. 266 p. UM 79-5662.

Survey covers 1,004 works. Music for brass ensemble is excluded.

* Glover, Stephen L. "Early Trumpet Music in Schwerin." *Brass Bulletin*, no. 23 (1978): 35-40.

Cited below as Item 1133.

1009. Gray, Robert. "The Trombone in Contemporary Chamber Music." *Brass Quarterly* 1 (1957-58): 10-19.

An overview prefaced by a brief sketch of the use of the trombone in earlier chamber music.

1010. Gregory, Robin. "The Horn in Beethoven's Symphonies." *Music and Letters* 33 (1952): 303-10.

Reviews the kinds of instruments employed and the manner in which Beethoven made use of them. Reprinted in *The Horn Call* 7, no. 2 (May 1977): 25-31.

* Henderson, Robert. "A Study of the Trumpet in the 17th Century: Its History, Resources and Use." M.A. thesis, University of North Carolina, 1949. 125 p.

Cited above as Item 346.

1011. Hildebrandt, Donald Jay. "The Bass Trombone in the Twentieth-Century Orchestra: Its Use in Twenty-Seven Representative Scores." Ph.D. dissertation, Indiana University, 1976. 207 p.

Presents an overview of the role of the bass trombone in twentieth-century music. Focuses on the types of instruments in use, the types intended for each of the selected works, the role of the instrument in the orchestration of the works, and the technical demands made by the composers.

1012.   Husted, Benjamin F. "Contemporary American Brass
        Quartets." *Brass Quarterly* 1 (1957-58): 147-54.

        Attempts to define the principal musical traits of
        more than fifty American brass quartets published
        after *ca.* 1940. Places special emphasis upon the
        employment of quartal harmonies.

*   Hyatt, Jack H. "The Soprano and Piccolo Trumpets:
        Their History, Literature, and a Tutor." D.M.A.
        dissertation, Boston University, 1974. 238 p.
        UM 74-20,473.

        Cited above as Item 349.

1013.   Isaacson, Charles Frank. "A Study of Selected Music
        for Trombone and Voice." D.M.A. dissertation,
        University of Illinois, 1981. 142 p. UM 82-3495.

        Examines the role of the trombone in the music of
        the fifteenth and sixteenth centuries. Includes a
        list of works.

1014.   Karstädt, Georg. *Lasst lustig die Hörner erschallen!*
        Eine kleine Kulturgeschichte der Jagdmusik. Hamburg:
        Parey, 1964. 136 p.

        Traces the history of music for hunting horn and
        its influence upon orchestral writing. Also see Item
        1015, cited below.

1015.   ————. "Die Verwendung der Hörner in der Jagdmusik."
        Bericht über die erste internationale Fachtagung zur
        Erforschung der Blasmusik, Graz 1974, edited by Wolfgang
        Suppan and Eugen Brixel. Tutzing: Schneider, 1976,
        pp. 197-215.

        An overview of the history of music for hunting horn
        from the Middle Ages through the early nineteenth
        century. Describes the kinds of hunting horns found
        in the seventeenth and eighteenth centuries and sur-
        veys their employment. Also see Item 1014, cited above.

1016.   Mahrenholz, Christhard. "Über Posaunenmusik." *Musik*
        und Kirche 1 (1929): 132-37, 163-73, 261-67.

        Argues for the use of trombone choirs in the church.

1017. Morisset, Michel. "Étude sur la musique pour trompette
       en France de Lully à Rameau." *Recherches* 13 (1973):
       35-55.

       Surveys the use of the trumpet especially in religious
       and dramatic works from the end of the seventeenth and
       the beginning of the eighteenth centuries.

1018. Piersig, Fritz. *Die Einführung des Hornes in die
       Kunstmusik und seine Verwendung bis zum Tode Joh.
       Seb. Bachs: Ein Beitrag zur Geschichte des Instru-
       mentation.* Halle: Niemeyer, 1927. 144 p.

       Focuses on the treatment of the horn only in German
       music. Bach's use is discussed in detail.

*   Pizka, Hans. *Das Horn bei Mozart/Mozart and the Horn.*
       Kirchheim: Pizka, 1980. 276 p.

       Cited below as Item 1186.

1019. Schaefer, Jay Dee. "The Use of the Trombone in the
       18th Century." *Brass Anthology.* Evanston, Ill.:
       Instrumentalist, 1976, pp. 471-76.

       A general survey.

1020. Schünemann, Georg, ed. *Trompeterfanfaren, Sonaten und
       Feldstücke nach Aufzeichnungen deutscher Hoftrompeter
       des 16./17. Jahrhunderts.* Das Erbe deutscher Musik,
       series 1: Reichsdenkmale, vol. 7. Kassel: Bärenreiter,
       1936. 80 p.

       Brings together a large number of trumpet signals,
       monophonic sonatas, toccatas, etc., from German sources
       of the sixteenth and seventeenth centuries. Preceded
       by sketch of the musical background and followed by a
       discussion of the music.

1021. Smithers, Don L. "Seventeenth-Century English Trumpet
       Music." *Music and Letters* 48 (1967): 358-65.

       Describes a number of English works for trumpet from
       the late seventeenth century together with English
       manuscript copies of works from the continent. Notes
       that English writing for trumpet tended to be more
       conservative than continental writing.

1022. Tarr, Edward H. "Monteverdi, Bach und die Trompeten-
       musik ihrer Zeit." *Bericht über den internationalen
       musikwissenschaftlichen Kongress Bonn 1970.* Kassel:
       Bärenreiter, [1971], pp. 592-96.

       Examines the toccata from *Orfeo* and argues persuasively
       that Monteverdi intended it to be played by a choir of
       five trumpets. Suggests also that Fantini's *L'Imperiale*
       should be played by a similar choir. Calls attention
       to identical trumpet figures in Bach's *Christmas
       Oratorio* and a sonata by Biber and proposes that the
       figure might well have been taken from a familiar
       trumpet call.

1023. ―――――. "Original Italian Baroque Compositions for
       Trumpet and Organ." *Diapason*, April 1970, pp. 27-29.

       A discussion of works by Girolamo Fantini and Giovanni
       Bonaventura Viviani.

1024. Tarr, Edward H., and Thomas Walker. "'Bellici carmi,
       festivo fragor': Die Verwendung der Trompete in der
       italienischen Oper des 17. Jahrhunderts." *Hamburger
       Jahrbuch für Musikwissenschaft* 3 (1978): 143-203.

       A thorough, carefully documented study. Includes an
       index of seventeenth-century Italian operas that make
       use of the trumpet.

1025. Wigness, C. Robert. *The Soloistic Use of the Trombone
       in Eighteenth-Century Vienna.* Nashville: Brass
       Press, 1978. 50 p.

       Mostly a description of trombone solos in a small
       selection of eighteenth-century works. The works lie
       mostly in flat keys, which suggests that the instrument
       in Vienna of the period was pitched in B flat.

                    4. Percussion Instruments

*   Bowles, Edmund A. "Nineteenth-Century Innovations in
       the Use and Construction of the Timpani." *Percussion-
       ist* 19, no. 2 (March 1982): 6-75.

       Cited above as Item 432.

1026.   Charlton, David. "Salieri's Timpani." *The Musical
        Times* 112 (1971): 961-62.

        Describes rather bold treatment of the timpani in
        three operas and notes the possibility of his influence
        upon Beethoven.

1027.   Geortzel Sandman, Susan. "Indications of Snare-Drum
        Technique in Philidor Collection MS. 1163." *Galpin
        Society Journal* 30 (1977): 70-75.

        Describes the drum parts in a manuscript from 1705.

1028.   Hochrainer, Richard. "Beethoven's Use of the Timpani."
        Percussionist 14 (1976-77): 66-70.

        A survey that stresses the dramatic and musical
        effects of Beethoven's treatment. Translated by
        Harrison Powley.

*   Kirby, Percival R. *The Kettle-Drums: A Book for
        Composers, Conductors and Kettle-Drummers*. London:
        Oxford University Press, 1930. 73 p.

        Cited above as Item 825.

1029.   Levine, David. "Percussion Instruments and Performance
        Practices in Beethoven's Music." *Percussionist* 15
        (1977-78): 1-6.

        Points out the instruments employed by Beethoven and
        notes his innovations in the use of timpani.

1030.   Longyear, Rey M. "Ferdinand Kauer's Percussion Enter-
        prises." *Galpin Society Journal* 27 (1974): 2-8.

        Describes the use of percussion in the orchestral
        and chamber music of Ferdinand Kauer (1751-1831), whom
        Longyear describes as "a pioneer in percussion writing
        through his introduction of new timbres and effects."

1031.   Pollart, Gene J. "The Use and Innovations of Percus-
        sion in the Works of J.S. Bach and Handel." *Per-
        cussionist* 13 (1976): 75-80.

        An overview and comparison that points out the expan-
        sion of the role of the timpani in Bach's music and
        Handel's innovative use of orchestral bells and gun-
        shot effects.

1032. Terry, Charles Sanford. "Bach's Kettledrums."
       The Musical Times 72 (1931): 119-21.

       Reviews Bach's rather limited use of the instrument.

XIV

DISCOGRAPHIES AND BIBLIOGRAPHIES OF BOOKS AND ARTICLES

1033. Agrell, Jeffrey. "An Indexed Bibliography of Periodical Articles on the Horn." *The Horn Call* 6, no. 2 (May 1976): 51-54; 7, no. 1 (November 1976): 45-51; 7, no. 2 (May 1977): 49-55.

    Includes articles from only two foreign-language periodicals.

1034. ————. "A Tentative Bibliography of Masters' Theses and Doctoral Dissertations." *The Horn Call*, 8 no. 1 (November 1977): 44-47.

    Lists fifty-one theses and dissertations dealing with the horn.

1035. Bahr, Edward Richard. "A Discography of Classical Trombone/Euphonium Solo and Ensemble on Long-Playing Records Distributed in the United States." D.M.A. dissertation, University of Oklahoma, 1980. 324 p. UM 80-16,922.

    A comprehensive list.

1036. Bowman, Jack W. "The Present State of Research on Construction of the Clarinet." *Journal of Band Research* 10, no. 1 (Fall 1973): 22-24.

    A brief, incomplete, annotated bibliography prefaced by an introduction decrying the state of the literature.

* Brixel, Eugen. *Klarinetten-Bibliographie*. Wilhelms-haven: Heinrichshofen, 1978. 493. p.

    Cited below as Item 1073.

*   Brown, Leon F. *Handbook of Selected Literature for
        the Study of Trombone at the University-College
        Level.* [Denton, Texas: North Texas State University],
        1972. 23 p.

        Cited below as Item 1124.

*   Brüchle, Bernhard. *Horn-Bibliographie.* 2 vols.
        Wilhelmshaven: Heinrichshofen, 1970-75. 272, 246 p.

        Cited below as Item 1125.

1037.   Cauchi, Gary S.M. "Clarinet Dissertations, 1970-
        June 1977." *The Clarinet* 5, no. 2 (Winter 1978):
        24-26.

        A list of fifty-nine items gathered from *Dissertation
        Abstracts International.*

1038.   ————. "The Clarinet Reed: A Comprehensive Bibliography."
        The Clarinet 3, no. 3 (May 1967): 20-21.

        Lists books, articles, and dissertations, mostly of
        a practical nature.

1039.   ————. "The Single Reed Mouthpiece: A Bibliography."
        The Clarinet 5, no. 2 (Winter 1978): 26-28.

        Lists ninety-six items, many of which are articles from
        Instrumentalist, The Clarinet, Woodwind, and *Woodwind
        World.*

*   Clark, David L. *Music for Wind Instruments: A Survey
        of Anthologies in Print with Notes on the Repertoire
        and an Annotated Bibliography.* London: Library
        Association, 1970. 321 p.

        Cited below as Item 1062.

1040.   Coover, James. *Musical Instrument Collections:
        Catalogues and Cognate Literature.* Detroit:
        Information Coordinators, 1981. 464 p.

        A comprehensive list of altogether 2,418 items.
        Partly annotated. An indispensable reference tool.

*   Dudgeon, Ralph Thomas. "The Keyed Bugle, Its History,
        Literature and Technique." Ph.D. dissertation, Uni-
        versity of California, San Diego, 1980. 262 p. UM 80-
        23,094.

        Cited above as Item 331.

1041. Ehnes, Fred Rickard. "A Guide to the Archive of the
       International Horn Society 1969-1977 at Alexander
       M. Bracken Library, Ball State University, Muncie,
       Indiana." D.A. dissertation, Ball State University,
       1982. 218 p. DA 82-19,443.

       Includes a short history of the society and lists of
       the contents of the collection.

1042. Errante, F. Gerard. *A Selective Clarinet Bibliography*.
       Oneonta, N.Y.: Swift-Dorr Publications, 1973. 82 p.

       Covers a wide range of material, from the most
       scholarly to the extremely rudimentary and superficial.

1043. Gilbert, Richard. *The Clarinetists' Solo Repertoire:
       A Discography*. New York: Grendallia Society, 1972.
       100 p.

       Includes 78-rpm recordings, a curious list of taped
       performances without any indication of where the tapes
       can be found, and brief evaluations of the work of a
       number of prominent (and not-so-prominent) players.
       Also includes a selection of excerpts from record
       reviews. A supplement (150 p.) published in 1975
       (New York: Grenadilla Society).

*   Gillespie, James E. *Solos For Unaccompanied Clarinet:
       An Annotated Bibliography of Published Works*.
       Detroit Studies in Music Bibliography, vol. 28.
       Detroit: Information Coordinators, 1973. 79 p.

       Cited below as Item 1082.

1044. Glover, Stephen L. *Brass Recordings Catalog No. 3*.
       Nashville: Brass Press, 1973. 10 p.

       Lists recordings available from U.S. publishers.
       Includes recordings of works for solo instruments and
       for ensembles.

1045. Gora, William A. "An Annotated Bibliography of Selected
       Materials Relative to the History, Repertoire, Acoustics
       and Pedagogy of the Saxophone." D.M.A. dissertation,
       University of Miami, 1975. 80 p. UM 76-4709.

       Includes a discography.

1046.   Hellwig, Friedemann. "The Care of Musical Instruments.
        A Technical Bibliography for Conservators, Restorers,
        and Curators." *Musical Instrument Conservation and
        Technology News* 1 (1978): 2-39.

        A valuable list.

1047.   Higbee, Dale. "Baroque Flute Discography." *Early
        Music* 7 (1979): 250-53.

        Lists out-of-print as well as currently available
        recordings.

*   Langwill, Lyndesay G. *The Bassoon and Contrabassoon.*
        New York: Norton, 1965. 269 p.

        Cited above as Item 84.

1048.   Messenger, Joseph C. "A Comprehensive Performance
        Project in Clarinet Literature with an Annotated
        Bibliography of Selected Books and Periodical
        Material about the History, Repertoire, and Acoustics
        of the Clarinet." D.M.A. dissertation, University
        of Iowa, 1971. 106 p. UM 71-30,467.

        Includes a list of relevant master's theses.

1049.   Meyer, Frederick. "Selected Books and Dissertations
        on the Double Reeds." *Woodwind Anthology.* Evanston,
        Ill.: Instrumentalist, 1976, pp. 296-97.

        An annotated list of ten books and an unannotated
        list of twenty-two dissertations. Originally published
        in April 1968.

1050.   Miller, Dayton C. *Catalogue of Books and Literary
        Material Relating to the Flute and Other Musical
        Instruments.*

        A comprehensive list of books mostly about the
        flute. Includes tutors. Items of special interest
        are annotated.

1051.   Myers, Anna. "A Bibliography of the Oboe and English
        Horn." M.Mus. thesis, Kent State University, 1972.
        25 p.

        Lists approximately 400 books, articles, and disserta-
        tions.

*   Pizka,Hans. *Das Horn bei Mozart/Mozart and the Horn.*
         Kirchheim: Pizka, 1980. 276 p.

         Cited below as Item 1186.

*   Rossing, Thomas D. "Musical Acoustics." *American
         Journal of Physics* 43 (1975): 944-53.

         Cited above as Item 470.

*   Smithers, Don L. *The Music and History of the Baroque
         Trumpet before 1721.* London: Dent, 1973. 323 p.

         Cited above as Item 369.

1052.   Snyder, John R. *A Partially Annotated Bibliography
         of the Clarinet.* 2 vols. N.p.: Snyder, 1979.
         798 p.

         Lists books, articles, dissertations, theses, and
         reviews written or published before 1976, with particular
         emphasis on American items. Valuable for its inclusion
         of items that appear only in out-of-the-way places.
         Marred by the inclusion of frequently worthless items
         (e.g., newspaper articles about the author or his
         friends) and by annotations that are sometimes more
         curious than helpful.

1053.   Taylor, Laurence. "Research for the Flute: A List of
         Theses." *Woodwind Anthology.* Evanston, Ill.:
         Instrumentalist, 1976, pp. 67-68.

         A list of thirty-two items . Originally published in
         1960.

1054.   Turrentine, Edgar M. "The History of Brass Instruments
         in Ancient Times: A Bibliographic Essay." *NACWPI
         Journal* 21, no 3 (spring 1973): 29-30.

         Points out a few sources that might otherwise be
         overlooked.

1055.   ———. "The Physiological Aspect of Brasswind Per-
         formance Technique: A Bibliographic Essay." *NACWPI
         Journal* 26, no. 2 (November 1977): 3-5.

         Lists recent research on the physiology of brass
         playing.

1056. Vinquist, Mary, and Neal Zaslaw, eds. *Performance
       Practice: A Bibliography*. New York: Norton, 1971,
       114 p.

       Indispensable as a source of access to the scholarly
       literature. Supplements appear in *Current Musicology*,
       no. 12 (1971): 129-49, and no. 15 (1973): 126-36.

*   Warner, Thomas E. *An Annotated Bibliography of
       Woodwind Instruction Books, 1600-1830*. Detroit:
       Information Coordinators, 1967. 138 p.

       Cited above as Item 925.

1057. Zimmer, Ulrich. "Bläsermusik auf Schallplatten."
       Der Bläserchor: Besinnung und Aufgabe, edited by
       Wilhelm Ehmann. Kassel: Bärenreiter, 1969, pp. 155-60.

       A discussion that cites and comments upon a number of
       recorded collections of brass music.

XV

BIBLIOGRAPHIES OF WIND AND PERCUSSION MUSIC

1. General

1058. Altmann, Wilhelm. *Kammermusik-Katalog. Ein Verzeichnis von seit 1841 veröffentlichten Kammermusikwerken.* 6th ed. Leipzig: Hofmeister, 1945. 400 p.

The fundamental bibliographic guide to published chamber music, available either as separate publications or in collections. Sixth edition covers music published from 1841 to June 1945. Supplemented by Richter, cited below as Item 1068.

1059. Brown, Merrill E. *Wind and Percussion Literature Performed in College Student Recitals (1971-72).* [Toledo]: Merrill Brown, 1974. 255 p.

Based on a survey of 273 schools. Reports the number of performances and the kind of recital (senior solo recital, graduate solo recital) on which each work was performed. Includes works for ensembles of various kinds.

1060. Brüchle, Bernhard. *Musik-Bibliographien für alle Instrumente.* Munich: Brüchle, 1976, 96 p.

A comprehensive list of bibliograhies of music. Includes theses, dissertations, and works in progress. Lists specialized journals and music societies together with their addresses.

1061. Chapman, James, Sheldon Fine, and Mary Rasmussen. "Music for Wind Instruments in Historical Editions, Collected Works and Numbered Series: A Bibliography." *Brass and Woodwind Quarterly* 1 (1966-68): 115-20; 2 (1969): 17-58.

A valuable list of the music found in 42 editions and series.

1062. Clark, David L. *Music for Wind Instruments: A Survey of Anthologies in Print with Notes on the Repertoire and an Annotated Bibliography.* London: Library Association, 1970. 231. p.

Includes an annotated list of monographs.

1063. Contemproary Music Project. *The CMP Library: Works for Band, Winds and Percussion: Solos.* Washington, D.C.: Music Educators National Conference, 1967. [Unpaginated.]

Lists music written as part of the Composers in the Public School Program. Includes all the works written for band, for solo wind and percussion instruments, and for wind and percussion chamber ensembles. Includes biographical sketches of the composers, sample pages, and descriptions of the works.

1064. Goodman, A. Harold. *Instrumental Music Guide.* Provo, Utah: Brigham Young University Press, 1977. 240 p.

Composed of short graded lists of ensemble and solo music for wind instruments.

*   Gorgerat, Gérald. *Encyclopédie de la musique pour instruments à vent.* 3 vols. Lausanne: Éditions rencontre Lausanne, 1955. 380, 452, 614 p.

Cited above as Item 41.

1065. Heller, George N. *Ensemble Music for Wind and Percussion Instruments: A Catalog.* Washington, D.C.: Music Educators Conference, 1970. 142 p.

A graded, classified list arranged alphabetically by title, except in the case of collections, which are listed by composer or editor. There is no index by composer.

1066. Helm, Sanford M. *Catalog of Chamber Music for Wind Instruments.* New York: Da Capo, 1969. 85 p.

A reprint, with corrections by the author, of the book published in 1952. Lists music for ensembles of three instruments and more. Once very useful but now superseded by more recent bibliographies, especially Richter's *Kammermusik-Katalog*, cited below as Item 1068.

1067. Kurtz, Saul James. "A Study and Catalog of Ensemble Music for Woodwinds Alone or with Brass from *ca.* 1700 to *ca.* 1825." Ph.D. dissertation, University of Iowa, 1971. 250 p. UM 72-8273.

Catalog includes published and unpublished works for three to *ca.* ten instruments, omitting music employing keyboard instruments and string instruments other than the double bass. Study traces the development of the wind ensemble. Investigates the meaning of such terms as *Harmonie, Harmoniemusik*, and *Musique militaire.*

1068. Richter, Johannes Friedrich. *Kammermusik-Katalog. Verzeichnis der von 1944 bis 1958 veröffentlichten Werke für Kammermusik und für Klavier vier- und sechshändig sowie für zwei und mehr Klaviere.* Frankfurt, Leipzig: Hofmeister, 1960. 318 p.

Supplements Altmann, cited above as Item 1058. An excellent classified list. A standard source.

1069. Vagner, Robert. "A Selective List of Choral and Vocal Music with Wind and Percussion Accompaniments." *Journal of Research in Music Education* 14 (1966): 276-88.

Lists music employing instrumental emsembles or solo instruments with and without an added keyboard instrument. Includes but does not designate arrangements.

1070. Weerts, Richard K. *Original Manuscript Music for Wind and Percussion Instruments.* Washington, D.C.: Music Educators National Conference, 1973. 42 p.

A highly selective graded list of approximately 400 works. Indicates, in the case of works not obtainable elsewhere (through the American Composers Alliance, for instance), the addresses of the composer. Includes arrangements for wind and percussion ensemble. Does not include works for unaccompanied solo instruments.

2. Woodwind Instruments

1071. Bartlett, Loren W. "A Survey and Checklist of Representative Eighteenth-Century Concertos and Sonatas for Bassoon." Ph.D. dissertation, University of Iowa, 1961. 247 p. UM 61-5544.

Includes an annotated list of more than 120 bassoon
sonatas and concertos from the period complemented by
a list of additional works not examined in the study.
Also traces the history of the bassoon through the
eighteenth century, placing special emphasis upon the
eighteenth century.

1072. Bedford, Frances. "A Survey of Twentieth-Century Music
       for Woodwinds and Harpsichord." *Woodwind World,
       Brass and Percussion* 15, no. 1 (January 1976): 16-17,
       23; no. 2 (March 1976): 7, 9, 14; 16 no. 2 (March 1977):
       8-9, 30; 17, no. 1 (January 1978): 10-12.

       Lists published and unpublished works.

*   Blake, Cevedra Marc. "The Baroque Oboe d'Amore."
       Ph.D. dissertation, University of California, Los
       Angeles, 1981. 677 p. UM 82-20,919.

       Cited above as Item 221.

1073. Brixel, Eugen. *Klarinetten-Bibliographie*. Wilhelms-
       haven: Heinrichshofen, 1978. 493 p.

       A nearly exhaustive list. Includes music for ensembles
       employing clarinet but does not include solo music for
       bass or sopranino clarinets. Also includes a list of
       books and articles about the clarinet.

1074. *Catalogus voor de fluit-literatur*. Amsterdam: Broekmans
       & van Poppel, [ca. 1974]. 30 p.

       A graded list by Jojo van Roy-Haanstra and Peter
       Quakernaat. Probably of little value, owing to citations
       that are both incomplete and ambiguous. Includes music
       for recorder.

1075. Copenhagen. Royal Library. *Catalogue of Giedde's
       Music Collection in the Royal Library of Copenhagen*.
       Copenhagen: Royal Library, 1976. 196 p.

       Compiled by Inge Bittmann. Lists the contents of an
       important eighteenth-century collection, which contains
       mostly flute music. The collection comprises 1,230
       items, many of which are rare or unique. Where necessary,
       the catalog includes incipits.

*   Dobrinski, Ingeborg. *Das Solostuck für Querflöte in
       der ersten Hälfte des 20. Jahrhunderts*. Regensburg:
       Bosse, 1981. 278 p.

       Cited above as Item 973.

*   Eberst, Anton. *Klarinet od A do Z.* Krakow: Polskie
         Wydawnictow Muzycnze, 1971. 214 p.

         Cited above as Item 89.

1076.   Fletcher, Richard W. "A Comprehensive Performance
         Project in Clarinet Literature with an Essay on
         Music for Bassoon and Small String Ensemble, circa
         1700-1825." D.M.A. dissertation, University of
         Iowa, 1974. 230 p. UM 74-21,958.

         Lists ninety-eight works written for solo bassoon
         and two or more strings. Excludes works with a key-
         board instrument or basso continuo.

1077.   Fridorich, Edwin. "The Saxophone: A Study of Its
         Use in Symphonic and Operatic Literature." Ed.D.
         dissertation, Columbia University, 1975. 709 p.
         UM 75-27,058.

         Includes a list of works employing the saxophone.
         Analyzes 246 works and notes the gradual decrease
         in the twentieth century of the use of the saxophone
         in the orchestra.

1078.   Gee, Harry R. *Clarinet "Solos de Concours," 1897-
         1980: An Annotated Bibliography.* Bloomington,
         Ind.: Indiana University Press, 1981. 118 p.

         Arranged chronologically. The annotations are
         distinguished by their length and the amount of infor-
         mation they contain. Prefaced by a sketch of the
         historical background of the *solo de concours.*

1079.   *General Catalogue of Flute Music.* London: Muramatsu,
         1972. 263 p.

         Includes etudes and methods, music for solo flute,
         for flute and piano, flute and orchestra, and for
         ensembles of various kinds. Titles given in Japanese
         and in the original languages.

1080.   Gifford, Virginia Snodgrass. *Music for Oboe, Oboe
         d'Amore, and English Horn.* Westport, Conn.:
         Greenwood, 1983. 431 p.

         Lists the extensive holdings of the Library of
         Congress. Includes chamber music as well as music
         for solo instruments and band or orchestra.

1081. Gillespie, James E. *The Reed Trio: An Annotated
       Bibliography of Original Published Works.* Detroit
       Studies in Music Bibliography, vol. 20. Detroit:
       Information Coordinators, 1971. 84 p.

       Lists works for oboe, clarinet, and bassoon that
       in 1871 were in print and that were written between
       1897 and 1968. Indicates degree of difficulty and
       timing and notes performance considerations. Pre- -
       faced by a historical overview of the reed trio.

1082. ————. *Solos for Unaccompanied Clarinet: An Annotated
       Bibliography of Published Works.* Detroit Studies in
       Music Bibliography, vol. 28. Detroit: Information
       Coordinators, 1973. 79 p.

       Includes works in print in 1972. Provides brief
       commentary on the works as well as information on
       recordings and reviews. Introduced by a discussion
       of the history of the medium. Also includes a discog-
       raphy.

1083. Gillette, John C. "An Annotated Bibliography of Works
       for Unaccompanied Bassoon." D.M.A. dissertation,
       Indiana University, 1976. 93 p.

       Indexed sixty-five works and lists 10 additional works
       without annotation. Indicates range, level of difficulty,
       and performance time for each work. Also notes tech-
       nical problems and describes the works generally.
       Lists recordings.

*   Girard, Adrien. *Histoire et richesses de la flûte.*
       Paris: Gründ, 1953. 143 p.

       Cited above as Item 69.

*   Gorgerat, Gérald. *Encyclopédie de la musique pour
       instruments à vent.* 3 vols. Lausanne: Éditions
       rencontre Lausanne, 1955. 380, 542, 614 p.

       Cited above as Item 41.

1084. Harriss, Elaine Atkins. "Chamber Music for the Trio
       of Flute, Clarinet, and Piano: A Bibliographical
       and Analytical Study." Ph.D. dissertation, The
       University of Michigan, 1981. 160 p. UM 81-25,122.

       Includes a graded list of 108 compositions.

1085. Heard, John M. "A Graded and Annotated Survey of Oboe Literature Currently Available in Modern Editions." D.M.A. dissertation, University of Texas, 1975. 161 p. UM 76-7987.

   Arranged according to historical period and performance difficulty. Includes an alphabetical index of composers.

1086. Hiscock, Sherrick Sumner II. "An Annotated Bibliography of Selected, Published Mixed Trios for One Clarinetist and Two Other Musicians." D.M.A. dissertation, University of Miami, 1978. 204 p. UM 78-18,727.

   A graded list of more than 400 items.

1087. Hopkins, Harlow. "The Clarinet in Latin-American Chamber Music: An Annotated Bibliography." D.M.A. dissertation, Indiana University, 1974. 189 p.

   Lists and describes seventy-five works, most of which were written during the past thirty years. Provides information about the difficulty of the works, the pitch ranges, and tempo indications. Also lists 118 additional works not examined.

1088. Hošek, Miroslav. *Oboen-Bibliographie.* Edited by Rudolf H. Führer. Wilhelmshaven: Heinrichshofen, 1975. 403 p.

   A comprehensive guide. Lists published works for oboe alone and in combination with one through fifteen other solo instruments, with and without orchestra. Includes a list of tutors and a brief list of books and articles.

*   Jansen, Will. *The Bassoon: Its History, Construction, Makers, Players and Music.* Buren: Knuf, 1978. 1818 p.

   Cited above as Item 83.

1089. Jones, William John. "The Literature of the Transverse Flute in the Seventeenth and Eighteenth Centuries." Ph.D. dissertation, Northwestern University, 1952. 519 p.

   Valuable especially for its extensive bibliography of music in original as well as in modern editions.

1090. Klitz, Brian K. "Solo Sonatas, Trio Sonatas, and Duos
       for Bassoon Before 1750." Ph.D. dissertation, Univ-
       ersity of North Carolina, 1961. 223 p. UM 61-6125.

       Includes a list of 159 sonatas preserved in European
       libraries.

*   Kölbel, Herbert. *Von der Flöte: Brevier für Flöten-
       spieler*. 2nd ed. Kassel: Bärenreiter, 1966. 249 p.

       Cited above as Item 70.

*   Kroll, Oskar. *The Clarinet*. Translated by Hilda Morris.
       London: Batsford, 1968. 183 p.

       Cited above as Item 90.

1091. Londiex, Jean-Marie. *125 ans de musique pour saxophone:
       Répertoire général des oeuvres et des ouvrages
       d'enseignement pour le saxophone*. Paris: Leduc, 1971.
       398 p.

       An exhaustive list of published and unpublished music,
       including 2,000 original works and over 1,000 arrange-
       ments. Notes the availability of tape recordings of
       the piano parts.

1092. Losch, Philipp. *Musikliteratur für Oboe und Englisch
       Horn*. Leipzig: Merseburger, 1914; reprint ed.,
       Wiesbaden: Sändig, 1972, and Buren: Knuf, 1978. 32 p.

       A comprehensive classified list. Includes methods,
       etudes, ensemble music, and transcriptions. Music for
       English horn and oboe d'amore is listed separately.
       Bound together with Bechler and Rahm, cited above as
       Item 78.

1093. McGowan, Richard A. *Italian Baroque Solo Sonatas for
       the Recorder and the Flute*. Detroit: Information
       Coordinators, 1978. 70 p.

       An annotated list of manuscripts and original publi-
       cations with their locations, together with a list of
       modern editions.

1094. Mellott, George K. "A Survey of Contemporary Flute
       Solo Literature with Analyses of Representative
       Compositions." Ph.D. dissertation, University of
       Iowa, 1964. 393 p. UM 64-7932.

       Includes a full list of works for solo flute published
       since 1930.

1095. Merriman, Lyle C. "Solos for Unaccompanied Woodwind Instruments: A Checklist of Published Works and Study of Representative Examples." Ph.D. dissertation, University of Iowa, 1963. 181 p. UM 64-3398.

Lists all known published works for woodwind solo as well as unpublished works available from the American Composers Alliance. Surveys music from the eighteenth and nineteenth centuries for solo clarinet and for solo flute and discusses in detail representative solo works from the twentieth century.

1096. Monsen, Ronald Peter. "Contemporary Norwegian Chamber Music for Clarinet." *Woodwind World, Brass and Percussion*, 14, no. 5 (November 1975): 10-11, 25, 51.

Lists published and unpublished works.

1097. *Music for the Flute*. New York: McGinnis and Marx, 1969. 204 p.

An extensive classified list drawn from publishers' catalogs. Includes methods, studies, some scores, and a few books. Compiled by Wayne Wilkins and Paul Solem.

1098. Oleson, Orval Bruce. "Italian Solo and Chamber Music for the Clarinet--1900-1973: An Annotated Bibliography." D.M.A. dissertation, University of Missouri, Kansas City, 1980. 185 p. UM 81-7986.

Lists ninety-six works for one to eight instruments. Sixty different composers are represented. Biographical sketches are included.

1099. Opperman, Kalmen. *Repertory of the Clarinet*. New York: Ricordi, 1960. 140 p.

A classified list of music, methods, and studies for soprano, bass, and contrabass clarinet. Does not distinguish between arrangements and original compositions. Includes a separate list of music for basset horn as well as a short list of books about or relevant to the clarinet.

1100. Pellerite, James, J. *A Handbook of Literature for the Flute*. 3rd ed. Bloomington, Ind.: Zalo Publications, 1978. 408 p.

A graded, superficially annotated list of works, etudes, exercises, and methods for piccolo, flute,

alto flute, and bass flute. Includes works for ensembles employing flute. Also includes a list of
reference material.

1101. Peters, Harry B. *The Literature of the Woodwind
       Quintet*. Metuchen, N.J.: Scarecrow, 1971. 174 p.

       A very useful bibliography. Includes more than
       1,500 works for woodwind quintet alone and for wood-
       wind quintet augmented by one to five additional per-
       formers.

1102. Pierreuse, Bernard. *Flûte litterature: Catalogue
       général des oeuvres édites et inédites par formations
       instrumentales*. Paris: Jobert, 1982. 670 p.

       The most comprehensive list of music and tutors for
       flute and piccolo. Includes transcriptions and arrange-
       ments. Lists altogether 35,000 published and unpublished
       works for flute or piccolo with orchestra, for flute or
       piccolo alone and in combination with up to twelve other
       solo instruments. In many cases indicates performance
       time. Includes brief but error-ridden lists of books
       and articles about the flute and about wind instruments
       in general.

1103. Pound, Gomer J. "A Study of Clarinet Solo Concerto
       Literature before 1850: With Selected Items Edited
       and Arranged for Contemporary Use." Ph.D. disserta-
       tion, Florida State University, 1965. 355 p. UM 65-
       9410.

       Identifies more than 300 works and locates copies of
       136.

1104. Prill, Emil. *Führer durch die Flöten-Literatur*.
       Leipzig: Zimmerman, 1899. 265 p.

       The fundamental bibliography. Lists more than 7,500
       items. Includes arrangements, music for piccolo, and
       flute method books. A supplement (166 p.) was published
       in 1913.

1105. Rasmussen, Mary, and Donald Mattran. *A Teacher's Guide
       to the Literature of Woodwind Instruments*. Durham,
       N.H.: Brass and Woodwind Quarterly, 1966. 266 p.

       A complement to Rasmussen's guide to brass literature
       (Item 1153). Includes a discography and a selective
       bibliography of books and articles.

*   Rehfeldt, Phillip. *New Directions for Clarinet.*
         Berkeley: University of California Press, 1977.
         135 p.

         Cited above as Item 949.

1106.   Ricker, Raymon L. "New Music: Electronic in General,
         Clarinet and Tape in Particular." *Woodwind World*
         10, no. 4 (September 1971): 13-14, 17.

         A list of music with addresses from which the music--
         parts and tapes--can be obtained.

1107.   Risdon, Howard. *Musical Literature for the Bassoon.*
         A Compilation of Music for the Bassoon and as an
         Instrument in Ensembles. Seattle: Berdon, 1963.
         24 p.

         Lists approximately 1,000 published works. Does not
         distinguish arrangements from original compositions.

1108.   Sacchini, Louis Vincent. "The Concerted Music for the
         Clarinet in the Nineteenth Century." Ph.D. disserta-
         tion, University of Iowa, 1980. 401 p. UM 80-22,063.

         Includes an inventory of 139 works, including a newly
         discovered concerto by James Hook.

1109.   Stanton, Robert E. *The Oboe Player's Encyclopedia.*
         [Uneonta, N.Y.]: Swift-Dorr, 1974. 48 p.

         Lists chamber works for oboe and English horn as
         well as works for oboe and English horn with orchestra.
         Also lists recordings and sources of double reed sup-
         plies.

1110.   Sumrall, Joel N. "The Literature for Clarinet and
         Voice and Its Historical Antecedents." D.M.A.
         dissertation, University of Illinois, 1974. 192 p.
         UM 75-11,883.

         Includes a list of the known works for altogether
         two or three performers.

1111.   Sundet, Jerold A. "Some Out-of-Print and Unpublished
         Compositions for Oboe with Small String Group ca.
         1750-1820." *Woodwind World* 11, no. 5 (December 1972):
         7-9.

         Lists forty-three works for three and four instruments.

1112. Swanson, Philip J. "Avant-Garde Flute Music." *Wood-
      wind World* 11, no. 5 (December 1972): 19-20, 22; 12,
      no. 3 (June 1973): 6-9.

      A classified list, prepared with the assistance of
      Charles W. King. Title is misleading in that a signifi-
      cant number of the works listed are by no means avant-
      garde.

1113. Titus, Robert A. "The Early Clarinet Concertos."
      Journal of Research in Music Education 13 (1965):
      169-76.

      Lists the surviving clarinet concertos from the
      eighteenth century. Includes a separate list of
      eighteenth-century composers thought to have written
      clarinet concertos that have not been found.

*   ————. "The Solo Music for the Clarinet in the
      Eighteenth Century." Ph.D. dissertation, University
      of Iowa, 1962. 619 p. UM 62-2412.

      Cited above as Item 989.

1114. Tuthill, Burnet, C. "The Concertos for Clarinet."
      Journal of Research in Music Education 10 (1962):
      47-58.

      An annotated list of more than 200 concertos.
      Includes some works originally written for another
      instrument.

1115. ————. "The Sonatas for Clarinet and Piano."
      Journal of Research in Music Education 14 (1966):
      197-212.

      An annotated list of more than 240 published and
      unpublished works, including arrangements.

1116. Vester, Frans. *Flute Repertoire Catalogue: 10,000
      Titles.* London: Musica Rara, 1967. 383 p.

      A comprehensive list. Also includes a short list
      of books and articles relating to the flute.

1117. Voxman, Himie, and Lyle Merriman. *Woodwind Ensemble
      Music Guide.* Evanston, Ill.: Instrumentalist, 1973.
      280 p.

      A classified list of music from 262 publishers.

1118. Waln, Ronald. "A Comprehensive Performance Project in Flute Literature with an Essay on Chamber Music for Solo Voices, Flute, and Keyboard or Continuo, and Including an Annotated Bibliography of Selected Literature." Ph.D. dissertation, University of Iowa, 1971. 182 p. UM 71-22,105.

Includes a list of 379 solo works and 34 duets for flute and voice. Also includes an overview of the genre.

1119. Weiner, Lowell Barry. "The Unaccompanied Clarinet Duet Repertoire from 1825 to the Present: An Annotated Catalogue." Ph.D. dissertation, New York University, 1980. 263 p. UM 80-17,535.

A graded, annotated list of music for clarinets in A and B flat.

1120. West, Charles W. "A Comprehensive Performance Project in Clarinet Literature with an Essay on Music for Woodwinds and Strings Five to Thirteen Players, Composed between *ca.* 1973; A Catalogue of Compositions, and Analyses of Selected Works by Composers Active in the United States after 1945." D.M.A. dissertation, University of Iowa, 1975. 275 p. UM 76-2204.

Traces the evolution of large ensembles of woodwinds and strings. Catalog includes 280 unpublished works. The title of the dissertation should not be taken as a model.

1121. Wilkins, Wayne. *The Index of Clarinet Music.* Magnolia, Ark.: Music Register, 1975. 143 p.

Limited to published works. Includes a short list of books. Periodically updated with supplements, 1975-.

1122. ————. *The Index of Flute Music, Including The Index of Baroque Trio Sonatas.* Magnolia, Ark.: Music Register, 1974. 131 p.

Limited to published music. Includes methods and studies.

3. Brass Instruments

1123. Anderson, Paul G. *Brass Solo and Study Material Guide*.
       Evanston, Ill.: Instrumentalist, 1976. 237 p.

       Lists published study materials and solos.

*   Baker, David. *Contemporary Techniques for the Trombone*.
       New York: Colin, 1974. 2 vols. 482 p.

       Cited above as Item 930.

1124. Brown, Leon F. *Handbook of Selected Literature for
       the Study of Trombone at the University-College
       Level*. [Denton, Texas: North Texas State University],
       1972. 23 p.

       A graded list. Includes books of warm-ups, scales,
       clef studies, jazz studies, and orchestral studies,
       as well as methods, solos, and books about the trombone.

1125. Brüchle, Bernhard. *Horn-Bibliographie*. 2 vols.
       Wilhelmshaven: Heinrichshofen, 1970-75. 272, 246 p.

       A comprehensive classified list of music. Vol. 2,
       which supplements and amends Vol. 1, indicates the
       availability of recordings, citing record labels and
       numbers. Each volume also lists books and articles
       about the instrument.

1126. Carnovale, August N. "A Comprehensive Performance
       Project in Trumpet Literature with an Essay on
       Published Music Composed Since *ca*. 1900 for Solo
       Trumpet Accompanied by Orchestra." D.M.A. disserta-
       tion, University of Iowa, 1973. 197 p. UM 74-16,703.

       Includes an annotated list of 201 compositions written
       between 1900 and 1971.

1127. Chesebro, Gayle M. "An Annotated List of Original
       Works for Horn Alone and for Horn with One Other
       Non-Keyboard Instrument." D.M.A. dissertation,
       Indiana University, 1976. 100 p.

       Annotations include indications of difficulty, the
       ranges of the parts, and duration of the works.

1128. Cramer, William F. "An Annotated List of Sonatas for Trombone and Piano." *Brass World* 4 (1968): 386-90.

Lists fifty-nine works. The annotations are very brief.

1129. Day, Donald K. "A Comprehensive Bibliography of Music for Brass Quintet." *Brass Anthology*. Evanston, Ill.: Instrumentalist, 1976, pp. 649-56.

A graded list of published and unpublished works. Where possible, cites published reviews.

1130. Everett, Thomas G. *Annotated Guide to Bass Trombone Literature*. Nashville: Brass Press, 1973. 34 p.

Includes unpublished compositions and a list of books and articles related to bass trombone performance.

1131. ————. "Solo Literature for the Bass Trombone." *Brass Anthology*. Evanston, Ill.: Instrumentalist, 1976, pp. 587-90.

A graded, annotated list of works originally intended for the bass trombone.

1132. "General Brass Catalogue." *Brass Bulletin*, no. 16 (1976): 3-8; no. 20 (1977): 3-19.

First installment lists current publications of music from six publishers together with Claves recordings. Next installment lists publications by eleven publishers as well as Crystal recordings.

* Gifford, Robert Marvin, Jr. "A Comprehensive Performance Project in Trombone Literature with an Essay Consisting of a Survey of the Use of the Trombone in Chamber Music with Mixed Instrumentation Composed since 1956." D.M.A. dissertation, University of Iowa, 1978. 266 p. UM 79-5662.

Cited above as Item 1008.

1133. Glover, Stephen L. "Early Trumpet Music in Schwerin." *Brass Bulletin*, no. 23 (1978): 35-40.

Includes a list of eighteenth-century and early nineteenth-century music for trumpet that is preserved in the Mecklenburgische Landesbibliothek in Schwerin (East Germany).

1134. Gray, Robert, and Mary Rasmussen. "A Bibliography of Cham-
       ber Music Including Parts for More Than One Different
       Brass Instrument." *Brass Quarterly* 3 (1959-60):
       141-54.

       Of use probably more to teachers than anyone else.

1135. ————. "A Bibliography of Chamber Music Including
       Parts for the Trombone." *Brass Quarterly* 3 (1959-
       60): 93-102.

       Includes published and unpublished works.

1136. ————. "Three Bibliographies of Nineteenth- and
       Twentieth-Century Concertante Works." *Brass Quarterly*
       6 (1962-63): 10-16.

       Lists works with parts for solo trumpet, solo trom-
       bone, and for two or more different solo brass instru-
       ments.

*   Gregory, Robin. *The Horn: A Comprehensive Guide to
       The Modern Instrument and Its Music.* New York:
       Praeger, 1969. 410 p.

       Cited above as Item 112.

*   ————. *The Trombone: The Instrument and Its Music.*
       New York: Praeger, 1973. 328 p.

       Cited above as Item 107.

1137. Hummel, Donald A. "A Selected and Annotated Bibliog-
       raphy of Original Works for Trombone Trio." D.M.A.
       dissertation, University of Missouri, Kansas City,
       1976. 149 p. UM 76-25,147.

       Lists fifty-three original works for trombone trio.
       Includes, where possible, published reviews.

*   Isaacson, Charles Frank. " A Study of Selected Music
       for Trombone and Voice." D.M.A. dissertation, Uni-
       versity of Illinois, 1981. 142 p. UM 82-3495.

       Cited above as Item 1013.

1138. Kagarice, Vern L. *Annotated Guide to Trombone Solos
       with Band and Orchestra.* Lebanon, Ind.: Studio P/R,
       1974. 177 p.

       Lists 135 works. Distinguished by lenghty annotations.
       Indicates range for the solo part of each work, the length
       of the work, and its level of difficulty. Includes a
       separate list of transcriptions.

1139. Kagarice, Vern L., et al. *Solos for the Student Trombonist: An Annotated Bibliography.* Nashville: Brass Press, 1979. 51 p.

A graded, annotated list.

* Miller, James E. "The Life and Works of Jan Vaclav Stich (Giovanni Punto)--A Checklist of 18th Century Horn Concertos and Players." Ph.D. dissertation, University of Iowa, 1962. 2 vols. 259 p. UM 62-4986.

Cited above as Item 668.

1140. Miller, Robert M. "The Concerto and Related Works for Low Brass: A Catalogue of Compositions from c. 1700 to the Present." Ph.D. dissertation, Washington University, 1974. 299 p. UM 75-6612.

A classified list of approximately 600 works. Includes a historical introduction.

1141. Morris, R. Winston. *Tuba Music Guide.* Evanston, Ill.: Instrumentalist, 1973. 60 p.

An annotated list of original works and arrangements. Includes methods and books of orchestral excerpts. Also lists recordings and suggests a basic library of tuba music and study material for the college tubist.

* Overton, Friend Robert. *Der Zink.* Mainz: Schott, 1981. 260 p.

Cited above as Item 103.

1142. Rasmussen, Mary. "A Bibliography of Chamber Music Including Parts for Horn, as Compiled from Thirteen Selected Sources." *Brass Quarterly* 2 (1958-59): 110-12, 146-57; 3 (1959-60): 12-20, 73-81, 103-13, 155-64; 4 (1960-61): 18-29, 64-74, 113-41, 159-67.

Lists published and unpublished works.

1143. ————. "Bibliography of Chamber Music Including Parts for Horn." *Brass Quarterly* 5 (1961-62): 18-33.

Indexes the bibliography cited above as Item 1142.

1144.   ————. "A Bibliography of Chamber Music Including
        Parts for Trumpet or Cornetto, as Compiled from
        Sixteen Selected Sources." *Brass Quarterly* 3 (1959-
        60): 40-72.

        Lists published and unpublished works.

1145.   ————. "A Bibliography of Choral Music with Horn
        Ensemble Accompaniment, as Compiled from Eleven
        Selected Sources." *Brass Quarterly* 5 (1961-62):
        153-49.

        A list primarily of nineteenth-century music.

1146.   ————. "A Bibliography of Choral Music with Trombone
        Ensemble Accompaniment, as Compiled from Eleven
        Selected Sources." *Brass Quarterly* 5 (1961-62):
        109-13.

        Lists published and unpublished works.

1147.   ————. "A Bibliography of Nineteenth-Century-
        and Twentieth-Century Music for Male Voices with
        Wind- or Brass-Ensemble Accompaniment." *Brass
        Quarterly* 7 (1963-64): 67-77, 124-32.

        Lists published and unpublished works.

1148.   ————. "A Bibliography of 19th- and 20th-Century
        Music for Mixed Voices with Wind- or Brass-Ensemble
        Accompaniment." *Brass Quarterly* 6 (1962-63): 120-
        30, 179-86; 7 (1963-64): 34-44.

        Lists published and unpublished works.

1149.   ————. " A Bibliography of *Symphonies concertantes*,
        Concerti grossi, etc., Including Solo Parts for
        the Horn, as Compiled from Twenty Selected Sources."
        Brass Quarterly 5 (1961-62): 62-68.

1150.   ————. "A Guide to Brass Ensemble Literature."
        Brass Quarterly 1 (1957-58): 160-67, 226-31; 2 (1958-
        59): 8-11, 78-82, 113-16, 167-73.

        A generously--if sometimes curiously--annotated list.

1151.   ————. "An Introductory Index of Contemporary Chorale
        Settings for Brass Instruments." *Brass Quarterly* 6
        (1962-63): 47-81.

        Lists the contents of seven collections.

1152. ————. *A Teacher's Guide to the Literature of Brass Instruments.* [2nd ed.] Durham, N.H.: Appleyard Publications, 1968. 104 p.

A selective bibliography of methods and studies, solo and ensemble music, and books and articles. For the music, indicates the pupil age groups for whom the works are suitable. Also includes essays surveying each category of music.

1153. Sansone, Lorenzo. *French Horn Music Literature with Composers' Biographical Sketches.* New York: Sansone Musical Instruments, 1962. 80 p.

Sometimes cited but of little value. Provides scanty information about the music and the composers.

1154. Schuller, Gunther. "The Horn Literature." *Woodwind* 4, no. 1 (September 1951): 6-7.

The first of twenty-four annotated lists of music, the last of which appeared in 1955, when the magazine ceased publication. The annotations are sometimes rather breezy but usually valuable and invariably interesting.

1155. Schumacher, Stanley E. "An Analytical Study of Published Unaccompanied Solo Literature for Brass Instruments." Ph.D. dissertation, Ohio State University, 1976. 275 p. UM 77-2497.

Includes a list of sixty-one works.

1156. Senff, Thomas E. "An Annotated Bibliography of the Unaccompanied Solo Repertoire for Trombone." D.M.A. dissertation, University of Illinois, 1976. 318 p. UM 76-16,919.

Includes a list of recordings and a brief discussion of the solo trombone repertory.

1157. Shoemaker, John R. "A Selected and Annotated Listing of 20th-Century Ensembles Published for Three or More Heterogeneous Brass Instruments." Ed.D. dissertation, Washington University, 1968. 199 p. UM 69-9009.

*   Smithers, Don L. *The Music and History of the Baroque Trumpet before 1721.* London: Dent, 1973. 323 p.

Cited above as Item 369.

1158. Wilkins, Wayne. *The Index of French Horn Music.*
Magnolia, Ark.: Music Register, 1978. 120 p.

Includes a list of books and scores.

4. Percussion Instruments

1159. Percussive Arts Society. *Solo and Ensemble Literature
for Percussion.* Knoxville: Percussive Arts Society,
1978. 93 p.

An unrivalled list of published solo and ensemble
music, indicating in many cases the general degree
of difficulty.

1160. Snider, Robert. "A Guide to Percussion Excerpts."
Percussionist 16 (1978-79): 153-76.

An index to the excerpts found in thirteen collections.
Classified according to instrument.

1161. Vincent, David W. "Commercially Available Excerpts for
Percussion." *Percussionist* 15 (1977-78): 40-44.

A list of excerpts included in tutors and collections.

XVI

MISCELLANY

1162. Abondance, Florence. *Restauration des instruments de musique.* Fribourg: Office du livre, 1981. 129 p.

A good introduction to the restoration of musical instruments. Focuses mostly on string instruments but includes discussion of other instruments as well. Generously illustrated with photographs.

1163. Anfinson, Roland E. "A Cinefluorographic Investigation of Selected Clarinet Playing Techniques." *Journal of Research in Music Education* 17 (1969): 227-39.

Investigates the movement of the tongue and adjustments made in the throat opening as tonguing speed changes. Also notes supralaryngeal adjustments made to accommodate various kinds of tonguing as well as the effect of throat opening and tongue placement in changing tone quality in the upper register.

1164. Baines, Anthony. *European and American Musical Instruments.* London: Batsford, 1966. 286 p.

A pictorial catalog of 824 items "intended primarily for collectors and curators who are not already specialists in musical instruments, as a help to identification of types and varieties of the non-keyboard instruments of Western Society from the Renaissance onwards."

1165. Baker, Nicholson. "Playing Trombone." *Atlantic*, March 1982, pp. 39-58.

An outrageously funny short story that chronicles the life and brief career of the most remarkable trombonist ever described. Contains a fine set of illustrations by Alexandra Grace.

1166. Baltimore Museum of Art. *Musical Instruments and
       Their Portrayal in Art.* Baltimore: Museum of Art,
       1946. 48 p.

       A guide to an exhibition held during the spring of
       1946. Includes a list of seventy-nine paintings
       depicting instruments.

1167. Battipaglia, Victor A. "The Double-Lip Embouchure in
       Clarinet Playing." D.M.A. dissertation, University
       of Rochester, 1975. 103 p. UM 75-29,845.

       Includes a discussion of the history of the embouchure
       up to the nineteenth century.

1168. Bernier, René. "Le Congrès mondial de saxophone à
       Bordeaux." *Bulletin de la classe des Beaux-Arts
       de l'Académie Royale de Belgique* 56, no. 10 (1974):
       145-51.

       Reports the activities of the Fourth World Congress
       on the Saxophone, held at Bordeaux on July 3-6, 1974.
       The program was notable for its inclusion of a number
       of saxophone quartets, British and American as well
       as French.

1169. Bonanni, Filippo. *The Showcase of Musical Instruments.*
       New York: Dover, 1964. 309 p.

       A collection of extremely attractive engravings
       taken from the revised edition of Bonanni's *Gabinetto
       armonico* (1723). Provided with a new introduction
       and captions by Frank Lloyd Harrison and Joan Rimmer.
       A valuable source of information, especially about
       unusual instruments.

1170. Boyden, David. "Nicholas Bessaraboff's *Ancient
       European Musical Instruments.*" *Notes* 28 (1971):
       21-27.

       Traces the history of the book cited above as Item
       686 and sketches the fascinating background of its
       author.

1171. Bragard, Roger, and Ferdinand J. de Hen. *Musical
       Instruments in Art and History.* Translated by Bill
       Hopkins. New York: Viking Press, 1968. 281 p.

       Interesting especially for its photographs and des-
       criptions of unusual instruments, including a 20th-
       century percussion instrument by Baschet and a "crystal
       trombone," also by Baschet.

1172. *Brass Anthology.* Evanston, Ill.: Instrumentalist, 1976. 701 p.

A collection of articles related to brass instruments and brass performance that were originally published in *The Instrumentalist* between 1946 and 1974.

1173. Denis, Valentin. *De Muziekinstrumenten in de Nederlanden en in Italie naar hun afbeelding in de 15e-eeuswsche kunst.* Antwerp: Standard-Boekhandel, 1944. 352 p.

An account of the musical instruments depicted in Italian art works of the fifteenth century. Includes twenty plates.

1174. Farkas, Philip. *A Photographic Study of 40 Virtuoso Horn Players' Embouchures.* Bloomington, Ind.: Wind Music, 1970. 41 p.

A collection of singularly unattractive photographs showing the embouchures of experienced French horn players, including only one woman.

1175. Florence. Galleria degli Uffizi. *Mostra di strumenti musicali in disegni degli Uffizi.* Florence: Olschki, 1952. 47 p.

An annotated catalog, by Luisa Marcucci, of drawings from the Uffizi Gallery that depict musical instruments. Prefaced by a selection of pertinent excerpts from past writers, many from the Renaissance. Includes reproductions of twenty-five drawings.

1176. Florence. Galleria degli Uffizi. *I disegni musicali del Gabinetto degli "Uffizi" e delle minore collezioni pubbliche a Firenze.* Florence: Olschki, 1951. 233 p.

A catalog, by Luigi Parigi, of 1,382 drawings and watercolors with musical subject matter. Includes an index of the instruments depicted.

1177. Geiringer, Karl. "Haydn's Trumpet Concerto." *The Musical Times* 81 (1949): 83.

An account of the first radio broadcast of the concerto, which the author was largely responsible for and which led to the first recording of the work.

1178. Hall, Jody C. "A Radiographic, Spectrographic, and
       Photographic Study of the Non-Labial Physical Changes
       which Occur in the Transition from Middle to Low and
       Middle to High Registers during Trumpet Performance."
       Ph.D. dissertation, Indiana University, 1954. 313 p.
       UM 10-146.

       Investigates the function of the tongue and of the
       oral cavity in the production of trumpet tone. Indicates
       that the shape of the oral cavity as formed by the player
       is more significant than the difference among instruments.

1179. Klerk, Magda. *Répertoire internationale d'iconographie
       musicale: European Musical Instruments on Prints and
       Drawings*. [Zug, Switzerland]: Inter Documentation,
       [1976]. 16 p.

       Indexes forty-four microfiches published as a project
       undertaken as part of RIDM. The fiches reproduce 600
       prints and drawings in the collection of the music de-
       partment of the Gemeentemuseum in The Hague.

*   Leppert, Richard D. *The Theme of Music in Flemish
       Paintings of the Seventeenth Century*. 2 vols.
       Munich: Katzbichler, 1977. 388, 218 p.

       Cited above as Item 148.

1180. Lonnman, Gregory G. "The Tuba Ensemble: Its Organiza-
       tion and Literature." D.M.A. dissertation, Univer-
       sity of Miami, 1974. 63 p. UM 75-12,870.

       Reports a survey showing the presence of tuba ensembles
       in more than two dozen colleges and universities.

1181. Malm, William P. "A Computer Aid in Musical Instrument
       Research." *Studia instrumentorum musicae popularis*,
       vol. 3: *Festschrift to Ernst Emsheimer on the Occasion
       of His 70th Birthday January 15th 1974*, edited by
       Gustaf Hilleström. Stockholm: Nordiska musikforlaget,
       1974, pp. 119-22.

       Describes the Musinst data bank, established to facili-
       tate the search for and exchange of organological infor-
       mation.

1182. Naylor, Tom L. *The Trumpet and Trombone in Graphic Arts
       1500-1800*. Nashville: Brass Press, 1979.

       A splendid collection of plates, taken mainly from wood-
       cuts and engravings. Annotations, some brief and some
       relatively extensive, follow at the end.

1183. Otterbach, Friedemann. *Schöne Musikinstrumente.*
Munich: Schuler, 1975. 127 p.

A collection of photographs, largely in color, linked
by a non-technical narrative.

1184. Paganelli, Sergio. *Musical Instruments from the Ren-
aissance to the 19th Century.* Translated by Anthony
Rhodes. London: Hamlyn, 1970; reprinted London:
Hamlyn, 1974. 157 p.

Intended for the general reader. Short on text but
long on attractive color photographs.

1185. Perdue, Robert W. "Arundo donax--Source of Musical
Reeds and Industrial Cellulose." *Economic Botany*
12 (1958): 368-404.

A full, clearly written account of the history of
the use of reed cane together with a description of
reed making and cane production. Discusses the present
and future industrial utilization of the cane and the
possibilities of its production in the United States.

1186. Pizka, Hans. *Das Horn bei Mozart/Mozart and the Horn.*
Kirchheim: Pizka, 1980. 276 p.

Primarily a collection of facsimiles of the original
manuscripts of Mozart's works for horn, including arias
with prominent horn parts from *Così fan tutte* and
Idomeneo. Describes the works briefly, provides caden-
zas, discusses natural horn-playing, and provides detailed instructions for playing the concerto K. 447 on
natural horn. Includes a short dictionary of players
and a discography, prepared with the assistance of
Curtis Blake.

1187. Porter, Maurice M. "Dental Aspects of Orchestral Wind
Instrument Playing with Special Reference to the
'Embouchure'." *British Dental Journal* 93 (1952):
66-73.

Principally a discussion of the muscular mechanism of
the embouchure. Well illustrated with drawings and
photographs.

1188. ————. *Dental Problems in Wind Instrument Playing.*
London: British Dental Association, 1968. 56 p.

A collection of twelve articles that appeared in the
British Dental Journal in 1968 and 1968. Reports the
results of a comprehensive study of the problems en-
countered by players both amateur and professional.

*   ————. *The Embouchure.* London: Boosey and Hawkes,
         1967. 144 p.

         Cited above as Item 834.

1189. Rauch, Wolfgang. "Restaurierung und Pflege historischer
      Holzblasinstrumente." *Glareana* 20, nos. 1-4, 21,
      nos. 1, 3-4 (March, June, December, 1971; March,
      December, 1972): 1-2; 12-16; 29-32; 5-10; 31-41.

      Describes the repair and reconstruction of old wood-
      wind instruments.

1190. Ripin, Edwin M. *The Industrial Catalogs of Leopoldo
      Franciolini.* Hackensack, N.J.: Boonin, 1974. 201 p.

      A facsimile reproduction of the catalogs of the
      notorious Florentine dealer in musical instruments
      together with a discussion of his methods. Includes
      the texts and translations of documents and reports
      relating to his trial for fraud in 1910 as well as a
      selection of photographs.

*   Schrammek, Winfried. "Gadanken zur Restaurierung histori-
      scher Musikinstrumente." *Festschrift für Walter Wiora
      zum 30. Dezember 1966*, edited by Ludwig Finscher and
      Ludwig Mahling. Kassel: Bärenreiter, 1967, pp. 62-65.

      Cited above as Item 914.

1191. Sidorfsky, Frank M. "A Critical Study of Books on the
      Clarinet." D.M.A. dissertation, University of
      Rochester, 1973. 195 p.

      Analyzes and compares the books by Dunbar, Kroll,
      Rendall, Stein, Stubbins, Thurston, Tosé, and Willaman.

1192. Veselack, Marilyn Sue Warren. "Comparison of Cell and
      Tissue Differences in Good and Unusable Clarinet Reeds."
      D.A. dissertation, Ball State University, 1979. 136 p.
      UM 81-2480.

      Reports the results of microscopic examinations of reeds.
      Describes in detail the differences in cell and tissue
      characteristics of good and unusable reeds. Offers rec-
      commendations regarding the growing and harvesting of cane.

1193. Weigel, Johann Christoph. *Musicalisches theatrum.*
Nuremberg: Weigel, [*ca.* 1772]; facsimile reprint,
edited by Alfred Berner, Kassel: Bärenreiter, 1961.
12 p.

Includes thirty-six plates of engravings that depict
the playing of instruments, singing, and conducting.
Each picture is accompanied by a short, light-hearted
verse. The facsimile edition includes an afterword
by Alfred Berner.

1194. Winternitz, Emanuel. *Musical Instruments of the
Western World.* New York: McGraw-Hill, [1967]. 259 p.

A collection of remarkably beautiful photographs
by Lilly Stunzi, many of which are in color, together
with descriptions and introductory essays by Winternitz.
Originally published as *Die schönsten Musikinstrumente
des Abendlandes* (Munich: Seysersche Verlagsbuchhandlung,
1966).

1195. *Woodwind Anthology.* Evanston, Ill.: Instrumentalist,
1976. 905 p.

Brings together articles that were originally published in the *The Instrumentalist* during the years
1946-76. The articles, grouped according to instrument,
are mostly of a practical nature.

INDEX OF AUTHORS, EDITORS, TRANSLATORS

INDEX OF SUBJECTS